BANGLADESH MIGRANTS

BANGLADESH MIGRANTS

A Threat to India

P.K. Mishra

GYAN

ISBN: 978-81-212-1218-2

Price: ₹ 910

First Published 2014

Published by
Gyan Publishing House
23, Main Ansari Road, Daryaganj,
New Delhi - 110002
Phones : 23282060, 23261060
Fax : (011) 23285914
E-mail: books@gyanbooks.com
website: gyanbooks.com

Laser Typesetting: Rajender Vashist, Delhi
Printed at: G. Print Process, Delhi

Cataloging in Publication Data--DK
Courtesy: D.K. Agencies (P) Ltd. <docinfo@dkagencies.com>

Mishra, P.K.
Bangladesh migrants : a threat to India / P.K. Mishra.
p. cm.
Includes bibliographical references and index.
ISBN 9788121212182

1. Bangladeshis--India. 2. Illegal aliens--India. 3. Border security--India. 4. India--Emigration and immigration. 5. Bangladesh--Emigration and immigration. I. Title.

DDC 304.80954 23

“Dedicated to my beloved mother Shrimati Shakuntala Mishra for whose love and guidance I became what I am. Also dedicated to my wife Seema Mishra who spent her first few years with me just after marriage in border outposts of Geetaldah, Sahibganj, Chowdhurihat and Changrabandha in Indo-Bangladesh Border and accompanied me on foot to various enclaves in Coochbehar border and Bangladesh BDR BOPs close to the border. She was the force behind me to pen what she had also seen in Indo-Bangladesh border during her stay in the border outposts with me from 1978 to 1985.”

Contents

Padmashri
Prakash Singh
(Formerly Director General; BSF, DGP UP and DGP Assam)

3C Super Deluxe Flats,
Sector-15A, Noida -
201301 (U.P.)
Phone: 0120-2512165

Foreword

One of the biggest problems facing India and having a direct bearing on the country's economy and security is that of the continuing illegal migration of Bangladeshis into India. The factors which have been encouraging the influx from Bangladesh side are: steep rise in population with increasing pressures on land and mounting unemployment; recurrent natural disasters like floods and cyclones, uprooting large segments of humanity; better economic opportunities in India; religious persecution of Hindus and discrimination of tribals; Islamic interests encouraging expansion of territory, organised immigration by touts and anti-social elements; and porous and esily negotiable international borders.

The bulk of the Bangladeshi immigrants are in the states of Assam, West Bengal, Bihar, Delhi and the north-eastern states. The Task Force on Border Management which was headed by Madhav Godbole and submitted its report in August 2000. Considering that twelve years have elapsed since then, the figure must have reached at least two crores.

The Supreme Court of India, in a landmark judgement (July 2005), while repealing the notorious IMDT Act, observed that "there can be no manner of doubt that the states of Assam is facing external aggression and internal disturbance on account of large-scale illegal migration of Bangladeshi nationals" and directed the Union of India "to take all measures for protection of the states of Assam from such external aggression and internal disturbance as enjoined in Article 355 of the Constitution."

A parliamentary panel expressed the view (April 2008) that "the large presence of illegal Bangladeshi immigrants poses a grave threat to the internal security and it should be viewed strongly". The Government of India unfortunately continues to drag its feet in the matter and has not initiated any definite measures to throw out the illegal migrants.

As observed by an expert, it is important to take "perceptions and fears seriously and not dismiss them as irrational, xenophobic, or paranoid", India will be ignoring the dangers to its communal harmony, economic well being and, above all, security at its own peril. The Task Force indicated the political establishment for brushing the problem under the carpet in the following words:

"There is an all-round failure in India to come to grips with the problem of illegal immigration. Facts are well known, opinions are firmed up, and operating system is in position. But the tragedy is that desire this, nothing substantial happens due to catharsis of arriving at a decision in this regard due to sharp division of interest among the political class".

Mishra's book on the subject contains a wealth of information on the subject throwing light of the background of the problem, the complexion before the liberation of Bangladesh in 1971 and after that the feeble attempts to deal with it, and its security implications. One can only hope that it opens the eyes of the political class to the seriousness of the problem and provides them with some motivation to deal with it in a manner which would lessen, if not obviate, the gravity of the demographic problem and its security implications.

Prakash Singh

Preface

The longest land border India has with any country is that of Bangladesh which is of 4096.7 kilometre in length but the problems faced by our country with that of Bangladesh cannot be compared to that with China, Pakistan, Afghanistan, Myanmar, Nepal and Bhutan. The migration may be for any reasons, continued even from pre-British Period and will never end as practically the border with Bangladesh cannot be sealed, being totally impossible. What has been brought out in this volume is the real entry of the migrants from Bangladesh to India through various land and riverine routes which were witnessed by the writer who remained in Indo-Bangladesh border from 1972 to 1985. A special emphasis has been given to the entry of Bihari Muslims from Bangladesh to Indian border in Kishanganj and Islampur belt. The position is very precarious as a number of Bangladesh nationals coming to India with valid passports are reported to be missing whose numbers are more than those who are crossing the land border now unauthorisedly. The crossing of ISI agents in Tripura and Assam border with Bangladesh has been clearly reflected by the names of ISI agents apprehended in the last few years which show the shortfalls in the border management. The reasons for the delay in fencing and floodlighting of Tripura, Mizoram and Khasi belt of Meghalaya border remain as a problem. The border is not a straight line and is porous. The border people are quite indifferent in their attitude towards the border guarding forces and the BSF, till today, is not accepted fully to the border people. We have about 86 vulnerable BOPs whose areas are prone to crossing and there are about 115 gaps in the fencing in Indo-Bangladesh border. The cutting of barbed wire fence by smugglers, the demographic change of the border areas, the relation between families of both sides of the border, the position of char islands in river Brahmaputra, losing natural resources of Khasi and Jaintia Hills and the rampant corruption existing in the border belt pose maximum threat to the peace and tranquillity in these areas. The release of BADP and CAP funds for the development of border areas are too meagre which require to be ten times more. The ratification by the Parliament of India for exchange of adverse possession lands and enclaves is still pending from the time of Indira-Mujeeb Treaty, 1974. The demographic change in Assam and West Bengal is a warning for all of us to introspect and take action without losing any time. The border requires political, social, economic and security development in every respect and the interest of the border population, particularly the ethnic people, the tribals and the Indian Muslims need to be taken care of, or otherwise, more massacres like that reported at Neille and Kokrajhar will recur. The rising of Muslim fundamentalist groups in north-east, particularly in Assam, Manipur and in West Bengal will enhance security-related expenditure of our country. The mushrooming of number of mosques and madrassas in border districts of North 24 Parganas, Nadia, Murshidabad, Maldah, West Dinajpur, Dhubri, Cachar and Karimganj require security vetting.

The most important aspect is the demoralisation of the border guarding force for being ordered not to open fire and to use non-lethal weapons against the intruders even at night. This has emboldened border criminals and Muslim migrants and a number of casualties of the border guarding force have been reported. However, we are maintaining a better relation with the present Bangladesh government but the past episode of the firing resorted to by the BDR at

Pridwa in Meghalaya border and killing of 16 BSF personnel by Bangladesh villagers and the BDR in Boraibari should not be forgotten. The election in Bangladesh, if will be held again, and if, Begum Zia comes to power, we will again face a strained and hectic scenario in Indo-Bangladesh border and all these militant camps which were existing opposite to our border in Bangladesh, will resurface and the game of ISI and DGFI to destabilise our country will become easier. The congregation of various Muslim fundamentalist groups in the Maidan at Kolkata in March, 2013, the demolition of Hindu and Buddhist temples in Chittagong and Cox's Bazaar in September 2012, the killing of Hindus (who are in minority in Bangladesh), burning of their houses in hundreds and vandalising Hindu temples in Dhaka, Barisal and Khulna after the judgement of war criminals by Bangladesh court clearly give an indication to all Indians to rise to the occasion and take all precautionary measures against such actions of the fundamentalists. All political parties must come together in finalising the course of action to be adopted towards the presence of Bangladesh Muslim migrants in India and their fresh entry.

P.K. Mishra

Acknowledgements

Ever since I started working on this book, a year back, help has been pouring generously for me in doing justice to my work. I am indebted to the individuals who helped me in my mission and I am grateful for their cooperation.

First and foremost, I am grateful to Shri Ajit Doval, the Director (VIF), who inspired me and guided me to proceed with the writing of this book. I also thank Shri Sanjay Singh who provided materials from library, which were extremely handy to me.

I also thank Professor Makkhanlal, Prof. Dilip Chakraborty, Shri RNP Singh and Dr. N Manoharan who took the trouble of guiding me every day in infusion of the inputs.

My grateful thanks also go to Shri O P Kundu, IPS, IG BSF, Shri S S Chahar, DIG BSF, Shri Surjeet Singh, DIG BSF and Shri Yashpal Chouhan, Dy. Commandant BSF whose wholehearted support helped me in my work.

I shall fail in my duty if I do not mention my appreciation and applause to Shri Harshit Pandey who remained with me throughout the period in preparing copies of the same.

At the end, I also thank other copyright holders and the managers of the Wikipedia whose notes were very valuable to me.

P.K. Mishra

Abbreviations

AAGSP	All Assam Gana Sangram Parishad
AAMLF	All Assam Muslim Liberation Front
AASU	All Assam Students Association
AIUDF	All India United Demographic Front
AMULFA	All Muslim United Liberation Front of Assam
ARIFM	Arakan Rohingya Islamic Front of Myanmar
BADP	Border Area Development Programme
BDR	Bangladesh Rifles
BFSR	Battle Field Surveillance Radar
BGF	Border Guarding Force
BGB	Border Guards of Bangladesh
BLT	Bodo Liberation Tigers
Bn	Battalion
BNP	Bangladesh National Party
BOP	Border Out Post
BPL	Below Poverty Line
BSF	Border Security Force
BTAD	Bodo Territorial Autonomous District
BTC	Bodoland Territorial Council
CCTV	Close Circuit Television
CHT	Chittagong Hills Tracts
CM	Chief Minister
Coy	Company

CPMF	Central Para Military Force
CRPF	Central Reserve Police Force
DGFI	Director General of Forces Intelligence
DHD Jewel	Dima Halam Daogah Jewel
DHD-BW	Dima Halam Daogah Black Widow
FICN	Fake Indian Currency Notes
GoM	Group of Ministers
HHTI	Hand Held Thermal Imager
HujiB	Harkat-ul-Jihad I Islami Bangladesh
HuM	Hizbul-ul-Mujahiddens
IB	Intelligence Bureau / International Border
ICP	Integrated Checkposts
ICS	Islamic Chhatra Shibir
IMDT Act	Illegal Migrants Determination by Tribunal Act
ISI	Inter Services Intelligence
IURPI	Islamic United Reformation Protest of India
J&K	Jammu & Kashmir
JEI	Jamat-e-Islami
JuM	Jamat-e-ul-Mujahiddens
LBA	Land Boundary Agreement
LET	Laskar-e-Toiba
LIA	Lead Intelligence Agency
LORROS	Long Range Reconnaissance and Observations System
MHA	Ministry of Home Affairs
MLTA	Muslim Liberation Tigers of Assam
NBCC	National Building Construction Corporation Limited
NEC	North East Council
NEFA	North East Frontier Agency
NEHU	North East Hill University

NGO	Non-governmental Organisation
NPCC	National Projects Construction Corporation Limited
PDS	Public Distribution System
Pl	Platoon
R and AW	Research and Analysis Wing
SDPI	Social Democratic Party of India
Sec	Section
TOI	Times of India
UAV	Unmanned Aerial Vehicle
UG	Under Ground
UNHCR	United Nations High Commissioner for Refugees
UPA	United Progressive Alliance
VIF	Vivekananda International Foundation
WPI	Welfare Party of India

1

The Problem

Illegal immigration from Bangladesh to India has been a perennial problem. There are various reasons attributed to this influx. India has a long and porous border with Bangladesh and people on either side of the border have socio, cultural, religious and linguistic affinity. These factors, along with availability of better economic avenues in India, are mainly responsible for the large inflow of illegal migrants to India. In the initial years, the migrants used to settle in the Border states adjoining Bangladesh. Later on, they started spreading out into the interiors of the country. Illegal migration has not only disturbed the demographic profile of our Border states adjoining Bangladesh, but has also affected the political set-up. Today, there are many constituencies in some of the Eastern states, where most of these illegal migrants decide political future of a number of candidates. The *modus operandi* adopted by these migrants is not confined to clandestine sneaking, but also in the form of overstaying their visas. Many touts and criminals are also making a fortune out of this illegal human trafficking. The forces guarding border are trying to contain this menace to the best of their abilities, not only by preventive action, but also by resorting to firing on the intruders, though at present, due to a directive from the Ministry of Home Affairs, firing on intruders even during the night time along the Indo-Bangladesh border had been disallowed. Earlier, because of the firing, many intruders were killed while crossing over to India and while cutting the barbed wire fence.

2

Demographic Profile/ Geography/Availability of Land in Bangladesh

In the year 2011, Bangladesh was having a population of 152,518,015 out of which 76,350,518 were males and 76,167,497 were females. By the end of 2012, the population has increased to 164.4 million in an area of 144,000 sq km i.e. 55,599 sq miles. 98 per cent of its people constitute Bengalis. It consists of 90 per cent Muslims, nine per cent Hindus, and one per cent Buddhists and Christians. Bangladesh is one of the most densely populated country in the world. It has third largest Muslim population and the seventh largest overall population in the world. The density of population of Bangladesh is currently around 1,237.51 persons per sq km.

The country is vulnerable to high risks of dengue fever and the hygiene and sanitation standards there, are extremely poor. The water pollution level too is very high. The local clinics and hospitals are generally of a very poor standard. The content of arsenic is very high in ground water as a result of which Bangladesh is facing acute health problems.

At present, Bangladesh's per capita income has gone up to 1900 dollars per year i.e. about 10,000 takas per month. Bangladesh possesses a large labour force of 75.42 million who mostly go to Saudi Arabia and other Muslim countries, including India, where the demand for cheap labour is high. Forty per cent of its population is underemployed and they work on meagre wages, 31.51 per cent of the population are below poverty line and its inflation rate is 10.7 per cent.

The entire Bangladesh land is low-line with catastrophic flooding. There is threatening effect of global warming in Bangladesh as the sea level is rising slowly. There is every reason for skilled Bangladeshi workers to come to India as their requirement in Bangladesh is very less. Only 39.8 per cent women in Bangladesh are literate. Mere 19.9 per cent students go to higher secondary school. It is understood that corruption is very much rampant in Bangladesh. As poverty persists and is steadily increasing; in the years to come, a major demographic problem may occur in Bangladesh, which will comprise of a population with sickly elders. The population of women in fertility age group is much higher in Dhaka.

Illiteracy is highest in slums and amongst women. One-third of its slums do not have cot / bed and there is heavy crowding in each household. The phenomena of divorce, separation, widowhood is very common. Matriarchal householders are more commonly to be found. Reports of high prevalence of teenage marriages and teenage pregnancies amongst slum women are very common. Mostly, people use tube well water for drinking purpose. Only one, out of twenty persons, have access to private toilets and 50 per cent people are compelled to use common toilets. Pregnant women in younger age group are much higher. Unwanted pregnancies are also reported in urban areas. The infants do not get adequate food and have high rates of mortality, which comes to about 138 per thousand of population. The menace of diarrhoea is very acute and people have insufficient healthcare. Crime rate is very high along with high incidence of over-all population growth, both in urban and rural areas. Bangladesh is facing very poor housing problems with very high gross area density. Every room has three or more than that adults. They do not have proper drainage or sewerage systems. Reports of inadequate water supply in urban areas are heard of. The administration has failed in effecting sanitation, including garbage disposal. There is heavy demand for housing, schools, and health centres. About 55.3 per cent people are illiterate in slums, and 34 per cent of people live in very poor households with no access to electricity. Amongst the women, six per cent are employed in garment-making and 5 per cent work as housemates. 27 per cent of females are unemployed. There is high proportion of divorced women because of high rate of teenage marriages. Marriages in slums are being solemnised even before onset of puberty. There is high risk of teenage childbirths. However, Bangladesh has higher per cent of women labour force available. Their possession of household goods is very poor, crowding per room is extreme, and they subsist in substandard living conditions bereft of potable water, sanitation, and food security.

Lack of hygienic toilet facilities prevail all over Bangladesh. It has very small percentage of unwanted pregnancies ending with MR/abortion. There is appreciable occurrence of diarrhoea, food and water-borne diseases, hepatitis A and E, typhoid, fever, dengue and malaria.

3

Causes of Immigration from Bangladesh

Mostly people decide to go out due to economic reasons. As for Hindus, they left because of religious oppressions. The non-availability of resources, unemployment, poor health care, problem of education/literacy, security of children and their future are main reasons for migration of population from Bangladesh. The basic needs, i.e., food, shelter and clothing is not available in Bangladesh. People do not get better wages. They do not have better living conditions and the country is finding difficult to sustain such a large density of population. The population density in the border areas of India is just one-third of that of Bangladesh in north-east. The environment crisis too has a major role to play for migration from Bangladesh. The scarcity of land, scarcity of drinking water, rapid population growth together with the factor of environmental change, constrain people to find their alternative place for migration. The unequal resource distribution, weak development of rural areas, declining wages/income and degradation of human habitats are playing major role in respect of Bangladeshis to disperse out of their motherland, which is economically impoverished. The climatic changes occurring every year and the situation in coastal areas have caused problems for the poor rural Bangladeshis to the extent that they have no other option but to migrate.

The factors that attract the migrants from Bangladesh to India, particularly in the states of Assam, West Bengal and all the border districts alongside Bangladesh are the similar geopolitical, social, cultural, racial, linguistic linkages and easy accessibility to the states bordering Bangladesh. All those who came, have neither returned back, nor is Bangladesh interested to take them back. The migrants after coming to India from Bangladesh have become a *de facto* force in decision-making, whether it is political or even social. The changing socio-economic, political, ecological and communal conditions in Bangladesh were the forces behind the migrations. The historical, social affinity, the geographical contiguity and the economic superiority of India were the main allurements for these new settlers who were welcomed first, but have now become aliens in the whole of north-east. In the first phase, all these migrants have naturalised themselves in West Bengal. In the beginning, whether it was in West Bengal or Assam, it was in the shape of a peasant migration due to the conditions in Bangladesh. They received political patronage—both from government of West Bengal and from government of Assam. They got relief from the problems of non-availability of land, hunger, population pressure and adverse environmental conditions prevailing in Bangladesh and received a warm welcome everywhere in India.

The partition of India had also forced Hindus to migrate. The presence of kins, friends and relations in Indian side of the border, facilitated in providing them with the shelter. They received grand political support and were welcomed due to the ethnic affinity and fellow-feeling. Easy acquisition of citizenship, voter's card, ration card, lease of land and naturalisation helped them in settling in the place of their choice. The Hindu migrants considered India as their own motherland. The bright economic prospects existing in India were the significant forces behind this move. It is not only that they came from neighbouring districts of Bangladesh but migrated from all over Bangladesh to our border districts and to their pleasant surprise, the government of West Bengal went ahead with arranging for their inhabitation in border areas of Kalyani of Nadia district and Bijpur of 24 Parganas. A big camp, each at Taltala at Kalyani and Mallickbagh colony at Bijpur, came up under auspices of the government as settlement colonies in the vacant lands available.

They were given financial help and funds for roofing at Bijpur and *patta* for land at Kalyani camp. That was the time when there was no border fencing and practically no vigilance at the borders. Migrants received security of their lives in this country. Other pull-factors were the social network, proper educational facilities to their children, the war of 1971, better economic opportunities and availability of a job to support their families. At various places in India, they could purchase land for cultivation, obtained citizenship certificates, voter cards, ration cards, *pattas*, shelter and political support. The ethnic affinity at both sides of the border forced these two state governments of Assam and West Bengal to have sympathetic attitude towards them. Availability of schools, colleges, technical education facilities, daily labours, contract labours, jobs in business farms, offices and agricultural farms provided them job security. Ladies were employed as tailors, shopkeepers apart from working as helps in labour markets and households. They became a workforce for cultivators and agriculturists. The skilled labours like carpenters, traders, machinists, shopkeepers, tailors, barbers, blacksmiths, businessmen, fishermen, physicians, housemaids, three-wheeler drivers, students and primary teachers flocked in all border districts alongside Bangladesh. They got active support of the locals who ensured them peace, security of life and kept them as their relatives. They earned good income with minimum risk. The West Bengal was their main attraction; its pull-factors were the language, the culture, the food, home-ethnic climate, economic prospects, job opportunity, economic security, geographic proximity, shelter, cordiality, fellow-feeling, and lastly, the whole of West Bengal populace accepted their demographic change. Their aim was achieved by getting economic stability, social security, political patronage, communal harmony, democracy, proper law and order and last but not the least in manipulating names in voter list, getting ration cards, and job security for their children in our states.

Presently, India has a population density of 365 per sq km. If we see the migration of Bangladeshis to India in the areas of North Bengal, West Bengal, and border districts of West Bengal, the density of population of these areas has tremendously gone up which is evident from the data mentioned below:

West Bengal	1030 per sq km
North Bengal	790 per sq km
South 24 Parganas	819 per sq km
North 24 Parganas	2463 per sq km
Nadia	1316 per sq km
Murshidabad	1334 per sq km
Maldah	1071 per sq km
South Dinajpur	753 per sq km
North Dinajpur	956 per sq km
Darjeeling	585 per sq km
Jalpaiguri	621 per sq km
Coochbehar	833 per sq km

This is the result of huge migration to the border districts of West Bengal. The lebensraum continued in all north-east states as West Bengal was packed to capacity. The population density of the north-east states of India are as under:

Assam	397 per sq km
Sikkim	86 per sq km
Manipur	122 per sq km
Meghalaya	131 per sq km
Mizoram	52 per sq km

Nagaland	120 per sq km
Tripura	350 per sq km

This also shows that migration had an effect in Assam and Tripura States, which had more pull factors with them, as they are contiguous to Bangladesh. No human effort or fencing can stop this outflow from Bangladesh to India.

Illegal migration into India is one of the biggest security threats to the country and it had its effect in the political scenario, demographic pattern, economic condition, cultural imbalance, and insurgency-related problems. Though India has migration-related issue with a number of countries, yet, at present, the illegal migration is continuing from Bangladesh to north-east of India only. The number of Hindu refugees reported to be arriving from East Bengal and Pakistan to India are quite less in number; mostly their entry is to take asylum permanently in this country, which is because of persecution by Bangladesh fundamentalists.

No doubt, there is a serious lebensraum crisis in Bangladesh due to natural calamities; too much population growth is incommensurate with the availability of the land for the people to live in. In another 10 years or so, due to global warming, the sea level, in and around Bangladesh islands, will rise by one metre. So, most of these small islands which are hugely populated, and are just within 1 metre height from sea level, will all get submerged; further, being one of the most densely populated country in the world, this surplus population will have to find a place to survive. There is not a single year in Bangladesh, which passes without any flood. Heavy rains in Cherrapunji, Mysurram, Khasi and Jaintia hills of Meghalaya, and the hills of Tura and Garo, allow all the rainwater to flow through various channels to Bangladesh. One can see from Mankachar hill areas and Dawkie, Pridwa, Cherrapunji hill tops in the monsoon that the whole of Bangladesh is completely inundated by floods, with the worst scenario in Sylhet areas. Therefore, the lebensraum theory is applied here every year and the people rush to India for seeking health, shelter, accommodation, education and work. They are ready to leave their motherland and to accept nationality of some other country either by force or on their own will. It has already generated serious political, economic, social, communal tensions and conflicts not only in Assam and other north-east states of India but also in West Bengal and to some extent in other metro cities where they have already landed in significant numbers. Even though in the beginning, they were welcomed by the Britishers, the tea planters, Assamese and various political leaders of Assam and West Bengal and even now by few political leaders of Assam, yet, such heavy migration triggered agitation first in Assam by all India Assam Union which wanted their entry to stop and made various efforts for about six to seven ears in the eighties. Despite the Assam accord of 1985, no action could be taken on the ground either by government of Assam or their political leaders so far. This issue has remained and will never be solved, as there is no political will and the Bengali Muslim migrants' silent demographic invasion will persist in the whole of north-east, particularly in Assam for years to come, if proper political will is not coming up. The judiciary has instructed several times to contain this illegal migrantions in India, whether it may in Delhi, Kolkata, Rajasthan, Punjab or that in Assam. Various political parties have converted these Hindu migrants as their vote banks. Now they are vying among one another as to which side the migrants will take. The situation in Assam is quite different from that of West Bengal. Assam is a state where, in various districts, the demographic change has already taken place and political pattern is favouring these Muslim migrants. Though none of the political leaders in Assam have ever spoken against these migrants, yet, it was only one of the Governors of Assam— General S.K. Sinha— who highlighted in his report to the honourable President of India on 8th November, 1998 which, in fact, opened the eyes and ears of not only the central government but also those of the entire judiciary, various NGOs and various security agencies all over India. This brief of General Sinha had no effect as far as government of Assam is concerned. A number of steps were taken on the recommendations of General S.K. Sinha and few are still pending.

The General very clearly indicated in his report that this silent demographic invasion of Assam may result in the loss of the geostrategically vital districts of lower Assam. The influx of these migrants is turning these districts into a Muslim majority region. It will be then only be a matter of time when a demand for their merger with Bangladesh may be made. The rapid growth of international Islamic fundamentalism may provide the driving force for this demand. Bangladesh has since long discarded secularism and has chosen to become an Islamic State. Loss of lower Assam will sever the entire landmass of the north-east from the rest of India, and the loss of rich natural resources of that region, will be a blow to the nation economically.

Similar trend has been witnessd in various other states of the north-east, particularly, in Tripura and Meghalaya, which share the border with Bangladesh. In Tripura, the Bengali migrants from Bangladesh have already reduced the local Tripurites population to a minority. Thus to save their culture and ethos, the ethnic locals have formed insurgent groups like that of ATTF (All Tripura Tiger Force) and NLFT (National Liberation Force of Tripura). These Bangladeshis have also changed the demographic pattern of the entire border districts of India with Bangladesh excluding that of Mizoram. Their presence in numbers have been conspicuously felt in Manipur, Nagaland, Meghalaya, Sikkim, Delhi, Rajasthan, Bombay, Pune, Hyderabad, MP, UP, Bihar and Arunachal Pradesh also. Now, they are seen as potential threat bearers as it has been proved in Bombay, Pune, Hyderabad and Bangalore. Some of these migrants give shelter to Bangladeshi militant groups and their Huji leaders, Jamati leaders, the ISI linkmen, the Laskar-e-Toiba, Harkat-ul-Aansar, to name a few. They are the link between the DGFI, the ISI and the Indian Mujahideen. They have also become drug traffickers from Bangladesh, Nepal and Myanmar to India as these migrants have also flooded the Indo-Nepal border in Nepal area and the Indo-Myanmar border in the Myanmar side. The 'golden triangle' and the 'golden crescent' are famous for production of opium and preparation of drugs; similarly, caches of drugs are coming from Pakistan to Bangladesh by Air and by Sea. These drugs find entry into India through the migrants. I well remember a case in which I was travelling on foot from Balurghat Hilly Road to Kalamati Border outpost in North Dinajpur district where the IB is about seven to eight kilometres from the road ahead. I found a person coming in a cycle with a plastic bag in his carrier towards hilly Balurghat road. On being stopped by us, he gave his address as Balurghat but it was quite clear that he was from Bangladesh. To my utter surprise, when I opened the plastic bag in his carrier, I found seven kgs of opium in that. It was a case in the year of 1973, and in all probability, the drug smuggling must have been continuing from all these border areas even till now. The Bangladeshis, particularly the PULF fundamentalists, at a place called Kwakta, in between Moirang and Churachandpur of Manipur state, are involved in getting drugs from Myanmar through Moreh border, which is totally unfenced, and passing on to the hinterland. A number of such consignments from Churachandpur to Kolkata and other parts of the country were seized earlier. These unabated influx of illegal migrants from Bangladesh has not only made perceptible changes in the demographic pattern of Assam and reduced Assamese people into minority in their own state, but also in the case of Tripura reducing its ethnic population into minority. If we see the border adjoining sections of the districts of 24 Parganas, Nadia, Murshidabad, Malda, North Dinajpur, Jalpaiguri and Cooch Behar of West Bengal, we find that the demographic pattern of these areas have already undergone a considerable alteration. In the beginning, in border areas, one could find hundreds of thatched cottages in vacant field, which have been now converted to proper homes with the constructions gradually coming up. These Bangladeshi migrants are now permanent residents of border districts of West Bengal. They are already in possession of voter cards, ration cards and own landed properties. We notice that in

Guwahati and Dispur, many Bangladeshi migrants—who were earlier working as labours and home maids in the houses of residents of these areas—have purchased land and houses from these Assamese owners. They are hard working and earn more, while the Assamese, by and large are lethargic and office-oriented babus, who shirk doing menial jobs. Karimpur is a block and police station in Nadia district in West Bengal, opposite to Khulna and Jessore border of East Bengal. A block before it is Tehetta, and next to it is, Jalangi of Mushidabad. Here you do not think that you are in India. It gives the impression of a place in Bangladesh with associated culture. The border of Tura at Mahendraganj gives a feeling of Pakistan. This mass migration of Muslims to Assam was the core issue behind Assam Student Movement, and thus, was the main contributory factor in mushrooming of various insurgent groups in this state. Until now, Assam conundrum remains unsolved and the whole border of Assam can never be fenced, neither 100 per cent floodlighting can be done, nor can 100 per cent check on illegal migration be made. The Assam students' agitation, the Assam problem, the Assam political atmosphere, the violence in Assam (whether the infights between militant groups or civilians versus migrants), is a matter of grave concern and there is a complete political, bureaucratic and security failure in that state. This illegal migration to Assam now is not a matter that the Assamese or the state will have to deal, rather, it is a matter to be taken up by the centre and all other states together as this malady will spread all over India and it is likely to become a sinus. However, there will be increase in catalysts to add more fuel to fire.

If one travels now from the border of Raiganj through Kaliaganj, Radhikapur, Bindol, Karandighi, Rashakhowa, Borah, Kukradah, Phulbari, Siripur, Patagora, Moragati, Dhanirhat, Haptiaghach, Gowalgachh and Chopra through the West Dinajpur Bangladesh border, one will never get a feeling that he is in India. The atmosphere, the terrain, the culture of the people will by itself appear as if Bangladesh's effect is predominant in all these border areas.

4

What is the Impact

The illegal immigration into India is not only from Bangladesh, but also from Afghanistan, Pakistan, and Chakmas from Rangamati areas of Bangladesh, Burma, Bhutan, Nepal, Tibet, Somalia and Sri Lanka. Yet, the migration of Muslim immigrants from Bangladesh stands as one of the major security concerns for our country. This migration is reported from eastern and north-eastern parts of India from Bangladesh. The situation is expected to worsen further on increase in the frequency of natural disasters in Bangladesh with each passing year and the climate change will necessarily affect Bangladesh in its first phase. The illegal immigration from Bangladesh has led to a demographic upheaval and has generated serious communal, political, social, and economic tensions and conflicts in various cities of our country. The worst affected states are Assam, Meghalaya and Tripura. The lesser threatened are all other north-east states, West Bengal, Sikkim, UP, MP, Maharashtra and Bihar. The unabated influx of illegal immigrants from Bangladesh into north-east, particularly in Assam, and the concomitant change in the demographic pattern of the states, including that of Tripura, are a matter of concern. It has already relegated

Assamese people and ethnic tribals of Tripura to a minority in their own state. The trend of population overflow from Bangladesh is reflected in the words of Sadique Khan, "A natural overflow of population pressure is, therefore, very much on the cards and will not be restrainable by barbed wire or border patrol measures. The natural trend of population overflow from Bangladesh is towards the sparsely populated lands of the south-east in the Arakan side and of the north-east in the Seven Sisters' side of the Indian subcontinent". Abdul Momim, Ex-Secretary, External Affairs, further highlighted the problem of pressure on land in Bangladesh by saying, "Not only that Bangladesh has by far the highest density but also that others have several times more space to expand comfortably."

The Census Commissioner, C. S. Mullan, in 1931, described the infiltration of Muslims in Assam from East Bengal as a serious threat to the indigenous people of Assam. He said: "The whole structure of Assamese culture and civilisation has been threatened by the invasion of a vast horde of land-hungry Bengali immigrants—mostly Muslims, from the district of Eastern Bengal, and in particular, from Mymensingh...it is sad but non-violence in Kokrajhar appears improbable, and that, in another thirty years, Sibsagar district will be the only part of Assam in which an Assamese will find himself at home". (Politics of Regionalism in North-East India, p. 36).

In 1944, Dr. Rajendra Prasad, the first President of India, had also quoted the statement of Census Commissioner—C. S. Mullan, in his famous book 'India Divided', and expressed serious concern over the influx of Muslims in Assam from East Bengal.

5

What are Being Projected?

The core issue behind Assam agitation and all the violence that took place from 1993 onwards is the illegal immigration of Muslims from Bangladesh. It is the major contributory factor for mushrooming of all forms of insurgencies not only in Assam, but in other parts of the north-east too. The country has failed to adopt a decisive policy to contain this devastating migration. This cannot be treated as a regional matter affecting only the ethnic people of Assam, or the Assamese as a whole, but its dimension is much larger and the country has ignored the threat to its national security lurking out from the dangerous propositon of illegal migration of Muslims from Bangladesh. The long cherished motive of a greater Bangladesh making its inroads into Assam and all border districts of West Bengal and Tripura can lead to the shrinking of the entire habitable land of north-east (which is a rich resource of flora, fauna and minerals) from the rest of the country. It will lead to giving a disastrous strategic and economic blow to the country. As VIK Sarin puts it, "The illegal presence of aliens is indeed a national problem. But sadly, the untold hardships and sufferings undergone, and the sacrifice made by the Assamese during the prolonged agitation on the issue have neither moved the national leadership nor the general public in the rest of the country".

While preparing this report, I took into account the related issues at Kokrajhar, Manipur, Mizoram, Silcher, Tura, Khasi, Jaintia, Agartala border and interacted with various political groups, political leaders, Chief Ministers, bureaucrats, panchayat members, Heads of villages, journalists, doctors, lawyers, social workers, government officials, various NGOs operating in north-east, student unions, Meira Peibis, Advocate/MP Shri Sonowal and further visited Mahamaya Char, Mankachar, Borai bari, Dawki, Moreh, Parwa, Lawngtalai, Kawarpuchiah, Hilly, Sutarkandi, Akhwara, Lunglei, Mahendraganj, Changrabandha, Sahebganj, Dimagiri, Kukradah, Islampur, Patagora, Karimganj, Jalangi, Jhaukutty, Satrasal, Petrapole, Radhikapur, Sunderbans, Hamjapur, Balurghat and Karimpur. I also discussed with various Christian missionaries, members of various apprehended militant groups operating all over the north-east— both hill and valley-based—like, NSCN-IM, NSCN-K, ULFA, PLA, PREPAK, MPLF, MULTA, ANVC, NDFB, DHDJ, KLNLF, AASU, few Mullahs of madrasas, tea estate workers in Silchar, Meities from Imphal, ZRA, HMAR, Kuki groups, KYKL(O) and Rohingya Muslims. I had also discussed the issue with locals—opposite Manipur border— towards Myanmar, Chakmas— opposite Mizoram, in Bangladesh side, the BDR(BGB), Bangladesh police, villagers and boat owners of various char islands like Masalabari, Saitanbari, Majuli of 13/14 districts of Assam in river Brahmaputra by boat. I also met landowners of adverse possession cases (land of Bangladesh in India and India in Bangladesh), villagers of Bangladesh enclaves in India like Dahagram, Teen bigha, Kuchlibari, etc. Similarly, I visited extensively all the customs and ICP's, excise and border police stations, and Border outposts of BSF along Indo-Bangladesh border, Indo-Myanmar border and in the states of Nagaland, Manipur, Tripura, Meghalaya, Assam, West Bengal, Mizoram including holding discussion with the field officers working there. I also had the chance of supervising border fencing and floodlighting works along Indo-Bangladesh border in Assam, Meghalaya and Mizoram, including holding Barak valley of Silchar area, the Tura border and also few permanent Char Islands inside river Brahmaputra where, as a very special case, the demarcation has been made through border fencing, putting floodlights and carrying all those heavy equipments and machineries during monsoon in river Brahmaputra on number of open boats tied up in making a single vessel. I extensively toured border areas of Assam contiguous with Bangladesh, Nagaland with Myanmar, Manipur with Myanmar, Mizoram with Bangladesh, Meghalaya with Bangladesh and Tripura with Bangladesh. I also made visits to hundreds of border outposts of BSF and studied the ethnic, cultural, socio-economic, terrain and customs of the people living at the border. My recommendations and views are absolutely realistic as I also had a chance to visit Kokrajhar, Chirang, Udalguri, Baksa, Sonitpur—riot affected districts, and the entire Bodo areas in 2010 for about three months witnessing all the refugee camps sheltering about 2.5 lakhs people of various communities in Kokrajhar, Baksa, Udalguri, Chirang, Sonitpur and Dhubri districts. Most of the aspects connected with the illegal immigration have been examined. The recommendations given are based on my own experience at the border from 1971 until 2009. All the tactical steps, whether soft or harsh, that need to be taken to effectively arrest the ongoing influx of illegal immigrants and its adverse effects on national security, and the practices now to be followed for checking large scale illegal immigration, which has already taken place, have been penned. Large-scale migration from East Bengal / East Pakistan / Bangladesh has made the situation very complex.

ILLEGAL IMMIGRANTS AND REFUGEES IN INDIA

An illegal immigrant is a foreigner who enters India without proper passport or travel documents or enters India with valid documents but remains beyond prescribed / permitted period.

A refugee is a person, who, owing to well-founded fear of being persecuted for the reasons of his race, religion, nationality, membership of a particular social group or political opinion, is outside the country of its nationality and is unable, or owing to such fear, is unwilling to avail himself of the protection of that country, or who, not having a nationality and being outside the country of his formal habitual residence, is unable, or owing to such fear, is unwilling to return to it. Refugee is more or less a political term. A refugee can be a migrant. It can be his/her personal choice to be a refugee. However, a migrant is not necessarily a refugee. We have a number of ecological and environmental migrants. Forced migrants of one State are generally refugees in the other.

We have in our country refugees and illegal immigrants from Tibet, Pakistan, Bangladesh, Afghanistan, Bhutan, Myanamar, Sri Lanka, Somalia, and specifically, Chakmas from Bangladesh.

Tibetan Refugees

As far as Tibetans are concerned, since 1959, Dalai Lama and thousands of his followers entered India and are living in exile. The first wave of Tibetans in 1959 was termed as 'exoduses' by U.N general assembly in 1961. Dalai Lama and others, who came in the first group were not given the status of refugees, even though they were treated as refugees in our country. As far as their legal status is concerned, they do not qualify as refugees and remained legally as Stateless persons under Indian law. We have about 1.5 lakhs of Tibetan refugees staying in India. All the refugees (about 25,000) who came in the first 'exodus' in 1959 along with Dalai Lama were given full logistical support, financial help, and aid from various NGOs, including houses and land. All Tibetans who entered India between 1950 to 1960 were accorded informal refugee status. India is not a party to 1951 United Nations convention relating to status of refugees, or the 1967 protocol. The Tibetans have been given residence permit and few of them got formal employment and have been issued with registration certificate (RC) from the Central Tibetans Administration. The RCs do not give Tibetan refugees any formal legal status; it only permits these Tibetans to settle at different settlement camps in various states of India. All the scattered communities of Tibetans live in these designated camps under the CTA at Dharmshala where the headquarters of Dalai Lama is situated. Mostly, all the Tibetan refugees are engaged in agriculture, agro-industries and handicraft business. Tibetans are also issued with identity certificates (IC) which enable them to enter India legally. However, the IC has to be stamped "no objection to return to India" on it. Some of the Tibetans, who are now entering India, are only given special entry permits (SEPs). It is meant for those who come for pilgrimage, education and various other activities involving few months. It is the government of Maharashtra which has opened a special camp at Bandhara for accommodating Tibetans. These refugees have kept their art and culture intact and they have schools in Tibetan language for their children in the camp also. In 2011, Dalai Lama has handed over the political power he was enjoying, to Kalon Tripa. Recently, it has been rechristened from Kalon Tripa to Sikyong. The Tibetans are not in favour of asking for Indian citizenship, as they are quite confident that Tibet's political situation will change in future and those who are in exile will return to their homeland. In 2009, the Delhi High Court has passed a judgement supporting the right of a Tibetan born in India to claim Indian citizenship as per Indian Citizenship Act (CA) 3(1) (a) i.e. in the case of Namgyal Dolkar. It states that every person born in India on or after 26th January 1950, and before 1st July, 1987 shall be a citizen of India by birth. The government of Mysore/ Karnataka was the first state to have granted a large forest area for the settlement of Tibetans on being requested by the then Indian Prime Minister Pandit Nehru. [Refer note of Sri A K Doval (Director, VIF)]

Pak-Hindu Refugees

A number of Hindu families from Pakistan entered India during 1965 numbering about 1.15 lakhs. However, they were not given refugee status and a number of them had been staying in Jammu and Amritsar. It has been seen in last two or three years that a number of Hindu families started coming to take asylum in India. Out of them, 150 families are now at Amritsar. About 145 families entered India from Pakistan in 2010. 54 Hindu families were reported to have come in 2011. In mere last 12 months, 400 Hindus families have arrived from Pakistan. Earlier, Hindu refugees came from Pakistan's Sind/Punjab fearing persecution and harassment. Such penetration into India was also reported immediately after 1965 and 1971 wars. They also came in 1970, just before the war and in 1980. In 1992, after Babri Masjid demolition in Ayodhya, there was a backlash in Pakistan and Hindu refugees started leaving Pakistan to India. 1.15 lakhs Hindu refugees who arrived from Pakistan since 1965 are now habilitated in Rajasthan, Gujarat, and Amritsar but they are not being given refugee status. They do not have residence permit and face many difficulties to get employment. It was only in 2005/2006 that about 13,000 Hindu refugees from Pakistan were granted Indian citizenship.

Burmese Refugees

It was in 1988 that, about 3,000 refugees from erstwhile Burma, now Myanmar, have entered India and most of them are living in Mizoram. They were given refugee status by UNHCR.

Chakma Refugees

About 30,000 Chakmas migrated to Arunachal Pradesh after being persecuted in Bangladesh (erstwhile East Pakistan). This displacement took place due to communal violence against Chakmas in that region. Their present numbers in Arunachal Pradesh has grown to 60,000. They are not being treated as Indian citizens. Mostly, they were occupying areas in Chittagong hill tracts of Bangladesh. On 9th January 1996, Hon'ble Supreme Court in its judgement has passed a verdict directing the Arunachal Pradesh government that none of these Chakmas will be deprived of their life or liberty without due process of law. Government of India has given citizenship to Bangladeshi immigrants who came before 24th March, 1971, and it has been decided that they will not be evicted. In this case, the Chakmas had entered India in between 1964 and 1969. Though they are illegal migrants and had an unauthorised entry to India, but until today, they have not been granted refugee status. Arunachal Pradesh has given voting rights to 1500 Chakmas so far. The homeland of the Chakma tribe is the Chittagong Hill Tract. Chittagong Hill Tract was carved in 1860 and Britishers framed CHT Act in 1900. The migration to Chittagong was restricted by the Government of India Act, 1935. It was earlier declared as an excluded area. During partition, Chakmas thought that Chittagong Hill Tract would be annexed to India, as it had only three per cent Muslim population. Sardar Patel addressed a letter to Sir Radcliffe, the chairperson of the boundary commission between India and Pakistan to keep CHT annexed to India and not to East Pakistan. Both Sardar Patel and Jawaharlal Nehru took up the case with Viceroy Lord Mount Batten to retain CHT in India only. Liyakat Ali Khan first agreed to this proposal of Sardar Patel but, changed his mind later and claimed CHT for Pakistan. The Chakma issue could not be pursued further and Chakma remained in East Bengal as people with extra territorial loyalty. The construction of hydroelectric dam on river Karnaphuli deprived Chakmas of their fertile agricultural land. Because of torture in East Pakistan, 40,000 number took refuse in India in 1964 and about 1.4 lakhs Chakmas further came to India between 1964 and 1969. Out of these 1.4 lakhs, 15,000 Chakma refugees were sent to NEFA, now Arunachal Pradesh. Chakmas were not treated well by Bengali Muslims in East Pakistan neither during the period of Zia-Ur-Rehman nor that of Irshad. As regards Chakmas, who migrated to Arunachal Pradesh in 1964, the state is duty bound to protect the threatened Chakmas and carry out its legal obligations to safeguard the life, health and well-being of Chakmas in the state. No political party can forcibly evict or drive the Chakmas out of Arunachal Pradesh. The Chakmas shall not be denied domestic life and comfort in accordance with law. The applications for acquisition of citizenship of India by the Chakmas can be submitted to the collector or the DC as per the rules, who will forward the same to the Central Government for its consideration as per law.

Work permits are issued to Tamilians from Sri Lanka, Chakmas and Afghanistan at the point of entry while coming to India.

Somali Refugees

India has about 400 refugees from Somalia; and as per UNHCR mandate, they are enjoying refugees status.

Palestinian Refugees

India has about 160 Palestinian refugees and they have been accorded full refugee status as per mandate of UNHCR.

Afghan Refugees

India has about 70,000 Afghan refugees within its territory. Of these, 60,000 entered India after Soviet invasion in 1979. Similarly, 9000 more refugees, that are Afghans, entered India after 1992 when Nazibullah regime fell. These Afghan refugees are recognised and protected under UNHCR.

Bhutanese Refugees

About 30,000 ethnic Nepalese from Bhutan entered India in 1980. They are permitted to move freely across Indian border as per the Treaty, which was updated in 2007. They are not being treated as refugees in India.

Sri Lankan Refugees

Most of the Sri Lankan refugees are treated as illegal immigrants in India and they came to Tamil Nadu after crossing the Palk Strait, onto Rameshwaram area, where the government of Tamil Nadu opened 120 settlement camps and about 72,000 Tamil migrants were accommodated in these camps while 30,000 remained outside. Until now, their numbers are more than one lakh in India. They are being provided with education and health care only. No refugee status or political asylum has been given to such Tamil, Sri Lankan migrants.

Bangladeshi Immigrants

These immigrants have caused maximum worry to the government as their numbers are more than all refugees/ illegal immigrants combined, that are present in India, belonging to most of the countries of the world. Those who came during 1965 to 1971, after both wars with Pakistan, were settled in West Bengal, Dandakaranya in Malkangiri, Odisha, Barak Valley in Assam, Tripura, and Chittranjan Park in New Delhi. Even today, Hindu refugees from Bangladesh are fleeing to West Bengal. It is quite surprising that Shri Prakash Karat, the leader of CPI(M) has given a letter to the Prime Minister on 26th May 2012 to provide Indian citizenship to Bangladesh refugees and for amendment of the Citizenship Act. It was reported that until end of 1971, about 47 lakhs Hindu refugees entered India from Bangladesh. Due to terror of Pakistani Army and Pakistani Punjabis in East Pakistan, about 10 million of Hindus entered India. Since 1947, until 2001, the Hindu population in Bangladesh went down from 30 per cent to 10 per cent. If a census has to be conducted now, perhaps, Hindu population in Bangladesh might record a decline to five per cent as the influx is still continuing, remains unabated and it is possible for these migrants to come to West Bengal, both through riverine border and the Sundarbans. It is not only that the Hindu refugees have entered India; in fact, Bengali Muslims are also migrating to north-east in large numbers after 1975. Their first phase of migration was during British period and later during 1975, being the vote bank for the political groups in Assam. Their ultimate motive is for a greater Bangladesh, by increasing the population of Muslims not only in Assam but also in Tripura and all the border districts of India with Bangladesh starting from 24 Parganas upto Agartala.

Though most of the refugees from all these countries are treated as Stateless nationals in India, yet, because of political reasons and enormous presence of Bangladeshis, these people have an advantage in India in manipulating their citizenship and they were welcomed by various states like that of West Bengal and Assam.

There is no denying that New Delhi's task of furthering ties with Dhaka has been made more difficult following West Bengal chief minister Mamata Banerjee's pullout from the UPA. For example, the Teesta water sharing issue. Mamata had scuttled the Teesta deal once. Given the political games she likes to play, she may now try to go against the Land Boundary Agreement (LBA). The LBA, which will fully demarcate the India-Bangladesh land border and facilitate the exchange of enclaves, still awaits ratification in the Indian Parliament through a constitutional amendment. Both Teesta and the LBA are significant political issues in Bangladesh. Failure to deliver on either will be perceived as a setback to bilateral ties.

Both sides have signed agreements to combat organised crime and illegal drug trafficking and implement a coordinated border management plan. However, resources on the ground remain inadequate. Rectifying this is crucial to tackling crime and avoiding unnecessary deaths in the border areas.

Meanwhile, in gross violation of human rights, several Indian and Bangladeshi citizens continue to languish as under trials in each other's jails for years without any proper legal representation. According to estimates, there are 186 Indians in Bangladeshi jails whereas West Bengal alone has 309 Bangladeshi inmates in its prisons. Instituting a proper legal mechanism to assist those undertrials in each other's country would earn both New Delhi and Dhaka a significant amount of goodwill. Mutually beneficial ties with Bangladesh are crucial to India's Look East policy. With Bangladeshi leader of opposition Khaleda Zia's visit to India in October 2012, it was a good opportunity to improve ties with our eastern neighbour (Ref TOI editorial of 22nd October, 2012).

6

History

Colonial Period

Settlers: In 1912, Assam was carved out of East Bengal. During that time, mostly Assamese, allowed people from various states to pour into Assam including those from East Bengal on contract basis with a hope that after the end of the contract, these people would go back which did not happen. The inflow of population from Sylhet, Dhaka, Mymensingh and Rangpur increased to seek employment in the north-east area.

It was from 1826 to 1840, that the tea plantation in Assam was started by the Britishers, on being influenced by one Maniram Dutta Barua, an Assamese aristocrat, who first started the tea plantation. This trade was expanded and then the Britishers arranged tribal labourers for working in tea gardens. It attracted Bengali Muslims from East Bengal to settle in riverbanks all along Brahmaputra valley. Since then, after a century, the continuous unabated penetration of Bengali Muslims kept on occurring from Bangladesh to Assam. It resulted in change in demographic pattern of the state of Assam and its many districts, which had reduced the local people into minority. The migration initially was for economic reasons. Sir Syed Sadaullah, who ruled Assam in 1940s, has had a lot of missionary zeal to settle Bengal Muslims in Assam on a cover programme 'grow more food'. The then viceroy Lord Wavell described it as a 'grow more Muslims' campaign. The Bengali Muslim immigrants invaded Char island of undivided Goalpara district in 1921; their scouts first occupied the empty islands and a huge population followed closely after that. Thousands of Bengali Muslims practically tookover the district of Goalpara and wherever they found wasteland, those Mymensinghias occupied them. They seized all vacant areas in Assam valley without any fuss, without any trouble, and district revenue staff helped them in settling five lakhs of East Bengal Muslims into Assam valley in about 25 years.

It is only, then, the government of Assam is to be blamed for allowing this mass movement of Bangladeshi Muslims to its soil. Sibsagar was the only district where the Assamese revolted and grouped together to stop entry of Bangladeshis to that district.

Bengali-speaking areas comprised of the territory of Bangladesh and the Indian state of West Bengal as well as parts of Assam and Tripura. During the rule of Hindu Sena dynasty in Bengal, the notion of a Greater Bangladesh first emerged with the idea of uniting Bengali speaking people in the Odisha, Bihar, Assam, Tripura and Meghalaya along with Bengal. These areas were formed under Bengal Presidency, a province of British India that was carved out in 1765. Assam, including Meghalaya and Sylhet, were removed from the Presidency in 1874. Bengal Presidency was further partitioned in 1947 into Hindu Majority in West Bengal and Muslim Majority in East Bengal (Bangladesh). This was made to create a separate Muslim State of Pakistan and East Bengal became a separate province.

The partition was annulled in 1911 and Assam again became a separate province. The real invasion of north-east by East Bengal Muslims had commenced from 1940s. During that period, Assam had a Muslim League ministry headed by Sir Said Sadaullah, who was the pioneer in settling East Bengal Muslims in Assam under a programme known as "Grow More Food" which was described by then Viceroy Lord Wavell in his book "Viceroys Journal" as "Grow More Muslims" Programme. During 1931, the then Commissioner, C.S. Mullan gave a forewarning that Assamese are going to be "endangered species". This prediction of Shri Mullan can now found to be true as 40 per cent of the districts of Assam are now in Muslim majority and the Assamese have become minority in their own state.

When the Britishers occupied the north-east, the area was uninhabited and mostly the local tribals, having rivalries with one another, were available in various pockets. Initially under the British, the immigrants from East Bengal were welcomed and used for development of the north-east soil, for cultivation. However, these immigrants were considered as encroachers on the lands of local tribals and various ethnic groups as they took away all the reserve forest areas and forcibly occupied it affecting adversely the demography and ecology of a number of north-eastern states. In 1920, the British introduced inner line system to restrict Bengal Muslim immigrants from East Bengal but they were not successful in their effort. It is because of better economic prospects, shortage of local labour, and lack of sufficient mechanism, which were the main reasons for the influx of East Bengal immigrants.

Later on, the Indira-Mujeeb Agreement, 1972 defined the status of illegal immigration in India and it was agreed that those who came before 1971 operation were declared as Non-Bangladeshis. This Indira-Mujeeb agreement was badly resented by the people of the north-east and they started agitation against this Accord by their ethnic and tribal groups. Because of partition of Bengal in 1905, Assam was merged with East Bengal and the Assamese became a minority. Assamese have become minority in their own state now.

In January 1947, Sarat Chandra Bose resigned from the Indian National Congress in protest against the partition of Bengal. He wanted an independent Bengal separate from both India and Pakistan and formed his own party, the Socialist Republic Party. Hussain Shaheed Suhrawardy and Abul Hashem, the two leaders of Muslim League, comprising of both East Bengal and West Bengal, supported him. Akram Khan, a politician and Khawaja Nazimuddin of Muslim League wanted a united Bengal as part of Pakistan. Shri Shyama Prasad Mookherjee, the founder of Bharatiya Jana Sangh and Akhil Bharatiya Hindu Mahasabha opposed the idea of independent Bengal and they were concerned about both Sarat Chandra Bose and Hussain Shaheed Suhrawardy for favouring idea of making sovereign state of Bengal. Jawaharlal Nehru was also a force, in not taking the side of Sarat Chandra Bose, and opposed a united Bengal, i.e., to opt out of Union of India.

The process to check illegal immigration in the north-east, which started during the British period, remains unchecked despite various efforts made by the Central Government and the border states of the Government of India. When the Britishers occupied the north-east, the area was uninhabited and mostly the local tribals, having rivalries with one another, existed in various pockets. They were the better economic prospects, shortage of local labour, and absence of sufficient mechanism, which were the main reasons for the influx of East Bengal immigrants.

At the Time of Partition

Migrants: The problem of illegal immigration took a menacing turn after partition of the country. Since then, the East Pakistan government and Pakistani Army had made the life of Hindus miserable and insecure. As such, after partition, they began to migrate in large numbers from Sylhet to Assam.

During partition, Pakistan had visualised that it would comprise of Muslim majority provinces in the west and Bang-e-Islam, comprising Bengal and Assam, in the east. Mainul Haque Choudhury, then PS to Md. Ali Jinnah said to Jinnah that he will present Assam to him in a silver plate. Jinnah confidently declared in Guwahati that Assam was in his pocket. Mainul Haque Choudhury later on, became a minister in Assam and a minister in Union government.

The Cabinet Mission Plan placed Assam in group C with Bengal. Both the Congress high command and the Muslim League accepted the grouping plan but Gopinath Bardoloi vehemently opposed it, supported by Mahatma Gandhi and the plan could thus be foiled, and Assam was saved from becoming a part of Pakistan (now Bangladesh).

Pakistan's failure to get Assam was a source of heartburn in that country. Zulifikar Ali Bhutto, in his book 'Myths of Independence' wrote, "It would be wrong to think that Kashmir is the only dispute that divides India and Pakistan though undoubtedly the most significant. One, which at least is nearly as important as the Kashmir dispute, is that of Assam and some districts of India, adjacent to East Pakistan. To these, Pakistan has very good claim".

Sheikh Mujibur Rehman in his book 'East Pakistan: its population and economics' observed "Because Eastern Pakistan must have sufficient land for its expansion and because Assam has abundant forests and mineral resources, coal, petroleum, etc., Eastern Pakistan must include Assam to be financially and economically strong" (Assam in this sense included whole of northeast and not merely present Assam).

The desire of Muslims to annex Assam to East Pakistan during independence remained unfulfilled. Mainul Haq Choudhury, who was a minister in Assam government during independence, and worked with Mohd. Ali Jinnah, was the mastermind in getting East Bengal Muslims to Assam and helping them to settle in government vacant lands. It was more than the Muslim farmers who were brought during British regime to Assam particularly to Silchar belt for tea plantation.

In the year 1937, Sadaulla formed the minority Muslim League government and became the Chief Minister of Assam. During his tenure, he brought a huge number of Muslims from erstwhile East Pakistan, the present Bangladesh, to fill up the sparsely populated Bodo villages. As a result, Muslims up to a tune of 20,000, were brought to Dalgaon in a single day. Bangladeshi Muslims have started settling there since then, multiplying in a geometrical progression through polygamy. Again, in 1971, during the Indo-Pak-Bangladesh war, lakhs of Bangladeshi Muslims entered every nook and corner of Assam crossing the borders. Thousands of them came via Dhubri, got down virtually at every railway station, including Udalguri and Darrang districts. There were serious objections all over regarding the unending inflow of Muslims into Assam. The Assam government too was serious at that time and took up the matter with the central government. The then Prime Minister, Smt. Indira Gandhi, however, appealed that the people should consider it on humanitarian grounds, assuring that once the war is over, she would take up the matter with the Bangladesh Government to deport them back; which she never did. This was the root cause of the large scale "Assam Agitation" during the last seventees and eightees of twentieth century.

Pre – 1971 War: Refugees— When the Britishers left India; the north-east was not affected by riots. However, uncertainty prevailed due to influx of refugees, who came in droves from most of the districts of East Bengal to the border districts of India. Consequently, this large-scale migration had a social, economic, political and environmental effect leading to the people of north-east voicing their concern, whereas, in the beginning, the West Bengal kept on absorbing the Hindu immigrants. The explosive dimension, noticed soon after the independence, forced the centre to pass the Immigrant Act, 1950 in the Parliament stating people who were displaced because of civil disturbances in East Pakistan, could migrate to India. Due to Nehru-Liyakat Ali Khan Agreement of 8th April, 1950, the Indians who were deported until 31st December, 1950, were allowed to return to India. During the Indo-China War 1962, it was reported that some infiltrators came with Pakistani Flag. This resulted in adoption of the Prevention of the Infiltration of Pakistanis to Assam Plan (1964). Due to atrocities committed by Pakistani Punjabis in East of Pakistan before 1971 operation, Bangladesh refugees poured into India on a large scale. 'The Silent Invasion' by Hiranya Kumar Bhattacharyya, p. 6.

Way back in the fifties of the last century, Indira's favourite, if not blue-eyed boy, had without any reservation voiced his design in respect of the north-east of India; Sheikh Majibur Rehman in his 'Eastern Pakistan: Its Population Determination and Economics', which, briefly speaking, may be summarised as follows:

"The huge population of Bangladesh is an asset; Assam is full of forest resources. In addition, Assam has abundant resources in the coal and petroleum sector. Which is why, Assam must be a part of East Pakistan (Bangladesh was then yet to be born). Then only, the economy of East Pakistan would prosper..."

After 1971 : Illegal Migrants

Came with them about six lakhs of Bihari Muslims, who were earlier kept in various camps in Dhaka and its surrounding area by Pakistani Army and Pakistani Punjabis to help them in controlling Bangladeshis. Out of such 10 lakh population of Bihari Muslims, about six lakhs left the camp after 1971 operation when Pakistan Army left Bangladesh. These Bihari Muslims had desired to go back to Pakistan but Pakistan government did not allow them to enter. The new Bangladesh government and Bengali speaking Bangladeshis did not like them to continue to remain in Bangladesh. Such Bihari Muslims had their families entered India in Maldah, West Dinajpur, Siliguri border, crossing Mahananda river and the land border, both day and night, from 1972 to 1975. Mostly, their penetration was through Narayanpur, Radhikapur, Haptiyagach, Bindol, Kaliaganj, Raiganj, Khurka, Kaderganj, Bora, Dangapora, Phulbari, Sripur, Kukradah, Moragati, Patagora, Sonamati, Hatkhola, Chopra, Dhanirhat, Dalkhola, Siliguri, Islampur and Panjipara border. These Bihari Muslims first tried to go to western border to enter Pakistan but as they were apprehended, they refrained from going to Pakistan and settled in Purnea, Kishanganj, Panjipara, Dalkhola, and Islampur belt of Bengal-Bihar border. Even now, this area, cannot be ruled out as being a hub and activities having link with the Pakistani Army and ISI. This is a big patch near Siliguri corridor where all these Bihari Muslims can manage their link with ISI through Nepal border, which is very close from Kishanganj, Panjipara and Islampur. Their locations are in the borders of two states and very close to Nepal and Bangladesh border. The ISI finds it as a heaven for making it one of their best camps in India. These are some of the villages on both sides of the national highway who are not culturally similar to Biharis or Bengalis. As they were having their link in India earlier, their penetration after 1971 operation from Bangladesh through the border was very easy, and they could easily mix up with Indian population in Kishanganj and Islampur border as the terrain was very familiar to them. This was the lot whose penetration to India was facilitated by the old Bangladesh Rifles, as Bihari Muslims were earlier working with BDR, whose officers were all from Pakistani Army. I have personally seen such groups concentrating in these villages after crossing the border in 1972-73. They were not like Bangladeshi Hindu migrants but were quite rough and tough and used to speak in Hindi better than what Bengalis do. Their entry was not through touts but they found their own way and never bothered for both the border-guarding forces of Bangladesh and India. As even now, whatever foreign goods are available in Siliguri market and Nepal border of Siliguri; more better foreign products are available in Panjipara and Islampur markets. Bihari Muslims bring mostly the foreign goods from Bangladesh through their contacts in Chittagong, Cox's bazaar, Khulna and other ports of Bangladesh. Practically, border was free that time and no fencing, floodlights, or bundhs were available at the border. Even the border outposts were then of platoon or section strength, which were located at a distance of seven to nine kilometres from each other, thus keeping a long gap. Rainy season, winter foggy morning, winter night was the easiest time to cross the border because of lack of strength of border guarding forces then existing at the Bangladesh border.

Later on, the Indira-Mujeeb Agreement, 1972 defined the status of illegal immigration in India and it was agreed that those who came before 1971 operation were declared as non-Bangladeshis. This Indira Mujeeb agreement was stoutly resented by the people of the north-east and they started agitation against this Accord through their ethnic and tribal groups. Even after the creation of Bangladesh in 1971, the illegal immigration did not stop. Mostly, the Hindus in large numbers left their landed properties and all materials in Bangladesh and came in batches to India, particularly to West Bengal from 1971 to 1975. As a young officer, I have personally seen these Hindus refugees coming in hundreds and crossing the open border where there was no fencing just to seek protection, a place to stay, anything to work, and a handful of rice to eat. There were no provisions by Government of India that time even to feed these Hindu refugees coming in large numbers from Bangladesh through river Ichhamati, the Sunderbans, the 24 Parganas border, the Banpur / Petra pole areas, Nadia, Murshidabad, Maldah, West Dinajpur, Jalpaiguri, and Cooch Behar districts. There was even no vehicle available to carry them all from the border to hand over them to the border police station or the nearest police station. The officer-in-charge of the police station also had no funds with him to give food for 24 hours to these apprehended Hindu refugees. He also had no transport system to take them to the court and to submit charge sheet against them. He had no place in the police station to keep so many refugees. There were no working hands in police stations to prepare cases against all such refugees coming from Bangladesh under the Foreigners Act. There were children below eight or 10 years of age begging and crying for food. There were women with infants requesting for mercy to give a handful of rice to feed their child. There were young Hindu girls who came after being raped on the opposite side by criminals. The security system at the border was paralysed and was not efficient in tackling these problems at that time. Due to political reasons and suffering, being oppressed, such Hindu refugees were pouring not only at night, even during day time. I was an eyewitness to this and was completely helpless. I thought of bringing it open in a paper of mine. That was the time when about 10 millions of Hindu refugees *per force*, entered India from Bangladesh. There was no protection at the international border; they were welcomed in all over West Bengal and mostly all of these Hindu immigrants, by 1975, were settled in West Bengal itself as they had similar culture, ethnicity, social bond, and language.

Besides Hindus, the influx of Muslim migrants in lakhs was also reported more so after 1971, when Bangladesh was made, and again in 1975, after Sheikh Mujibur Rehman was assassinated. These Muslim migrations cannot be compared with that of the Hindu migration reported earlier from the West Bengal-Bangladesh border. The Muslim immigrants came with an ulterior motive and penetrated through the borders of most of the border districts of West Bengal, i.e., 24 Parganas to Cooch Behar and the entire north-east border of Assam, Meghalaya and of Tripura with Bangladesh. Their main fulcrum and target was Assam. Before independence, Muslim peasantry from East Bengal were crossing over to the fertile lands of thinly populated Brahmaputra and Surma valleys in the north-east of India. The All India Muslim League in Dhaka encouraged the migration to increase the Muslim population in Assam for political reasons. The alarming forecast of census superintendent, Shri C S Mullan, in his report of 1931, exposed this political design of Muslim League of Dhaka. He went to the extent of stating that the demographic feature of Assam will be destroyed permanently and these land-hungry Muslim immigrants from border districts of East Bengal will one day decide the future of Assam and ruin the Assamese culture and the civilisation. The Assamese are also to be blamed at their end to receive these Muslim migrants and welcoming them, employing them for their survival and providing them living space both in their houses and in government lands.

The situation of illegal migration worsened after Bangladesh was formed in 1971 and their economy was shattered, the administration was paralysed, the social structure was fragmented and the Bangladeshis could not decide about their future. Due to pressure of displacement of persons from coastal areas and flood-hit areas, the surplus people started their way to find space in India. On 9th May, 1975, it was stated in Rajya Sabha that due to severe floods in Bangladesh in 1974, which aggravated conditions of scarcity and hardships in certain areas, sizeable movements of persons was observed from Bangladesh into the neighbouring states, particularly to West Bengal, which started taking place from July, 1974. It was also stated in Rajya Sabha that the BSF succeeded in preventing the entry of 39,000 personnel from Bangladesh. Particularly, this discussion in Rajya Sabha may not be fully correct. All these 39,000 persons might have taken another way for their entry into India that time itself, as the border was completely open and porous without any barbed wire fencing and the distance of BOPs was more than seven kilometres and there was no technical up-gradation of BSF that time. I have seen during that period of 1974 and 1975, that in monsoon, most of the boundary pillars were submerged under water. The complete border was open to these Hindu migrants and that was not the time when the border guarding force could have guarded the border during night hours under seven to eight feet of water. As long as Sheikh Mujibur Rehman was in power up to August 1975, the government of Bangladesh was not putting official pressure on their people for migration to India. However, after the assassination of Sheikh Mujibur Rehman, the whole government machinery, Bangladesh Army, the Bangladesh Rifles and the Jamatis, including Muslim League, encouraged, both—Muslim migration for attaining their aim to make a greater Bangladesh, and eviction of Hindus, using pressure tactics.

Even Bangladesh tried to push a large number of people to enter India with permits, which were taken up with Bangladesh, but Bangladesh government dismissed the report of such exodus as baseless and misleading. They only replied that those Indian nationals, who migrated to Bangladesh sometime before 1971 operation, were allowed to return to India under special permits. People from Jessore and Khulna entered from Gede, Metehari, and Banpur border and availed direct train journey from Banpur to Calcutta/ Sealdah in thousands.

The illegal crossing continued from muddy paddy fields during dark hours, through riverine border and through Char Islands of river Brahmaputra. Thousands of Hindus left their homes in Barisal district and entered India. A number of Hindu migrants came from Khulna and Pawna district and entered through West Dinajpur border. In one case, my men apprehended one Odia family of Khurdha district coming from Bangladesh. I happened to interrogate this family at Hilly myself. It transpired that they had their own land in Pawna district since their ancestors and due to fear and oppression; they had no other option than to come back to India, to go to Odisha to meet and stay with their own relatives. However, this family was handed over as usual to Hilly police station and they disappeared like millions of migrants coming from Bangladesh to India. Until today, whatever Hindu migration is now taking place in small numbers, mostly is in the West Bengal border, that is, from 24 Parganas up to Krishnanagar. The Muslim migration, in hordes, invaded north-east, particularly Assam, after 1971 and mostly after 1975.

This continuous flow was from Khasi, Jaintia, Tura and Garo Hills border of Meghalaya, the whole of Karimganj border of Silchar belt, the whole of Tripura border and lastly the great Char Islands of mighty Brahmaputra, which till date are assessed to be as the biggest route of penetration of Muslim immigrants to the whole of Assam and north-east, particularly to Goalpara, Dhubri, Kokrajhar, Sonitpur, Udalguri, Baksa, Nagaon and Chirang districts. The influx of illegal migrants from Bangladesh increased substantially after 1971. The then Chief Election Commissioner of India, in the year 1978, had pointed out, "The influx has become a regular feature. I think it may not be a wrong assessment to make on this basis, of an increase of 34.95 per cent between the two censuses; the increase that is likely to be recorded in the 1991 census would be more than

100 per cent over the 1961 census. In other words, a stage would be reached when the state may have to reckon with the foreign nationals who may in all probability constitute a sizeable percentage if not majority population in the state."

Once these people managed to cross the international boundary, there was no system to track them in the hinterland. The border-guarding forces had no jurisdiction to prosecute these illegal immigrants and in most of the cases (from 1970 to 1980), the immigrants could not be prosecuted as they could not be handed over to police, nor could be charge-sheeted and produced before the court. In earlier days, in a single entry case, it was difficult to identify a Bangladeshi national due to passive and indifferent attitude of border population towards illegal migrants. We had a number of unauthorised and unlicensed boats in the riverine belts of the Indo-Bangladesh border, which facilitated ferrying illegal immigrants from Bangladesh to India. Out of 4,096 kilometres long Indo-Bangladesh border, 1,116.2 kilometres is riverine and 2,979.5 kilometres is land border. Only 719.16 kilometres of riverine border is feasible for erection of fence while remaining 397.04 kilometres is not feasible. Major rivers like Ganga, Brahmaputra, Gangadhar, and Jinjiram used to rapidly change their courses causing severe erosion in the area and making international border fluid. Each of these rivers has numerous channels. Riverine area, being interspersed with water-channels and cultivated fields, could not be covered by visual observation round the clock. The infiltrators easily sneaked through the blind gaps on the border in the absence of proper border fencing. The total riverine area and the Char lands were devoid of landmarks. Patrolling in riverine area and Char lands in general, caused serious navigational problem. The mobility in riverine area is restricted to boats.

These illegal migrants have made substantial perceptive changes in demographic pattern of West Bengal, Assam, Tripura and Sikkim. It resulted in outbreak of insurgencies in various states and now had become an issue of national security. The sense of alienation felt by the people of the north-east is best reflected in the words of Rajmohan Gandhi who said, "The rest of India does not see us. If seen, we are not recognised. If recognised, we are not remembered. And we are not heard. This has been the charge of the citizens of the north-east against the Indian majority." This feeling is even stronger in the state of Assam. As Myron Weiner puts it, "The Assamese often think of themselves as a 'forgotten' and 'neglected' state within the Indian Union and as a neglected people in danger of being overwhelmed by migrant people and absorbed by neighbouring states." The design of Greater Bangladesh will have a great impact on strategic and economic issues. Therefore, practical steps have to be taken for arresting ongoing influx of illegal immigrants, which has already taken place on a large scale and has posed huge economic, security and social problem for our nation. The border, since ages, remained porous, and until 1990, there was no fencing and when single lane fencing was constructed in West Bengal international border, it was only futile expenditure of money without getting any result, as, most of the time, the fencing remained submerged under water and at various places, they were washed away by heavy floods.

There was a reason for migration of immigrants from Bangladesh as it would outwit other countries because of unbridled population growth and they have no right to control it as it was against their religion. The runaway population growth in Bangladesh resulting in 'suffocating' density of population in a territorially small country presents a nightmarish picture—114 million then, within an area of 55,000 square miles constituting a density of 1,054 per square mile in 1990s. The inexorable growth swelled to 137 million by the year 2010. The population reached 160 million in 2012 with density as 1,230 per square mile. No other place, except few countries like, Singapore is so packed. Bangladesh population has been growing at the rate of 2.8 million per year. Every year, one-third of Bangladesh is inundated by floods displacing on an average 20 million people. 60 per cent of Bangladeshis live below poverty line. Thus, the circumstances explain reason for invasion of Bangladeshis to India, particularly to north-east.

North-east insurgents had lived by the motto 'enemy's enemy is our friend', and looked to East Pakistan for all helps.

Pakistan was quite eager to help north-east militants. The seed for this was sowed by AZ Phizo, the leader of Naga insurgents this was nurtured by Pakistan with care and caution, never allowing for a slip-up. During Bangladesh War of 1971, the ISI remained aloof, but after 1975, the ULFA again resumed their relationship with ISI, seeking their help and after Mujib's assassination, it became more powerful again in Bangladesh. Apart from Naga insurgents, but they were also able to mushroom number of insurgent groups all over north-east India, helping them in their finance and providing arms and ammunitions. The north-east leaders invariably looked their personal interest above national interest as the Bangladeshi immigrants provided full support to them. In the early stages, it was beneficial for Congress, the ruling party in both Assam and centre. The famous saying of Debkanth Barua—one of the All India Congress Presidents—was "so long as Alis (Muslims) and coolies (tea planters) are with Congress, it did not care for anybody". The massive movement of Bangladeshi Muslim immigrants continued during the period of few of the congress leaders which included Mainool Haq Choudhury, Faqruddin Ali Ahmed, Abdul Ghani Khan Choudhury, and Santosh Mohan Dev, to some extent. The Congress government in West Bengal under Siddharth Shankar Ray was also quite passive and remained quiet including the next CPM government and its leader Jyoti Basu supporting the cause of Hindu immigrants from Bangladesh and allowing them to settle in West Bengal.

In 1990, Hiteshwer Saikia had declared in Assam Assembly that there was not a single foreigner in Assam. In 1991, the Congress-I ministry that had 25 per cent Muslim ministers, was nicknamed as Muslim ministry. The Muslim migrants were both left and right hands of the Muslim leaders of Assam in tilting the election results in favour of Congress. It gave considerable boost to fundamental elements that became quite vocal and aggressive.

The rivalry between local ethnic groups and the migrant Muslims over possession of fertile cultivable land had added to the communal tension. During the Babri Masjid agitation, the Muslims had indulged in violence by way of killing, looting, and destruction of temples. Even though increase of large number of Muslims in Nadia, Murshidabad, Maldah, West Dinajpur, Jalpaiguri, Cooch Behar, Dhubri, Karimganj, Cachar, and Tripura border districts were reported after 1971, yet the largest increase was noticed in Assam state excluding Sib Sagar district. This contributed to communal polarisation in all the border districts of India with Bangladesh. The electoral roll division continued all over Assam and all the political parties, including ULFA, tried their best to ensure that the Muslim immigrants are given voter card.

In 1996, the Assam Gana Parishad came to power following same policy of winning the heart of Muslim immigrants of Bangladesh similar to that of the Congress regime. The force of Congress and the BJP was swelling the voter list. The people of north-east are generally lazy, lethargic, easy-going and are keen to adopt office jobs. For their day-to-day life, they wanted the help of these immigrants who were available to them at a very cheap rate. All the efforts of various security agencies to identity Bangladeshis, and to push them back, failed, as the locals did not help in identifying the real immigrants. North-east has about 2,000 kilometres of porous border with Bangladesh. All the infiltration could take place through the gaps in land border, riverine border, Char Islands, forests, hilly terrain, and as the Phase one fencing comprised of only single pole type, as a result, that also remained submerged under water for months together during monsoon. The touts were operating both the sides of the international border and both the border-guarding forces, whether the then BDR or the BSF BOPs, were in connivance.

Migration into India, particularly to north-east, has been taking place from the past 200 years. In the beginning, during British period, the migration was for economic reasons, but after the independence, and particularly after 1975, i.e., the assassination of Sheikh Mujibur Rehman, it acquired communal and political hue. It has now acquired an international dimension and poses a great threat to our national security. The Britishers developed tea industry in Assam. They encouraged Bengali Muslim peasants from the then East Pakistan to move into lower Assam for ploughing open land for cultivation. In 1911, the British government partitioned Bengal province and Assam was made a separate province, under charge of a Lieutenant Governor. The Assamese had threats from the Bengali Hindus dominating the administration of the state and the Bengali Muslims from East Pakistan altering the demography of the province. The migrant Bengali Muslims were hardworking peasants who occupied all the vacant land, cultivated them and tried to take the ownership of such government land and forest land, including Char Islands. As the agricultural economy of Assam progressed, the Assamese in the beginning welcomed such efforts of Bangladesh Muslim migrants. Sir Mohd. Sadaulla, during his Musim League Ministry, encouraged the migration of Bengali Muslims from East Pakistan to Assam for sheer political reasons.

After the partition, an international border came up and the population movement from East Pakistan, initially consisted mostly of Hindu refugees, fleeing due to religious persecution to West Bengal through various border routes in the Sunderbans, Baanpur, Gede, Karimpur, Jalangi, Farakka, Maldah, Hamjapur, Radhikapur, Bindol, Kukuradah, Patagora, Shripur, Hatkhola, Moragati, Phoolbaari, Chopra, Chowdhury haat, Gitaldah, Sahibganj, Jhaokutti, and Sattrasal areas. All these border areas were earlier having Hindu population who could receive them and guide them to go to the hinterland making the best use of these unfenced border areas. The deployment of border-guarding force that time was too weak, it was not modernised, they were without any training with old point 303 rifles, having no night vision devices, no fencing, and transport system. There was no floodlighting at the border.

There were open common haats all along the border where people from both sides could mingle and trespass; there were no border police, excluding that of Assam, and the local police never came to border areas.

Touts were available on both the sides of the border, collecting money from such Hindu refugees in East Pakistan, guiding them to the international border, handing them over to Indian touts and despatching groups of such refugees by trains and by buses to Kolkata, Howarh, Bardhaman, Midnapur, Siliguri, Maldah, Barrackpur, Balurghat, Murshidabad, Bankura, Srirampur and all such districts of West Bengal. It was that time when a number of such Hindu refugees from Bangladesh could manipulate and exchanged houses in Bangladesh with that of Kolkata and in other parts of West Bengal. Some Hindu refugees could manage to acquire land and building in various districts of West Bengal, both, during Congress regime and CPM regime. They were more tactful in becoming vote banks of earlier Congress government in West Bengal and then changed their allegiance to CPM government after Jyoti Basu came to power. Dhoti–kurta and chappal, liking for paan, interest in Nazrool sangeet, Rabindra sangeet, opera, rice and fish served as common factor of bond between the West Bengalis and the Bangladeshi Hindu refugees.

Neither the locals tried to give any information about migrants nor local police station in West Bengal tried to apprehend them nor any of the NGOs came forward in West Bengal against such penetration; no effort was made by the state government to push back such Hindu refugees consisting of large numbers to Bangladesh. It was only a *mela* like position "come you, come more and more, and we are here to garland you". In the west, the Hindu refugee influx from Pakistan continued in 1971 and 1972 only. It got reduced year-by-year after all such Hindus in Sind province decided to leave Pakistan immediately due to persecution just after 1971 war. However, in case of Bangladesh (East Pakistan), migration of Hindus continued for years and years, and even tilll today, they continue to arrive. The Hindu population in East Pakistan, which was

27 per cent in 1947, was reduced to 14 per cent in 1971, to 10 per cent in 1991, and perhaps, by now, there would be hardly 5 per cent of Hindus in Bangladesh.

During their entry, some could manage to sell their immovable properties like, land and building and could carry some of their ornaments. However, while crossing the borders, they lost everything to the touts operating on both sides of the border and in few cases, they left their immovable properties as it was, and fled. One could see the signs of hunger on their face when they were apprehended by security forces this side. How can one manage to feed such big groups of refugees entering through the international border? Perhaps, the local security agencies at the border thought it proper to leave them onto themselves and the mercy of the God; with the same old theory of 'survival of the fittest' applicable in their case. People have come crossing Mahananda River while it was on spate, they crossed river Ganges, river Ichhamati, just to find another home to lead their new lives in India. Along with Hindu refugees, Muslim infiltrators continued their migration into Assam for economic reasons. This economic migration was a continuous factor from 1947 until now. The movement of Hindu refugees to Assam and north-east was largely arrested due to anti-Bengali riots and because of violence in the wake of insurgencies in north-east. At present, the Hindu refugee movement from Bangladesh is directed to Tripura and West Bengal only.

Unlike that of West Bengal, the old ethnic tribal—Dev Barmas in Tripura—came into minority and thus emerged ATTF, the insurgent organisation of this ethnic group of Tripura. The demographic situation in 24 Parganas, Nadia, Murshidabad, Maldah, West Dinajpur, Jalpaiguri and Cooch Behar border districts of West Bengal got changed. All the vacant government fields, grazing lands, reserve forests, and open fields of these districts vanished in between 1970 and 1980. One could find rows of thatched houses in bunch suddenly mushrooming in all these open lands of border areas. One very important aspect was that the migrant groups settling in border districts of West Bengal were mostly Muslims. The Hindu refugees had their way to Kolkata and other interior districts like Bishnupur, Midnapore, Hoogly, etc. Illegal immigrants who came to Assam and north-east were mostly Muslims. One can see and visualise these penetrations through various islands of river Padma, all the Char Islands of river Brahmaputra, the hilly forest areas of Tura, Garo Hills, Khasi and Jaintia Hill, through Mankachar, Mahamaya Char, Dhubri, Satrasal, and Mahendraganj. The entry of Muslim migrants is due to economic reasons, political reasons and is also linked to fundamental activities in Assam, in the whole of north-east, and also, in most of the Muslim majority pockets of the country. Failure to get Assam included in East Pakistan in 1947 remained a source of resentment in that country. The wish of Zulfikar Ali Bhutto remained unfulfilled; the forethought of Sheikh Mujibur Rehman remained in his book only, whereas the prediction of Mr. Sadiq Khan, a former diplomat, who wrote in the book 'Holiday of October 18, 1991' that Bangladesh would face a crisis of lebensraum, had come true. Sadiq Khan could further visualise that borderless competitive trade of labour will better serve the consumer interests. He further added that international cooperation was needed to work out a plan to carry out population movements and settlement of Bangladeshis in order to avoid critical demographic pressure in pockets of high concentration. Due to global warming phenomenon, many small islands in Bangladesh used to get submerged in sea and thus displaced lakhs of population who had no other option but to expand and migrate to city areas on economic grounds and for bare survival too. A natural overflow of population pressure existing in Bangladesh cannot be contained by creating and establishing barbed wire fencing and concertina coils, and deploying guns for creating fear factor. The USA is helpless for the last many years in checking influx from Mexico; similar was the situation between Iran and Iraq, between South Vietnam and North Vietnam, between East Germany and West Germany, and between North Korea and South Korea. The surplus population of Bangladesh thus marched forward to the sparsely populated lands in south-east and the Seven Sisters of the north-east India. All the seven states in the north-east were having surplus land earlier (even in the past— in Assam), and not only it helped the migrants to settle, the economy of all the north-east states prospered and all the vacant lands which were unutilised and unfit for cultivation earlier, could be turned green. Abdul Momin, former Foreign Secretary and Bangladesh's first Ambassador to China, in "Holiday Magazine" issue of November 21, 1991 stated—"there is more population growth in Bangladesh resulting in suffocation, and raising the density of population in a territorially small country thereby presenting a nightmarish picture". Abdul Momin advocated that along with borderless circulation of food and commodities, there should be borderless competitive trade of labour. He proposed that if Bangladeshis integrate themselves with all the hill tribes within their border and adjacent to their borders, their bulging population might be welcome in adjacent land inhabited by kindered people. It proved to be correct. All the border districts and border states of India towards Bangladesh, in the beginning, welcomed such population pouring into their land, may be to West Bengal, may be to undivided Goalpara and Dhubri, may be towards Char Islands, to Assam, Manipur, Meghlaya, Tura, Dawki, Tripura, Murshidabad, Malda and 24 Parganas. Not only was it a social welcome by Hindus in West Bengal and Muslims in border districts of India towards Bangladesh, but also politically. Tripura, Assam and West Bengal failed to oppose this infiltration and most of the political leaders, whether Hindus or Muslims, kept on increasing their vote banks and future political prosperity. We may have the best of relation with Sheikh Hasina government now, but we have forgotten that the time will come very soon again for Begum Zia's regime (which may come up in the next election). There will be one more attempt of demographic invasion to India, and mostly whatever five per cent Hindus are available in Bangladesh, will permanently shift to India. All the insurgent camps, now closed opposite to our borders, and shifted to hinterland in

Bangladesh, will again be re-established and Bangladesh will not only pass on burden of migrants to us but would become another 'Afghanistan', where India will be involved directly.

This penetration of migrants to India was not accepted officially by any government of Bangladesh, even Sheikh Hasina. Both Begum Zia and Sheikh Hasina, have washed away their hands of the issue, and they have categorically told government of India that the government of Bangladesh is not behind this game plan of pushing their surplus labour to India. The immigration continued because of demographic disproportion, that is to say, the density of population of Bangladesh is, more or less, three times that of all the states in the north-east India put together. The immigrants provided cheap labour, domestic helps in homes, started pulling rickshaws, helped inflow of militants, of arms and ammunitions, of ISI agents, of drugs and gave shelter to militants coming from Bangladesh and Pakistan all overIndia, be it West Bengal, Assam, Sikkim, Tripura or Bombay, Pune, Maharashtra, Hyderabad, Jaipur, Bangalore, and Agra. Along with immigrants, touts got involved in women and child immoral trafficking. Even though the figure comes to around 30,000 women and girls of Bangladesh forced into prostitution in India by touts, yet the numbers are much more, as every year, in north-east and West Bengal border, such trafficking of women and girls is reported and a number of NGOs are helping security agencies in curbing this menace.

DG of BSF, Shri A K Mitra in October 2008, had revealed that 12 lakh Bangladeshis, who entered India legally between 1972 and 2005, had not returned back to their country and became traceless (India Policy Foundation).

As of now, provision contained in Foreigners Act, 1946 can only be applied for deportation of Bangladeshi immigrants, or while entering at the international border, they can be intercepted by border guarding forces and security forces so as to push them back, then and there. There is a motive to create a greater Bangladesh by expansion of territory comprising parts of West Bengal and Assam, and few other districts of north-east India along with Sikkim and Tripura.

Bangladeshis are able to take most of the jobs in the government. You find them in schools, colleges, courts, markets-practically everywhere. There are certain areas, which are forcibly occupied by the infiltrators in the market places. The entire local market is in their hands. They are also employed in tea estates and other agricultural activities. It is impossible to find a single rickshaw driver who is an Assamese. One wonders whether he is in Assam or in Bangladesh; the scale of infiltration has gone to that extent. The day is not far when Assamese will end up as refugees in their own state. If a Hindu kills one Muslim, the Muslims should retaliate by killing three Hindus and the Government would support ..." (Quoted from an electioneering campaign speech delivered on 10/2/1983 by Abdul Ghani Khan Choudhury at Mairabari while campaigning for the Congress (I) candidate during the infamous and bloody election of 1983) ['The Silent invasion' by Hiranya Kumar Bhattacharyya, p. 4].

Reference of the letter of ex-Governer of Assam to the President of India is given below as an instance.

Raj Bhawan, Guwahati D.O. No. GSAG.3/98/
November 8, 1998

Dear Adarniya Rashtrapatiji,

Large-scale illegal migration from East Pakistan/ Bangladesh over several decades has been altering the demographic complexion of this state. It poses a grave threat both to the identity of the Assamese people and to our national security. Successive governments at the centre and the state have not adequately met this challenge.

As Governor of Assam, I feel it is my bounden duty, towards both the nation and the state I have sworn to serve, to place before you this report on the dangers arising from the continuing silent demographic invasion. I have also formulated my recommendations for dealing with this issue of vital importance. I earnestly hope that this matter will receive due consideration and suitable action taken to avert the grave danger that has been building up for some time.

The concluding recommendations of the then governor General S K Sinha to the Honourable President of India are as follows:

1. Awareness should be promoted about illegal migration into Assam being not only a threat to the identity of the Assamese people, but what is more, being a grave threat to our national security.
2. Border fencing in Assam should be completed on war footing. Observation towers and lighting should be provided on the same scale as in Punjab.
3. BSF battalions deployed in Assam should not be given responsibility to hold unduly extended frontage of 30 km Additional BSF battalions should be provided for this purpose.
4. Diversion of BSF battalions from the border in Assam for other tasks, when the battle against infiltrators is on, must be scrupulously avoided.
5. All country boats, plying in the river near the border should be registered and their registration numbers marked on them.
6. Medium rafts for floating BOPs with adequate speedboats for the riverine sector should be made available as early as possible.
7. Multi-purpose photo identity cards should be provided to all our nationals. Districts bordering Bangladesh should be accorded higher priority.
8. Effective arrangements should be made for registration of births and deaths.
9. The National Register of Citizens (NRC) should be updated and computerised. A separate register of stateless citizens should also be maintained.
10. Vacant chars in the river should be handed over to the Forest Department and trees planted on them.

11. As far as possible, we should assist in the process of economic development in Bangladesh. Socio-economic programmes designed to improve the lot of women should be given priority due to their multiple beneficiary spin-offs improving the family's income, women's education, curbing population growth and educated women becoming a bulwark against the spread of Islamic fundamentalism.
12. Hindu illegal migrants who have infiltrated after 24th March, 1971 should not be given refugee status. They should be treated as illegal migrants.
13. While maximum effort must be made to stem the ingress of illegal migrants, those who have already infiltrated after 24th March, 1971 to date, may not be deported.
14. The IM(DT) Act should be repealed and replaced by a new legislation, which should provide for detection of illegal migrants in a just, fair and expeditious manner, with due judicial sanctity accorded to the process. Those identified as illegal migrants should be allowed to stay in the country as Stateless citizens with no voting right or the right to acquire immovable property.
15. Survey teams working under Magistrates on deputation from other States assisted by policemen of Border Organisation should identify illegal migrants in a fixed time-frame of short duration. Those identified as foreigners by these teams should be given the right of appeal to tribunals set up under the Foreigners Act.

With profound regards.

Yours Sincerely,

(Lt. Gen. (Retd.) S.K. Sinha, PVSM)

11. As far as possible, we should assist in the process of economic development in Bangladesh. Socio-economic programmes designed to improve the lot of women should be given priority due to their [illegible] beneficiary impact on improving the family's income, women's education, curbing population growth and educated women becoming a bulwark against the spread of Islamic fundamentalism.

12. Hindu illegal migrants who have infiltrated after 25th March, 1971 should not be given refugee status. They should be treated as illegal migrants.

13. While maximum effort must be made to stem the ingress of illegal migrants, those who have already infiltrated after 25th March, 1971 en masse, may not be deported.

14. The IMDT Act should be repealed and replaced by a new legislation which should provide for detection of illegal migrants in a just, fair and expeditious manner, with due [illegible] safeguards accorded to the people. Those identified as illegal migrants should be allowed to stay in the country as stateless citizens with no voting rights or the rights to acquire immovable property.

15. Survey teams working under Magistrates on deputation from other States assisted by policemen of Border Organisation should identify illegal migrants in a fixed time-frame of short duration. Those identified as foreigners by these teams should be given the right of appeal to tribunals set up under the Foreigners Act.

With profound regards,

Yours Sincerely,

(Lt. Gen. (Retd.) S.K. Sinha, PVSM)

7

Implications

Political: Vote-bank Politics

The vote-bank politics has taken a toll on the life of common citizens and the government at the centre has to mend its policies towards north-eastern states. The issue of Assam has assumed larger proportions because of the vote bank policies adopted by different political parties. If they are not stopped, it would have a disastrous impact on the state and the country as a whole. It can happen only in India, where vote-bank politics scores over national interest and the country's sovereignty. The centre and the Assam government disregarded the remedial measures suggested by two important Supreme Court judge

ments, which highlighted the demographic aggression faced by Assam from mass influx of illegal migrants. In 1971, India was complaining in the UN about the aggression it faced from the migrations from East Pakistan to its north-eastern part. Strangely, now, the illegal migrants have become an invaluable vote-bank for certain political parties, which avoid their identification and deportation, despite clear directions from the apex court in two rulings in 2005 and 2006. The vote-bank politics practiced by India's politicians has baned Assam with communal violence raging between the indigenous Assamese Bodos and the Bangladeshi Muslims who have settled there illegally. The violence in Assam has spread to all corners of India and instilled communal hatred in the minds of the people. The volatile situation of north-east is a "living volcano".

The Governor of Assam, in a secret letter to the central government in 2005, revealed that "up to 6000 Bangladeshis enter Assam every day" (then). According to various estimates, India is host to around twenty to thirty million illegal Bangladeshi immigrants now. Around seven to ten million illegal immigrants inhabit in Assam itself. The Indian politicians, for encouraging illegal immigration for the sake of vote-bank politics, prefer to sideline the interest of their own natives. This has grievous national implications. The Congress which has been the dominant political force, both at the central level and in Assam—post independence, has often been accused of encouraging this infiltration for political gains. Illegal migrants are mobilised to vote *en masse* for Congress candidates and get access to every national resource. In achieving political returns, the party and the Government have ignored the destabilising impact of the socio-economic situation arising out of this influx. No one likes the vote-bank to be disturbed, and therefore, national interests are being sacrificed till this day. Encouraged by the dubious approach of the governments, fundamentalists have started manipulating illegal migrants for their own gains. Fundamentalist Muslim leaders in Assam have already issued calls for 'jihad' if the indigenous Bodos involved in retaliation during the violence were not arrested. Even attempts by the Government of India to prepare a National Register of Citizens based on the 1971 rolls in the state for an authentic documentation of the population have failed to make any headway in the face of strong opposition from Muslim groups of Assam.

Fundamentalist groups are apprehensive about political power slipping away from their hands, once the process of identification of the illegal migrants is initiated seriously. The effort to prepare the NRC is abandoned at the slightest resistance from the vested interests which smacks of the connivance of the politicians with concerned quarters. After so much of violence and bloodshedding, migrants are still rushing towards Assam and government has no control over these intruders. All these migrants are Bangladeshi Muslims and are supposed to constitute a solid vote bank. There is a wrong notion that Muslims always vote for the Congress. They never voted more than 50 per cent in its favour. Now, even AIUDF is progressing ahead securing 18 seats in the present assembly, being supported by only the migrants. Illiteracy among Muslims and polygamy has to be blamed for the high growth rate among the community and outnumbering Hindu population in the state. The issue of illegal immigrants has become the biggest challenge and headache for the country. A long-term solution should be implemented to resolve this issue. Protection of national interest, interest of ethnic locals, retention of ethnic culture and their security should be of prime importance to all political parties and they must help in identifying and prosecuting all Bangladesh migrants and initiate action for their pushback.

The state government is doing nothing to stop this, not because there is a lack of avenues, fund or manpower, but because they don't want to. Free entry of migrants in Assam was the design of the state government from the days of Moinul Haque Chaudhury, B.P. Chaliah, Faquiruddin Ali Ahmed, Hiteswar Saikia, and Santosh Mohan Dev until now. The Congress party patronizes these immigrants, and instead of coming on them with heavy hand, they show them motherly affection. Phasewise they are issued ration cards, voter ID, and even BPL card, in due course of time. In a matter of couple of years, the Congress, in connivance with few of their supporting NGOs had already transformed these foreign refugees as our own citizens, bypassing even the Rajiv-Assam accord. This systematic approach at sabotaging our national integrity is going on for decades together. There are even instances of refugees standing for election, based on the official documents supplied to them. These migrants are in majority in many tribal parts of Assam. These same miscreants repeatedly reveal their true colours by pouncing on the ethnic Assamese in the name of their religion. Even though it is not that a big problem, the attitude of our government, every time such untoward incident happens, is a matter of regret. Always, there has been a late reaction to riots in Assam so far. Even the present Governor of Meghalaya, Shri Musaharry, who hails from Kokrajhar, has blamed the state government and the state administration for not taking prompt action when they had enough evidences in advance. One wonders; why a responsible government can allow this to happen? The answer is only the vote bank. There seems a clear role of dirty vote bank politics in the region for things to go out of hands. The migrants are in full knowledge of the central government and the authorities. Rather than throwing them out for illegal entry, they are nurtured and gracefully welcomed with shelters so that they turn into potential vote–banks of Congress party in the present and in future. Lakhs of voter cards are issued randomly to non-citizens despite realising the consequences in the long run. The consequences of such anti-national acts will be there for all Indians. Even the migrants are at times encouraged to take the law in their own hands, which has been noticed in Assam, Nadia, Maldah and Murshidabad border.

Not only Congress Party is using Bangladesh migrants in Assam for vote-bank politics but it goes to all other parties in opposition as well. They manipulate migrants from Bangladesh to illegally cross the porous border through various gaps, intrude in our country, be enrolled in the voters' list, and encroach on our lands. They all gain political mileage from these invaders. Blame goes to the Indians, who employ them at home and outside as they get them very cheap. The danger of vote bank politics is too real to be dismissed.

The most important point is whether political parties are ready to rise to the challenge at all. It is a million dollar question. It will be pernicious when the migrants will manage their own government in some states in future electoral process in 2019 and onwards.

Millions of Bangladeshi Muslim infiltrators 'invaded'

north-east silently and changed the demography of Assam and a few other border districts of India with Bangladesh. In pursuance of the cherished goal of various Muslim leaders, they became successful in changing the demography of entire north-east region, Assam in particular. In 1871, Muslim population of Assam was only five per cent. Continuous inflow of Muslims from East Bengal (now Bangladesh) has worsened the situation in Nadia, Murshidabad, whole of Assam and Tripura. Now the Muslim population in Assam is touching 35 per cent. At present, eight districts of Assam are with Muslim majority and three more will become so very soon. In 1947, no district of Assam had Muslim majority. Out of 126 Assembly constituencies, 46 are under political influence of the Bangladeshi Muslim population. In 2006, in the Assam Legislative Assembly, out of 26 Muslim MLAs, two were of Assamese origin and the rest 24 had their roots in Bangladesh. The Chief Minister of Assam in 1992, Shri Hiteshwar Saikia announced on 10th April, 1992 on the floor of the State Assembly that there were 30 lakhs of Bangladeshi infiltrators in Assam, even though Mr. Saikia withdrew his statement *per force*. We have the statement of the Hon'ble Home Minister of Government of India, Shri Indrajeet Gupta, who announced in Parliament on 6th May, 1997 that the number of illegal infiltrators has crossed more than one crore. Muslim Population in Assam had risen by 77.42 per cent till 1991 from what it was in 1971. Hindu population had risen by nearly 41.89 per cent in this period. In the case of Muslims, the Assam growth rate was much higher than All India rate. This suggests continued large scale Muslim illegal migration into Assam.

In 1970, the total population in East Pakistan was 7.5 crores, but in 1974, it had come down to 7.14 crores. If we take 3.1 per cent annual population growth rate of that period, the shortfall of 6 million people can be explained only by large-scale migration to India ['Emigration, Immigration and Diaspora Relations in India' by Daniel Naujoks, October, 2009].

Political scientist, Kamal Sadiq, has estimated the number of illegal migrants of Bangladesh to be between 15 to 20 millions, basing the number partly on documented growth of Muslim communities, and partially on unpublished government reports. Sadiq's research has found that many of these Bangladeshis adopt Hindu names and are able to obtain fraudulent documents that allow them access to government subsidies and even to cast vote in elections. Indeed, some Indian politicians have benefitted from votes by illegal resident Bangladesh migrants.

Political parties keep on encouraging and helping the migrants, be it the BJP or Congress, or that way CPM or TMC as they all need these people with them during elections. These hard-working migrants attract even educated people in the cities in working as domestic helps with lower remuneration. The educated and even business community accept Bangladesh migrants to work for them. We have corrupt officials, maybe in revenue, may be in district office, who can easily be bribed for giving various identity support to the migrants, including selling government land and reserve forests to the migrants as it has happened all over in Assam. Until today, one cannot charge government of Bangladesh to have connived for this migration but indirectly they are passive supporters to this as it solves their population problem, automatically taking away many administrative problems from the government of Bangladesh.

Shri L K Advani, the then Deputy Prime Minister of India, while addressing the conference of senior civil and police officials on 8th January, 2003 asked them to locate and throw out all the 20 millions Bangladeshis as they pose serious threat to the internal security of the country but the instruction remained on paper only. The identification and repatriation of millions of illegal migrants is not that easy. Only few of them could be pushed back from various states. Their numbers have not risen so far; neither the central govt, nor the state govts, will ever be successful in pushing them back. Any such plan to drive them back will create a major political problem and communal violence like that which occurred at Kokrajhar,

Bombay, Pune, and Hyderabad. Even though numerous proofs are available in India about this migration, but Dhaka has always refused to accept that there is any illegal Bangladeshi in India. During her visit to India in May, 1992, Begum Khalida Zia did not accept this version of India but only agreed to include the matter in the joint communiqué issued on 28th May, 1992 which said 'Taking into account the problems being caused due to large scale illegal migration of people across their borders, they (the Prime Ministers of India and Bangladesh) expressed their determination to stop illegal movement of people across the border by all possible means including strengthening of existing arrangements and mutual co-operation in this regard.'

Again Sheikh Hasina on her visit to India on 1st Aug, 1998 stated that "We do not accept that there is any Bengali speaking Bangladeshi National living in India. So the question of deporting any Bangladeshi national by the Indian government does not arise".

These migrants avail very easily the ration cards as proof of their citizenship; in few cases, government jobs, and are able to purchase lands at various places in India. The migrants not only can become a candidate for election to panchayat bodies but they are trying for membership in municipalities, assemblies and parliamentary constituencies (Journalist). It has come to such an extent that the migrants do not have any fear as they possess linguistic and cultural similarities, same food habits, homo-ethnic climate, belief of getting shelter, cordiality and fellow-feeling anywhere in India as their relatives are already available in all parts of hinterland in India, including all metro cities. They have started getting political patronage in a number of states in India including that of the capital. Now, they are not confined to the border districts of India, but have an eye on other parts since long, in which, they are becoming increasingly successful. Security of minority communities in Bangladesh and security to ethnic groups already existing since ages in our border states have to be given more preference. All illegal migrants must be given a photo identity card bearing their name, age, address, education qualification with blood group, and area of working in India printed on it, which should be issued from state intelligence authority only so that the duplication of the system could be made impossible and those found without these cards may be pushed back.

The Dolu border of Meghalaya state, the capital of Meghalaya — Shillong, the areas of Jaintia forests, after Jawai up to Silchar border, will give a nightmare of the presence of the Bangladeshis. Even though Mr. Mukul Sangma, the present Chief Minister of Meghalaya has taken up the case several times and spoken in various forums, but their state should come forward in detecting, and apprehending Bangladeshis, first in Shillong — in between NEHU (North Eastern Hill University) and NEC (North East Council), with the help of Khasis (their own people), take legal steps, and push them back to Bangladesh in their own border, if they want to save Meghalaya from the epidemic of migrants. Failure of political will to act on ground in taking the help of the Foreigners Act will clearly show that the political leaders in this state are using these migrants as their own vote banks and there is no reason as to why such Bangladeshis at Shillong cannot be identified, as their look is completely different from the Khasis.

Economic - Strain on Land and Other resources, Unemployment

Various estimates put the number of Bangladeshi illegal immigrants anywhere between two to three crores. The study reveals that environmental crisis caused by population pressure in Bangladesh and relatively greater economic opportunities in terms of higher lifetime income, acquisition of land and assets in Assam have been the primary motivations behind large-scale migration. However, they have put tremendous pressure on land, creating socio-political and environmental problems that have indirect adverse effects on the economy. Finally, the immigrants hardly contribute to the government revenue while the government spends a substantial amount to maintain this significantly large fraction of the population. It had its impact on the demography of all the border districts of India towards Bangladesh and the states of West Bengal, Assam and Tripura. This huge incursion of migrants caused economic problems in the whole of north-east of India and the per capita income of the ethnic Indians in these parts went down as the migrants provided cheap labour. It had its effect on the Indian labours coming from Bihar, Madhya Pradesh and Odisha. These migrants took away all the construction works (labours) in various parts of the countries. The whole of natural resources in the Sundarbans, Assam, Tura-Garo, Jaintia and Hill Areas of Meghalaya decreased. Similarly, the lime belt and coal belt of Meghalaya was completely dominated by these migrants. All the reserve forest resources in Assam in Goalpora, Baksa, Udalguri, Dhubri badly suffered. Most of the grazing fields for the cattle of Indian border population in the border districts were taken over. As a number of migrants became Indian citizen, the health problem of local population has been affected and the public health department in border districts have not been able to look after the health of the local population as sufficient medicines and doctors cannot be provided for such a big increase in the population. Similarly, Assam has seen the health problem of all the refugees who were sheltered in various camps in Kokrajhar areas in the last riot; particularly, the infants and the women faced acute health problems. Similarly, availability of woman doctors in border districts is still a problem. The availability of land in border district remains the same whereas the population of the border districts had a tremendous growth. Thus, the administrative tasks before the district machineries suffered badly. The proper policing for crime control became problematic. The public distribution system of whole of north-east and West Bengal had acute shortage of food materials and it was difficult for district authorities to supply food grains, kerosene, sugar, oil to such vast population, which included these migrants.

Similar was the problem in not only Mangoldoi constituency of Assam but also in various Assembly and

Parliamentary constituencies in West Bengal, Assam, Tripura, Bihar, MP, Manipur, Meghalaya, Nagaland and UP. The voters list kept on increasing and onus lies with various politicians. The crime—particularly theft, dacoity, and murder—witnessed an upward trend. Land grabbing became quite common. Polygamy and prostitution increased in those pockets where these migrants had their new colonies in India. There were social conflicts and cultural loss to the ethnic society due to these migrants in various border states and most of the border districts. It was difficult for the Government of India, the state government of West Bengal, the government of Assam, and the government of Tripura for arranging the settlement of millions of migrants. Very few government projects like those at Dandakaranya in Odisha could be managed for rehabilitating these migrants. As a result, they dispersed themselves to every city and town of the country.

The basic minimum infrastructure of health services is not available in border areas, particularly in Meghalaya and in Assam border. The Primary Health Centres are lying neglected without proper infrastructure, life saving medicines and good transport system for evacuation for PF malaria patients to district hospitals as a number of casualities are reported every year in border areas of states of Mizoram, Assam, Meghalaya, and Tripura due to incidences of malaria infecting brain, which require immediate medication. Similarly, primary and secondary schools for imparting basic education to the youths living in the border areas of Mizoram and Char Islands in Assam are too less, and this issue requires immediate attention. Polygamy is rampant in Murshidabad, Nadia, Dhubri, Cachar and Karimganj border areas. Due to maximum inroads of illegal immigrants, there is no development in peripheral areas of Manipur, Nagaland, Tripura, and Meghalaya, particularly, the border roads and lateral roads linking various villages from the town/cities. The ground water resources are very poor in Meghalaya, Assam and Mizoram. Similar is the situation in the Sundarbans. This also causes various ailments to the border population. The whole area of Mizoram, Meghalaya and a portion of Assam is lacking in horticulture, and mostly, they depend on forest products, timber and tea leaves. These areas are having very poor harvest and do not have proper market system. In irrigation sector also, north-east states suffer maximum and people have to depend upon the rain water and the water from various rivers as the only source. Assam, that way, has been facing floods since years like Bangladesh. Similar is the terrain in the Sundarbans, West Dinajpur, Murshidabad, and 24 Parganas border districts where erosion takes place every year and a number of villagers leave their houses and shift to safer areas for rehabilitation. Because of non-availability of proper border haats, the local people are facing problem to sell their produce in a nearby market because of the border fencing. To start with, Meghalaya, with the help of north-east council has opened two border haats, one at Dawkie and the other one at Bholaganj, which help the border population in selling their products. All three, Murshidabad, Assam and Mizoram are famous for handloom and handicrafts and they are suffering since long because of non-availability of raw materials. At present, the Ministry of Home Affairs and the Ministry of Commerce have opened new ICPs in Bangladesh border for proper trade and commerce with Bangladesh, of course excluding cattle. The inflow of fake Indian currency notes from Bangladesh has flooded border areas, the whole of north-east markets, banks in north-east, as also the border districts of Tripura and West Bengal. It is a matter of concern to keep a check on inflow of FICN through border roads from Bangladesh. Mostly, the transaction made by the cattle smugglers and coal mafias are through FICN only. We are loosing our revenue to Bangladesh in cattle smuggling and the price of cows and bullocks in our country have gone up tremendously because of lakhs of cattle being smuggled to Bangaldesh every year from various states of India through the whole of Indo-Bangladesh border excluding Mizoram. The funds released by Planning Commission and MHA through BADP and civic action programme are too meagre and it is not enough for development of border areas/border districts.

The studies on unstoppable and substantial inflow of Bangladeshis, both Hindus and Muslims, perpetually changed the demographic balance of West Bengal, Assam, Tripura, Sikkim, and they have started crowding Manipur, Nagaland, and Meghalaya. The newcomers indeed helped a number of Indians in solving the traditional shortage of labour but a gradual realisation of the danger of political patronage has started to instil a fear in the minds of public about their socio-economic requirements. It was only the youths in north-east, who rose to the occasion and a district named Sibsagar used peaceful means in disallowing migrants to settle there. The response against migrants was very poor as evident from the emerging scenario from the locals, the security agencies, the political leaders belonging border states and the central government.

The economic exploitation at the hands of these migrants gave heartburn to various ethnic groups in the north-east forcing some of the youths to take up arms when they found themselves swarmed by these Muslim invaders between 1947 to 1962, 1970 to 1974 and between 1975 to 1990. The voter lists in West Bengal, Tripura and Assam increased manifold. This increase was abnormal by national norms of increase in the number of voters.

North-east is connected with India by 14 km wide chicken-neck land between Nepal and Bangladesh with one railway line, which was earlier running between New Bongai Gaon to Guwahati, built by the Britishers. Since long, there was no railway bridge over Farakka that came only much later and people used to get down to one side of the river from train, cross the river through steamer and catch the train opposite side for New Jalpaiguri. Even as a child during 1962 and 1965, I have travelled on this line while going to Darjeeling from Bhubaneswar. I had to get into a new train after crossing the river at Farakka. Similar situation was there for the train line from Goalpara to Guwahati, which came much later, i.e., in the year 2000. Until today, there is no train communication to Manipur state and the whole state depends upon Dimapur in Nagaland, and they are at the mercy of NSCN-IM militant group, while the government has not yet been able to open the other route to Imphal from Silchar since last 20 years. Similar is the situation in Meghalaya state and the complete government machinery at the capital of Meghalaya—Shillong, has to take recourse of passage through the whole of Guwahati in Assam to reach to the other part of Tura and Garo Hills. Till today, Shillong is not capable of maintaining its road to Tura in their own land and depends upon the government of Assam for this purpose. The central government did not take interest in railways in developing the road communication or the industrial development of north-east. Even though central funds kept on flowing to states like that of J&K, auditing was not made properly. Assam had to spend about 70 per cent of the central funds towards payment of the salaries of their staffs and their pension. Similar is the situation in Manipur and Nagaland where a major portion from the government fund, earlier, were taken by either of the militants, such as NSCN-IM or ULFA or PLA or UNLF, from the source.

The mounting pressure of unemployment in the whole of north-east gave rise to militancy and it was aggravated by the entry of these migrants from Bangladesh. Unemployment was also one reason for migrants to leave Bangladesh. Even the educated Bangladeshi persons could not find jobs in their own country and thus managed their entry to India, Sri Lanka, Pakistan and Saudi Arabia. There is a direct relationship between migration and unemployment. The migrants were in search of livelihood and it is the Indians, particularly the Delhites, the Assamese, the Bengalis in West Bengal who gave employment to these migrants. In Assam, the youth are easygoing, lethargic and not hardworking. They refuse to do any work involving sweat or skills. Similar is the situation in all over north-east and West Bengal. There were no indigenous carpenters, cobblers, washermen, blacksmiths, plumbers, tailors and no one to till the land. An Assamese will never like to go to the field to do manual job. For day-to-day life, the Assamese used to depend upon Bangladeshis since ages. They were interested only in salary-paying jobs with more vacations and their expectations were very high. They only wanted shortcuts to reach up to five Star lifestyle level and were keen upon giving all the laborious jobs on contract to the Muslim migrants of Bangladesh. God only can save Assam. Their culture, tradition, identity were similar to that of Bangladeshis inasmuch as dhotis, white saree with red border, kurtas, gamchaas, chappals and sandals, pan/supari, dubi tabla, dholak, Rabindra Sangeet, and the like. Only exception was of Bihu.

The Assamese lost their culture, tradition and identity leaving aside Guwahati and a few districts. The Assamese culture is rarely to be found in all districts of Assam. Bihu comes once a year. The so-called Assamese gamchha, the brass paan pot and Bihu hat are symbols just only to be presented to VIPs and to be kept in the drawing rooms. This is how these migrants survived in West Bengal and Assam providing manual labour, carpenters, washermen, cultivators, cleaners, sweepers and rickshaw pullers. If one goes to Meghalaya border in Khasi and Jaintia, in Lafarge mining project, in Cherapunji border, all the coal mines and Jaintia forest area, one can find only Bangladesh labours on permit working there. The people from north-east are not interested in these jobs. A big project at Dandakaranya in Odisha was started where 35,000 families of Bangladeshi Hindu migrants were settled by providing with thatched houses and a pair of oxen to cultivate 5 acres of land each. The local ethnic Maria tribes at Dandakaranya felt neglected as the government helped foreigners free of cost leaving their own people at the mercy of god. These migrants cherished hope to become eminent citizens like doctors, engineers, filmmakers, singers and educationists, to name a few. The project failed as most of them left Dandakaranya, after selling their properties, for various cities in the hinterland in search of good education and a bright future. Even in the recent Bodo clashes, the BTAD faced problem to employ any of ethnic Bodos for manual jobs, as a Bodo youth charges Rs. 300 for an eight hour work, which he will not do it properly, whereas all these Bangladesh migrants employed there as labours were willing to work at just Rs. 90 per day for about 12 hours work. All over north-east, whether it is in Manipur, Nagaland, Mizoram, or Assam, the contractors are employing Bangladeshi labours with them for their construction work, as they are easy to handle, hard working, they charge less and are available in numbers. I have seen myself in Jammu that a number of contractors are keeping Bangladeshi labours with them for various construction works and mostly in all government projects, private buildings, construction of dams, subways, road construction and similar other jobs. Further, in north, Srinagar is having a Bangladeshi colony at Quamarwari near Safakadal. Bangladeshis were pouring into Assam because of economic compulsion, as it is close to the border and there was an environment in whole of Assam and north-east, both politically and fundamentally, to accept Bangladeshi Muslim migrants. One of the gravest threats to India from Bangladesh is migrants coming from Char Islands and the people living in chars. If you just visit by boat in river Padma or Brahmaputra, particularly, in autumn/winter, one can see numerous small and large chars with thatched huts all around. Maximum chars can be seen in Dhubri district in South Salmara and Mankachar subdivision. These people are floating around like nomads and their numbers are increasing in thousands, year-by-year.

Population of children between eight to fourteen years is about 50 per cent in Char Island. They have no other alternative than to opt for child labour, whether it is weaving, making boats, making roofs, fishing, cultivating or any other manual job. The people in the Char Islands counter poverty, ignorance of know-how, lack of education, lack of health care, economic care, unhygienic conditions but they persist with their belief to produce more children and to survive some how. This profuse multiplication of Bangladeshi migrants has caused a serious threat not only in north-east states or Assam but also in most of the cities in India where such pockets are there. Even after the order of Delhi High Court, not all Bangladeshis could be expelled out from Delhi and they can be seen in big camps, such as one near JNU. It is not only economic reason which is the primary factor for migration but also Bangladesh is one of the most densely populated countries of the world, with a figure of 1,250 persons per sq km approximately now. The growth rate of population in Bangladesh is about 2.2 per cent and the population gets increased by 2.8 million per year. A country where about 20 million people are displaced every year, when their area is inundated by floods, have to find a place for survival. Bangladesh is a country where poverty rate is as high as 40 per cent to 60 per cent, per capita income was about 14,400 takas per year, which comes to about 2,100 takas equivalent to Rs. 1,350 approximately per month as the value of taka is less than a rupee. It is 40 per cent of the per capita income of an Assamese.

At present, the Government of India, Ministry of Railways is helping Bangladesh in laying a railway line between Feni to Belonia. Similarly, the Akhaura-Agartala rail link is being restored. The commissioning of the railway line from Radhikapur towards Jessore is going to start again.

Social - Demographic Changes

Language prevailing on both the sides of the border

Bengali speaking people dominate the whole of West Bengal; it is the same language used in whole of East Bengal. Similar was the situation in Tripura and a part of Assam in Silchar, Karimganj and Cachar. The Bengali language gave the same culture and same tradition to both the Bengali speaking people in East Bengal and West Bengal, as earlier, during British period they were united. Those who came to Assam from Sylhet, *per force*, had to learn Assamese as they were called to evict Bengalis from Assam. Yet those, who never wanted to speak in Assamese and remain with Bengali speaking people, such Muslims, went to Barak valley in Cachar. All the tea plantation labours who came from Sylhet to Silchar tea gardens were more or less speaking in Bengali, so they could be adjusted easily with the local people. The Tripurites, more or less, depended on Bengali language; so those who came from Chittagong side to Tripura, found it much easier to mix up with local people and could educate their children in Bengali medium schools. When agitation started in Assam against Bangladeshi migrants, Mr. Chaliah, who used to favour the Muslim migrants, had to shift his constituency from Guwahati to Karimganj, as the Muslim migrants from Bangladesh in Karimganj were Bengali speaking and never gave preference to Assamese culture.

Both ULFA and AASU have organised physical attacks on Biharis and people from UP and on Bengalis living in Assamese dominated areas. More or less, first, it was against Bengalis as during British Period the Bengalis were dominating the Assamese in Guwahati and Shillong, occupied all the key posts in the state government and were better educated.

B P Chaliah, the then Chief Minister of Assam, bore nickname Badruddin Chaliah given to him by Assamese nationalists. Mainul Haque Choudhury always furthered Pakistani views and support for migrants from across the border and he helped B P Chaliah to be elected from Badarpur Assembly Constituency with Muslim support. The language issue first raised by Assamese went against them in most of the north-east states. Even in Assam itself, Bodos have their own language, the Karbies and the Rajbongshis do not follow Assamese language, and whole of Barak valley and Karimganj belt including Silchar, are not in favour of Assamese language.

If we take into account the Bihari Muslims, they were all Hindi speaking but could adjust themselves with Bengalis. Therefore, they wanted a place to speak in Hindi keeping both Bihari culture, Pak culture and to that extent, a little culture of Bengalis for which they got concentrated at Katihar, Purnia, Kishanganj, Daalkhola, Dhantola, Panjipara belt. It is only the jihadis who took the benefit of language problem in Assam and incited the Assam youth and fundamentalist groups to terrorise Hindi-speaking people in Assam as mostly, the Hindi-speaking people were controlling the economy of Assam as business persons, skilled manual workers and contractors of various projects. These attacks on the people of UP and Bihar in various parts of

Assam continued until 2010, and perhaps, it may go longer. Even though Assamese has been declared as the official language but the anti-Bengali violence, and the recent anti-Hindi violence in Assam, has only emboldened the militant groups and the extremists, including the jihadis and the ISI, in taking advantage of this situation. Till this day, the barbed wire fencing is not over in the entire Indo-Bangladesh border. Very little progress in floodlighting has been achieved up till now. There are few patches in Tripura-Bangladesh border where BDR/BGB objected to fencing on the border as the state government of Tripura wanted the fencing to come up on extreme point of international border and not leaving 150 yards as per policy. There was a meeting between BSF and BDR in which the BSF did put forward the points for having only a single line of fencing just near the borders of these patches so that the land of 150 yards from the boundary line can be utilised for cultivation. Matter was discussed again with Bangladesh border guards and the approval from headquarters from BGB has been obtained recently in few cases. Similarly, all the adverse possession cases have to be re-fenced.

Due to ethnic, linguistic, religious commonality of people at both sides of the border, it is very difficult to detect Bangladeshis while entering into India. The worst part is that, the Indian border people mostly keep quiet and do not help our border guarding forces and border police to trace Bangladeshis, especially those, who are coming from the side of Karimganj border, Cachar border, and the border of Dhubri district, that of Dawki, Mankachar, Tura, Mahendraganj and Dolu. Representatives of various political parties help in entry of Bangladeshis, give them shelter and guide them to come to hinterland in large numbers as they will constitute their vote bank. It has happened before 1975 and also after 1975. Until today, the government of Bangladesh has bluntly refused that they are involved in any of the migration cases and no migration has taken place to India nor their border guarding forces are accepting any Bangladeshis when they are handed over. In all court cases, the BDR/BGB, have made their stand very clear that such people do not belong to Bangladesh and their locations, as intimated by BSF to them, were contacted but no such person by that name were ever found to be residing in Bangladesh.

It is very difficult for the border police or the BSF just to push back them at night to Bangladesh as it has to be informed to the court that they were not only pushed back but handed over to some Bangladeshi authority, which never happens. Many such cases are pending in the border districts and the Bangladeshis are waiting in sizeable numbers whose cases were refused by BDR for acceptance. During the last mutiny of BDR, and just after that for few months, the border remained completely open from Bangladesh for about 3 months in 2009 until BDR was regrouped and renamed as BGB and all personnel involved in the mutiny were removed till Army got control over BDR fully. Those were the times when again a number of migrants entered to north-east from Bangladesh. It was also that the Assamese, for evicting Bengalis from Assam, depended more on Bangladesh Muslim migrants who preferred to accept Assamese as their mother tongue and voted for the rights of Assamese. Thus, the ULFA, for achieving their goal, remained the contact group between Bangladesh migrants and the settlement areas all over Assam. They contacted them well in hinterland in Bangladesh at Dhaka, Barisal, Chittagong, Rajsahi, Khulna, Sylhet, and guided them to their proper new settlement areas in most of the districts of Assam particularly Sonitpur, Guwahati, Nogaon, Hailakhandi, Karimganj, Dhubri, Goalpora, Udalguri, Baksha, Kokrajhar, and various Char Islands in river Brahmaputra. It is ULFA again, which manipulated ration cards, voter cards and identity cards for Bangladesh migrants and some of the lower level revenue officials of Assam in these districts were pressurised to transfer government lands in the name of such migrants. Assam was full of touts who were preparing false identity cards and made easy money.

If today we go to the BTC/ BTAD areas in Bodoland, the Bodos are not seen anywhere as labourers or rickshaw-pullers or working as home maids or cooks in someone else' houses. These hard-working Bangladeshi migrants have been provided menial jobs as an helping hand on payment to the lethargic Assamese at a very cheap rate. Thus, they found their supporters all over Assam i.e. from the social forum, contractors, government, politicians, and from militants. The Multa, the Mulfa, the NDFB, the ULFA, the Rohingya soil organisations, and ARIFM of Myanmar with the help of Hujis and Jamatis formed coalition for formation of a better and greater Bangladesh. The Bangladesh also helped ULFA of Assam, PLA of Manipur, NSCN-IM of Nagaland, HDFC of Meghalaya, NDFB of Assam and ATTF, and NLFT of Tripura to have their camps in Bangladesh and offered them land, weapons, ammunitions and training by both DGFI and ISI. The Centre for Women and Children Studies keeps an eye over the girls and women of Bangladesh who are brought to India and forced into prostitution. Their numbers are rising year-by-year.

Bangladesh also went on accusing India for supporting fundamentalist organisations in Bangladesh like Swadheen Bangabhumi Andolan and United People's Democratic Fund (UPDF). The ULFA leader Ranju Chodhury, Aurobindo Rajkhowa, and Anoop Chetia, all have been busy in training the ULFA groups in various camps in Bangladesh and keeping liaison with ISI. The Indira-Mujib agreement of 1972 defined the status of illegal migrants in India as it declared that all those who had come before 1971 were declared as non-Bangladeshis. This agreement was in a bad taste for the north-east people. Mushrooming of our own militant groups was the cause of such defective Agreements and defective Acts passed by the central government. To name a few, Indira-Mujib agreement, the IMDT act 1983, the Assam Accord with Rajiv Gandhi in 1985, etc. It is widely believed that Islamic militancy has been consolidating because of unabated Bangladeshi immigrations and these Islamic militant groups are not only spreading to other north-east states, but also, to each border district of Indo-Bangladesh border. The worst part of it is the present posture of Bangladesh government who are not accepting the deported people and asking India in every case to prove their Bangladesh nationality. The plight of 37,100 strong Indian population spread over 17,149 acres of 111 of our enclaves inside Bangladesh must find an end. They are more or less, stateless citizens. Since 1947, until now, the central government has failed to take a bold step to solve the problem; it could have been easily solved in 1971 operation which could not be done. The Tin Bigha is a strip of land inside India which was given on lease to Bangladesh for giving access to Bangladeshis to their Dahagram and Angarpota enclaves inside India. There is a possibility of criminals, militants, smugglers, extremists, and fundamentalists coming through Tin Bigha from Bangladesh to Dahagram enclave, then easily enter India, mix with the crowd, and reach Siliguri corridor. We also have a practical problem in constructing the barbed wire fence 150 yards away from the border, thus practically disallowing the real owners of the land in not cultivating such lands, as their movement to their land is channelised through various iron gates of the barbed wire fencing. Hundreds of villages, which remain on the other side of the fencing towards international border, are at the mercy of Bangladeshi criminals and they pass their nights in shadow of fear. Practically, they do not have any security cover from Indian border guarding forces except for facing harassment. Such villages slowly and slowly become the hideout of Bangladeshi militants and Bangladeshi criminals.

There is also a clash between the cultures and religions of these groups as Bangladeshis are mainly Muslim and Assamese mainly Hindu. The indigenous groups fear the loss of their identity through dilution of their culture by the influx of outsiders. Extremist groups, such as the NDFB, base persecution of refugees on what is termed 'nativism,' which occurs when a group claims "rights upon land, employment, political power and cultural hegemony that are greater than those people who are not indigenous" due to historical claims (Swain 1996). On the other hand, Bangladeshis can also claim this right because they also have ancestors that once settled in the area.

Conflict in Assam began in the late 1970s when a routine pre-election census in Mangaldoi revealed the presence of 70,000 Bangladeshi nationals. The incumbent Congress Party needed the migrants' votes to win power, so they did not actively attempt to deport them. Angry Assamese watching their resources dwindle and their identity disappear considered this inaction as complete government failure. Battles quickly erupted between native Assamese, led by the All Assam Gana Sangram Parishad (AAGSP) and All Assam Students Union (AASU), and Bangladeshi settlers, who also organised attacks in the face of some of aggressions. The violence cost more than 3,000 lives, culminating in a systematic attack on the Bangladeshi Muslim migrant village of Nellie by more than 8,000 native Hindu Assamese. That five-hour rampage cost over 1,700 lives. Attacks between the groups continue to this day and are intensifying with calls for ethnic cleansing by extremists.

The conflict also benefits extremist groups that have historically pursued secession from India of their own state. The strain on resources caused due to the vast number of illegal migrants in Assam has created bitterness in a greater portion of the population and ethnic groups took up violence to cleanse their area of foreigners.

Growing power and threats from Hindu organisations led to massive deportation of the Bangladeshi Muslim migrants in 1992. Unfortunately, Bangladesh did not want them either, as the Foreign Minister of Bangladesh made clear when he refused to accept them without documented proof of Bangladeshi citizenship, halting the deportation process.

We have already undermined our national security in not giving proper attention to this illegal immigration, which was ignored for about 20 years from 1972 to 1990. The long cherished design of Pakistan nationalists for having Greater East Pakistan and then the design of Bangladesh leaders, including some Muslim leaders of Islam, to have a Greater Bangladesh in getting fulfilled gradually as a result of change of the composition of population one-by-one of all the north-east states may come true.

Deportation of Bangladeshis—The Indian Express (10.9.2012) wrote 'according to figures placed in the Assembly in July, 2012, various Tribunals (Initially, IMDT Tribunals and Foreigners' Tribunal, and from 2005 onwards, Foreigners' Tribunal) have, between August 15, 1985 and April 30, 2012, declared 54,500 persons in Assam as foreigners from Bangladesh who had illegally entered the state. While the Government claimed it had deported 2,431 to Bangladesh during these 27 years, 39,287 have absconded with the government machinery not being able to trace them."

Muslims, having a soft corner for the migrants, dominate the complete border areas and they give them shelter. We have a number of villages at the opposite side of the fence towards Bangladesh within the international boundary, and these villages during night time, are at the mercy of Bangladeshi militants and Bangladeshi criminals. Perhaps, they are alien to us and they belong to a third country as for organising a marriage function in their village they cannot invite their relations from hinterland and they are not free even to cultivate their land during day time, as security cannot be provided to them 24 hrs. Similarly, there are many factors, which play role for the migrants' entry. The government sanctioned a second line border guarding police i.e. Prevention of Infiltration Force for Assam with the strength of 4,000 led by one Additional DG police rank but the complete force is idle. Excluding handing over of few Bangladeshis to BSF for repatriation through court order, perhaps, this force has nothing to do. Situation in the north-east is worse than that in Kashmir. Here, we are losing Assam day-by-day as the indigenous people are losing their identity and soon it is going to be followed by Meghalaya, Tripura and Nagaland. The Chief Minister of Meghalaya, Mr. Mukul Sangma has already started speaking for stopping infiltration from Bangladesh whereas, he has forgotten that the fencing in Meghalaya was delayed for years together for non-cooperation from government of Meghalaya. It did not permit the CPWD to erect fencing in Khasi and Jaintia border and asking the border district collectors to earmark and handover the land for erection of the fence. It happened in this Congress regime in last 5 years. Tura sector had come up with fencing, even though it has forest and hilly terrain, but Khasi and Jaintia portion remained pending as the coal mafias never wanted the fencing to come up.

Much of the large-scale infiltration can be attributed to inaction and apathy of the people coupled with disinclination for skilled work or manual labour. The officials were only willing to enrol Bangladeshi voters in our electoral roles and to register landed property in their names. This news greatly facilitated the influx. However, there were sections who felt dispossessed of inalienable rights because of infiltration. Most of these migrants in a short duration of time occupied all the government lands and grazing fields in the border areas and turned out as poor tenants in Bengali Babus' and Assamee Babus' residences. This penetration brought a strong undercurrent of ethnic tension in the tribal inhabited area. Migrants never entered those areas where they faced opposition like, Sibsagar and Karbianglong, but were welcomed by most of the Hindu and Muslim communities in all the border states. The migrants spread to safer areas where the people were friendly. Gaining strength over a period of time, fundamentalist militant groups sprouted with ISI support. Their objective was to carve out an Islamic Republic in the north-east and a Greater Bangladesh by slicing of the whole of West Bengal. The central government, after 1971 operation, never thought that Bangladesh would create more problems to India than East Pakistan. Until the interference of ISI in the north-east of India, the Centre neglected the entire region, which caused mushrooming of militancy and rising of mosques and madrasas in all over Indo-Bangladesh border.

Similar is the situation in Mankachar, Tura Belt of Meghalaya where crossing of border is very easy as it was the main root of supply of arms by ULFA to Assam through various couriers and touts. Assam is full of natural resources, oil, forest, limestone, coal, timber and it gets a good rainfall for paddy cultivation. Since independence, both in 1947 and then in 1971, when it was separated from Pakistan, Bangladesh is having an eye on the rich resources of Assam and is playing the game to detach it from India. The way the migration is taking place and their progeny are proliferating rapidly their names and also find inclusion in the voter list of Assam, time is now ripe, that like Kashmir, this entire mass will raise their voice in favour of Bangladesh and Pakistan, as their numbers are increasingly swelling in the Assembly.

The Jatiya Sansad in its report on 24th Nov., 1998, brought out that any move by India to deport anyone on the plea of a Bangladeshi national would be unacceptable. Similarly, most of the papers including 'Bangladesh Observer' have brought out that BDR had foiled various attempts of India's BSF to push back Bengali speaking Indian nationals from Dinajpur to Satkhira. This indirectly means whoever we push back as Bangladeshi national are reported to be Indian nationals and Bangladesh does not own them up and the authorities over there are very happy that the burden of population growth in their country is shared to some extent by India. These large-scale migrations of Bangladeshis to Assam, West Bengal and Tripura have had an impact on the political atmosphere of the states.

We have in our record the statement made by Sri Hiranya Kumar Bhattacharyya, who has served the Government of Assam as Deputy Inspector General of Police. It transpires from his statement that according to the official claims, three lakhs foreigners are already deported. However, even the names of those deported foreigners who have been enrolled as voters are not deleted from the electoral rolls. "Neither there is, nor any reason can be as to why under-populated regions in the developed world cannot make room for planned colonies to relieve build-up of demographic disasters in countries like Bangladesh..." [Extract from the report of the Mehta Commission appointed by the Assam State Freedom Fighters Association for enquiring into the circumstances leading to the holocaust before, during, and after the forcefully imposed General Elections of 1983."

Despite the general optimism surrounding current India-Bangladesh relations, the momentum in bilateral ties between the two neighbours appear to be slowing down. Two-days Home secretary-level talks in Dhaka in second week of October, 2012 once again saw both sides kick the can down the road on vital issues. With general elections in Bangladesh only a year away, the Awami League-led government in Dhaka is getting jittery. Notwithstanding New Delhi's political compulsions, there is an urgent need to infuse the India-Bangladesh relationship with fresh energy and work towards concrete results.

Sri Bhattacharya DIG, Police, Assam earlier reminded the AGP leaders that, the AGP leaders are now reluctant to speak about the Accord fearing that they might lose the vote of the foreign nationals. [The Assam Tribune, August 13, 2000]

The Chief Minister of Meghalaya, Sh. Mukul Sangma, said that new mechanism to identify illegal immigrants and robust comprehensive border management system is required which should include upping economic activity across the border by promoting trade and commerce between both neighbouring countires which is necessary to proactively upscale living condition on both sides of the border, so as to reduce tendency for illegal migration. The Meghalaya government has organised two border haats to promote trade across the border. It could be replicated all along the Indo-Bangladesh border, which he informed to Shri Sushil Kumar Shinde, the Home Minister of India, during his visit to north-east [Times of India, 14th August 2012].

Thus, the penetration of migrants, even now, continues. The socio-economic conditions in Chars are worse during monsoon. These people shift themselves to high-rise bundhs or to boats and again start their life in new Char Islands. This has led to political turmoil in whole of Assam, particularly in changing the demographic pattern of Dhubri, Goalpara, Sonitpur, Baksa, Chirang, Udalguri, and Kokrajhar districts. Even though, every one in Char Islands is a foreigner, but they are enjoying Indian citizen status.

The political parties during every monsoon receive them as displaced persons, provide opportunity to mix with the crowd, and they go missing, avail ration card, identity card, and voters' card on payment. There are touts all over Char Island and in Karimganj border where even ration cards and identity cards are provided on payment well in advance to the migrants before they start their journey from Bangladesh hinterland. The migrants because of socio-economic factors like poverty, lack of infrastructure, education and health problems, prefer to find a place to settle themselves in urban areas rather than rural areas. In Char Islands, there are mostly Muslim communities, and even a small family has four to five children with two to three girls and polygamy is rampant which is another reason for the high growth rate of children in Char Islands.

We are heading for a disastrous strategic and economic fallout in Assam, which is the showpiece of whole of north-east.

Missing of Bangladeshi Nationals coming to India with Valid Passports

Over 80,000 Bangladeshi nationals who entered the country with valid documents have disappeared during the last three years in India. On a day when the debate over illegal infiltration rocked the Parliament, the Home Ministry admitted in Rajya Sabha that 82, 585 Bangladeshi nationals, with valid travel documents have gone missing in India.

In 2011, some 21,274 Bangladeshi nationals disappeared without a trace. The highest number of 32,644 Bangladeshis had gone traceless in 2009, though the figure came down to 28,667 the next year.

According to Home Ministry's records, 67,945 foreign nationals hailing from different countires have disappeared in India, but the highest number belongs to Bangladesh followed by nationals of Afghanistan [The Assam Tribune-11.8.2012].

Following volatile situation in Assam, the governments of USA, Canada, Britain and Australia warned their visiting tourists in India against visiting Assam and other north-east states (Asomiya Pratidin, 27.7.2012).

Peak Period of Bangladeshi Migration

There was a Hindu backlash during 1964-65 due to Indo-Pakistan war. In this incident, the first big migration took place from Bangladesh to India excluding that of the tea planters who came during British period and then the Mymensinghias who came to the undivided district of Goalpara Assam. Later, the biggest migration of Hindus, Bihari Muslims and few Muslims took place in 1971-72, just before and after the war operation, which was the sharpest peak period. Just after the assassination of Sheikh Mujibur Rehman on 15th August 1975, another peak period of Hindu migration from Bangladesh was noticed. The Hindu migration to West Bengal was again noticed during Zia-ur-Rehman tenure from 1975-81, and that of Begum Khalida Zia from 1981-96, when Muslim fundamental groups in Bangladesh became very powerful and threatened Hindus. Out of fear and insecurity, the Hindus had to leave that country.

Another reason for the Hindu migration from Bangladesh with a peak period was just after demolition of Babri Masjid in which a number of Hindu temples were destroyed in Bangladesh and Hindus were forced to convert themselves to Muslims. Due to lack of proper employment for Hindus in Bangladesh, the males migrated to West Bengal for permanent settlement and the females left Bangladesh facing sexual abuse and molestation. These migrants were mostly uneducated, were not aware of family planning methods due to which child population increased, wherever these clusters settled in India.

They lived in unhygienic conditions without proper nutritous food, non-provision of feed to their children, no resource for health care, no money to get hospitalisation, absence of potable water, poverty, illiteracy, absolutely new surrounding in the new world for them in India and faced child mortality to a great extent. However, their entry to India helped the agricultural sector as farming improved in

West Bengal and Assam and household industries also made development.

The slums in every part of India increased and small *jhuggi bastis* developed every nook and corner of the country including Delhi where, even in one room, ten number of such migrants could get shelter. They became very close to our politicians as their names were entered in the voter list and they manipulated to remain as best friends of our politicians.

Every political leader, irrespective of any party, whether it is in north-east, or in West Bengal, or in Delhi were in their favour and recommended their presence in their areas. There is no political or social will to oust them out to Bangladesh.

Such migrants who entered India, also got involved in smuggling, prostitution, robbery, begging, other crimes, and trafficking of women and children. Slowly and tactfully, they managed to grab land from Indian owners and from revenue authorities. Like that of Meghalaya government, which has issued work permits to these migrants as daily labours, similar solution can be brought out in Kokrajhar and Bodo areas. Deporting millions of Bangladeshi migrants, even, who came after 1971 or even after 2011 census, is practically impossible, and it will lead to violence like Hindu-Muslim riots, tension in Indo-Bangladesh border, political battles, uprise of Muslim fundamentalist organisations all over India, and open protest by Muslim-dominated areas against the government. Even though resident permit to illegal immigrants should not be granted in India, yet there is a question about the children who are born to them in India and also having one of their parents to be an Indian. There will be two states viz. West Bengal and Assam, which will come forward to announce that it will be inhuman to send these Bangladeshi migrants back. Due to religious persecution in Bangladesh, and as Bangladesh is an Islamic State, the Hindu migration from 1971, until now, remains unabated and for the time being, they remain in this country as stateless citizens. The economic depression, lack of employment opportunities, forced grabbing of land from

Hindus in Bangladesh, economic insecurity, poverty, struggle for livelihood, and lack of industrialisation forced these migrants to come to India which is not economically depressed as poverty is not that a big issue in our country. Even though agriculturally, Bangladesh is in a good position, but due to density of population and non-availability of sufficient land for cultivation, its men fail to look after their families.

Bangladesh is full of low-income group families whether they are Hindus or Muslims. They are supposed to migrate like in Mexico from high density area to low density area. The over population of Bangladesh has to find its way to spread as it crosses all the barriers. The worst phenomenon in Bangladesh is that they do not follow birth control policy, and child marriage and producing children profusely is rampant everywhere in its territory and same holds true for all the places whereever they are located in India.

The Hindus could not educate their children in the schools following Islamic preaching and the Hindu girls were humiliated, were forced to become Muslims; and Hindu husbands went to the extent of mortgaging their wives to get a small work. Those girls who belonged to better families, fled to India. Bangladesh has seen political instability since 1971 where riots were too common and terrorism had become a part of life even in Dhaka whether by Jamatis, by Muslim fundamentalists, by Hujis, Al-Qaedas, or by ISI and few political parties. A number of intidimidation incidences of Hindu voters were reported in Bangladesh elections and most of them either sold their properties or were forcibly asked to leave Bangladesh. The fundamentalist section, particularly Jamaat-e-Islami, played an important role in bringing Pakistan close to Bangladesh and creating anti-India atmosphere there. Pakistan always projected Bangladesh as not being a vital unit politically, strategically, or economically and, as such, manipulated to overpower the country through religious and fundamental means. The card of religion played by Pakistan had a sentimental impact on the psyche of Bangladeshis excluding few factions of Awami League. Few groups of the Bangladesh army, the people of Bangladesh, all Muslim parties, all political parties and fundamentalists are in favour of Pakistan and against India. Being a Muslim country, Bangladesh has maintained common bond with Pakistan. Gen Zia-ul-Haq gave a statement that "the law of a Muslim country for another Muslim country cannot be snatched away" (Daily News, 21st August, 1982). Similarly, Gen Zia further added that Bangladeshs' sorrow is Pakistan's sorrow and Bangladesh's joy is Pakistan's joy (New Nation, 6th June, 1985). Both Pakistan and Bangladesh have adopted pro-U.S. and pro-China policy and a hardcore anti-India, anti-soviet posture. Even during the present new regime of China under Xi Jinping in the second week of November 2012, the policy of Bangladesh towards China is maintained with same status without any change. Similarly, Xi Jinping had promised during Khalida's visit to China recently to provide all technical help to Bangladesh in future. China has already achieved diplomatic victory in expanding relations with Bangladesh at the expense of both India and Soviet Union and upgraded technical equipments and weapons for Bangladeshi troops, which are procured from China. The presence of PLA training camps in Bangladesh to train Indian insurgent groups and despatch of Chinese-made pistols and weapons to north-east insurgents and left-wing extremist groups is in the knowledge of Bangladesh.

China has set-up arms and ammunition factory in Bangladesh at Joydevpur. Bangladesh has steadily improved her relations with the U.S.A, China and Pakistan. Even though the present regime of Sheikh Hasina is having a pro-India stance, yet, it's most political parties and fundamentalist groups are not in favour of India as they are totally influenced by Islamic radicalism which has entered their blood and has permeated to all the border districts of India through their migrants.

The Huji-B attacked the American Centre in Kolkata on 22nd January, 2002 in which four police officers were killed and 17 were injured. The interrogation of arrested persons in this case revealed Hugi-B's links with Lakshar-e-Toiba, JEM and Huji of Pakistan. Similarly, Farhan Mallik

Illiyas Aftab Ansari, a Hugi-B activist of Bangladesh abducted Calcutta-based businessman Partha Prateem Roy Burman on 25th July, 2001 who was released on 30th July 2001 after payment of a ransom of 37.5 million rupees through Hawala Route (Bangladesh, the next Afghanistan by Hirenmay Karlikar).

Few of the other Jihadi groups, which are functioning with Huji and JuM, Harkat-ul-Ansar, Taliban and Al-Qaeda are Jagratta Muslim Janta Bangladesh, Hizbul-ut-Tahrir, Oikya Jote, and the Islamic Chhattra Shibir.

Khalida Zia's period aroused considerable insecurity feelings amongst Hindus in preaching religious Islamic curriculum in educational institutions. The lack of democracy in Bangladesh is an open fact. It always enhanced political terrorism. Excluding that of the capital and few cantonment areas, the law and order situation in Bangladesh is the worst. Even police stations do not register FIRs submitted by Hindus against their difficulties being faced from the fundamentalists. The Bangladesh police take the side of the criminals in cases where Hindus are involved and the complaints received from minority Hindus always go unnoticed. It was quite a routine in Begum Zia's time. That is why the Government of India is trying its best to remain in touch with Begum Khalida Zia's group, as the election in Bangladesh will be held in December, 2013 and Begum Khalida Zia visited Delhi from 28th October to 3rd November, 2012 on the invitation of the foreign minister of Government of India. During her visit, she met the President of India, the Leader of Opposition, the External Affairs Minister, the National Security Advisor Shri Shiv Shankar Menon, the Foreign Secretary Shri Ranjan Mathai and important members of the cabinet. The Awami League is sensitive to India's security concern, whereas, the BNP does not have empathetic views, as their vote banks depend upon anti-India stance. Yet, during her last tenure, the BNP favoured business communities in both sides. Her recent visit to China was very successful. BNP may take China's help for their infrastructural development. BNP since last three tenures had anti-India partners like

Jamat-e-Islami. Even then, as per an article "Bangladesh-India relations strategic analysis" of October 2012, Begum Zia wrote, "there are forces in both our societies who have played, and continue to play, on this fear psychosis to perpetuate mutual suspicion and thereby keep us apart. The need of the time is a changed mindset". BNP wants to dispel the popular notion that India is close to Awami League only and BNP is always anti-India. She favours greater economic engagement with India. Begum Zia has stated that she will try to connect the north-east part of the India to the ports Chittagong and Cox's Bazaar for trade and commerce purpose. She also emphasised improvement in bilateral relations between both the countries and further added that religious extremism is a living concern for both countries and we should make joint efforts to fight it (29th Oct 2012, The Daily Star). Khalida kept on adding that she will not allow terrorists to use Bangladesh land to harm India. However, she has contacted China and made them agree to construct the 2nd bridge over river Padma ('New Nation' of 1st November, 2012). China also has agreed to make the rail and road link from Chittagong to Kunming. A deep-sea port at Sonadia in the Bay of Bengal will also be constructed by China for Bangladesh, which is a matter of concern, and this will help China in its domination of Bay of Bengal. Begum Khalida Zia has already met the Prime Minister Shri Manmohan Singh and leader of opposition in Lok Sabha Smt. Sushma Swaraj. She made it very clear to them that the border killings of Bangladeshi personnel along Indo-Bangladesh border by the Border guarding force of India must stop as it creates a hostile feeling against India in the minds of Bangladeshis.

She also mentioned in her conversation with the leader of opposition here that the change of enclaves between both the countries must be made, which is pending for ratification in Indian Parliament, without displacing people. She also wanted full share for Bangladesh of Teesta waters and was happy on formation of a sub-committee of Indo-Bangladesh joint river commission of Tipai Mukh project on river Barak in Manipur. In Sinha earth blog of 30th

October, 2012 and Delhi new nation, South Asian monitor of 30th October, 2012; it has come out that both the countries should adopt a common approach to all the problems. Bangladesh may prefer 'twin India policies', one for dealing with all the border states of India towards Bangladesh, and the second with the central government.

Excluding industries of cottage, jute, cotton fabrics and that based on export of leather and fishes, the trade of Bangladesh with India in other sectors is negligible. All political parties enriched their vote banks and helped migrants with ration cards as a proof of citizenship. A number of them got government jobs. Few of them were recruited as doctors even in security organisations, who came from Bangladesh and had medical education certificate from Bangladesh in support of them.

We also have undocumented migration from Bangladesh even today. Hundreds of Bangladeshis have now started coming within official channels along with proper passport and visa through various border checkposts and airports. A number of them go missing in this vast country; they destroy their passport and visa and remain with the relatives or get a shelter from their known persons in some corner of the country, and it is an extremely tedious task to verify, notice and apprehend all such vanished migrants of Bangladesh. In fact, this is the only way, now, by which the militants are coming from Bangladesh and Pakistan to India using false passport and get a shelter by their men here. Weapons and ammunitions are available in plenty with their contacts in India to carry out their tasks, assigned to them either in Bangladesh or in Pakistan.

There is absolute absence of democratic rights to Hindus in Bangladesh, full Muslim domination and no political help to Hindu minority group. In India, whether it is Hindu, or Muslim migrants, they get a better standard of living. The political patronage was available to them earlier also in 1947, and it is there even today.

The present Chief Minister of Assam has gone to the extent of giving a statement on 20th October, 2012 at

Guwahati that, Muslim migrants to Assam is not the biggest issue for his government. He agreed that they are in sizeable numbers in Assam. He also agreed that the number of migrants in Assam kept on increasing but gave rise to other problems of Assam in the area of agriculture, revenue, education, unemployment and potable water for solution on priority basis (Navbharat Times, Guwahati, Hindi Edition, October 20, 2012). To give few examples, again in BTC area of Kokrajhar, two personnel were shot dead and were hacked to death on 10th November, 2012. Similarly, one more farmer was shot dead at Kokrajhar on 13th November, 2012 (TOI of 14th Nov., 2012). The violence will erupt repeatedly in Kokrajhar if this migrant issue is not solved (Times of India, 10th November, 2012). Similarly, on 12th November, 2012, one more farmer was killed in Kokrajhar. It shows that Muslim fundamentalists and other fundamentalist groups have become active again in BTC areas. To supplement this, one more casualty was reported on 15th November, 2012 at Kokrajhar on account of which Assam Government has declared curfew in BTC areas and the Army have been deployed to maintain peace. No one knows how 4.5 lakhs of displaced personnel who took shelter in various camps (TOI of 16th November, 2012) were settled by Assam government. India in future will remain as an economic pull factor for attracting migrants from Bangladesh as it gives lower level job opportunities to them, and the displaced Bangladeshis, whether Hindus or Muslims, will keep on coming to India for better economic opportunities, job opportunities, economic security and better health and education of their children.

The demographic similarity between Bangladesh and Indian north-east states, the social similarity and geographic location of north-east states will favour Bangladeshis to enter India even in future. If Assam is saturated, they will move to other north-east locations like Manipur, Nagaland and Meghalaya, where they are already getting social security, that is, at Shillong, Garo Hills, and Khasi in Meghalaya; Lilong, Kwakta, and Moreh in Manipur; and Dimapur in Nagaland.

It is high time we should not play with economic harmony of our border states and border districts. The undocumented migration of Bangladeshis has to end and during the present ongoing census; their numbers have to be seriously noted so that it will be easier to keep a trace of their movement all over the country. It requires a quantitative and a qualitative survey not only in border areas of Assam, Tripura, Meghalaya, and West Bengal, but in most of the states where they have taken shelter.

So far, no comprehensive study has been made on undocumented migration from Bangladesh to India. There are various statements and various publications on this issue by a number of authors, and there are several statements from politicians and Ministry of Home Affairs, quoting different figures.

On 21st March, 2012, Shri Mullapally Ramachandran, Hon'ble Minister of Government of India gave a statement to Press Information Bureau that Dhubri area has 75 per cent Muslim population out of which 70.07 per cent speak in Assamese and 24.15 per cent speak in Bengali, whereas in Barak valley, particularly in Haila-Kandi and Karimganj districts, 40 per cent Hindus are reported, but most people in these two districts speak in Bengali.

There was a meeting at Dhaka between both the chiefs of border guarding forces of India and Bangladesh in September 25, 2012 in which maximum focus was given to illegal migration and various measures to counter it. The Home Secretary level meeting of both the countries were held at Dhaka on 15th and 16th October, 2012 between Shri R.K. Singh, the Home Secretary of India and Shri Manjoor Husain, the Home Secretary of Bangladesh. Both of them visited new land customs checkposts at Akhaura, Tripura. They had discussions on smuggling of narcotics and drugs between both the countries, identification of vulnerable crossing points, repatriation of ULFA Leader Anup Chetia to India, inflow of FICN from Bangladesh, extradition treaty and combating terror (Anup Chetia, the General Secretary of ULFA, is in Bangladesh since 1997). Our Home Secretary also took up the case of human trafficking with Bangladesh and camps of north-east insurgent groups in Bangladesh. It was further discussed that the fencing on Indo-Bangladesh border was made up to extent of 75 per cent and the Indian side faced problem on 115 points to erect the fencing. These were mainly relating to opposition from Bangladesh border guards and shifting the fencing from the restriction of 150 yards up to the zero line so that maximum number of villages coming in between these zones could be benefitted and cultivable land can be saved. It was also informed to Bangladesh authorities that the BSF has been asked to use pump action and stun guns, non-lethal weapons in place of rifles while dealing with Bangladeshis crossing over to India. It was also brought out to the knowledge of Bangladesh authorities about menace of cattle smuggling in border areas, breaching of fence, inflow of FICN and shelter of north-east Indian insurgent groups in Chittagong Hills Tracts.

The border police force of Assam with a strength of four thousand, which is performing the duties under one additional director general of police, is more or less defunct and that has to be energised. They should be trained to provide a second line of defence behind the Border Security Force and work in cooperation with them as Assam is the only state where Bengali Muslim migrants are penetrating, followed by Meghalaya.

Neither the BSF, nor border police organisation of any border state of India, can prevent this large-scale illegal immigration from Bangladesh. Prompt action must be taken to close these 186 gaps reported to be existing within the fencing areas and the Bangladesh border guards and local population have to be taken into confidence. Similarly, the fencing has to be constructed on the zero line of the border. In such cases, where the villages are located within 150 yards from the IB, houses through which the boundary line passes must be shifted to interior areas giving the individual proper compensation to rebuild his house. The fencing should not be given a free access to the people to cross.

The political patronage shown by various political parties towards these migrants must stop in national interest, similarly, all Muslim fundamentalist organisations like that of SIMI, HUM, HUJI, Lashkar-e-Toeba, and Harkat-ul-Ansar should remain banned and their members be arrested. Any new mosques and madrasas coming up in border areas must be promptly reported by border guarding forces and border police organisation to the state authorities, and either they should be properly registered, or they should not be allowed to come up. Action should be initiated against all such mosques and madrasas which are getting funds from abroad and not only a watch has to be kept over such funding, but this funding business has to be stopped and not allowed by the Government of India.

Like that of Mangaldoi in Assam, the constituency in which 70,000 Bangladeshi migrants were enrolled as voters on the behest of political parties, nowhere in India these migrants be given voter cards and all those that have been issued, should be cancelled. It should start from Delhi itself where, more than lakhs of Bangladeshi migrants are camping in various 'jhuggi bastis' and get the support of political parties.

It is not possible to deport cent per cent Bangladeshi migrants who entered India after March, 1971. They have to be declared as stateless citizens, not to be given refugee status, should not be allowed to own landed property in India, and should not get government jobs. They may be, however, given work permits in India, all of them should be registered, and get the identity cards showing them as Bangladeshis. Any contractor or any civilian employing such Bangladeshis without any work permit should be penalised. The BSF, which is deployed in Indo-Bangladesh border, should not be shifted away from border guarding job for any internal security duties, which tends to remove them from the border in the process. It is only those BSF battalions, which are there as reserves, that can be deployed for such purpose, if required. First preference for the reserve battalions is to give relief to the battalions deployed at border and then to rotate them for annual training. This is in consonance with the policy and recommendations of Group of Ministers which is, however, not being followed on the ground. Even during changeover of BSF battalions, another reserve battalion has to be deployed in that area instead of asking training companies of various BSF battalionjs, otherwise, the flanking units have to cover that gap, which really is not effective and that is the route, mostly followed by the migrants and militants during such changeover of BSF units. Similarly, there are about 86 vulnerable border outpost areas in the entire stretch of Indo-Bangladesh border, which are easy to cross. These vulnerable areas have to be strengthened and the gaps have to be covered along with Sundarban areas, the Padma and the Teesta river border. Brahmaputra should have more number of medium crafts and speedboats, with marine troops attatched to them, under BSF to keep a watch over its riverine border.

Sufficient funds have to be kept with the border guarding force to ensure that all these boats are water worthy and ply in all weathers, including monsoon. Whatever migrants have already entered through Brahmaputra have to be taken into account and fresh entries from Bangladesh to temporary Char Islands should not be permitted and such temporary Char Islands, when reappear, be handed over to the forest authorities for plantation and should not be auctioned to Dewans to further lease it to Bangladeshis again in future. Further steps are to properly register the names of people permanently staying in big permanent Char Islands like Masalabari, Shaitanbari, that lie in India and Bangladesh, both. Any new person entering Indian side of these combined Char Islands be evicted and pushed back then and there, instead of apprehending him, bringing him by boat to Dhubri and producing him before the court and court ordering him to be pushed back. At the end, BGB, after three to four months, on being contacted, will come up with a reply that he is not a Bangladeshi but rather an Indian Muslim, and will refuse to accept it. One can see the mockery of the entire set-up, thus. Because of religious issues, Government of India cannot take a decision to have a cattle trade with Bangladesh. This is the only type of smuggling through which maximum portion of the border fencing is breached and militants keep on crossing along with cattle smugglers and transaction of FICN and drugs increase in these gaps. Either the troops need to be told to allow cattle smuggling and open the gates for that or we have to stop it by force. If the Government of India is not inclined to earn revenue in exporting cattle, the Bangladesh personnel can be allowed to purchase the cattle from border haats and be allowed to pass through proper gates rather than this skewed policy which demoralises the troops. The troops do not know, at times, what action they have to take. Similar is the effect of instruction passed on to the border security personnel for not using guns to open fire even at night against the person coming through the fence. In lieu of guns, BSF has been asked to use non-lethal weapons like stun guns, which are known to Bangladesh criminals. This has resulted in BSF border patrolling personnel being injured by Bangladeshi criminals.

Even recently during the visit of Khalida Zia to Delhi from 28th October to 3rd November, she has reiterated this point that there should be no killing at Indo-Bangladesh border. This was also the earlier stand taken by Sheikh Hasina, and thus, the Indo-Bangladesh border is now dominated more by Bangladeshi criminals and less by the Border Security Force. Even though, recently, BSF has opened a new frontier at Guwahati and a new sector headquarters at Dhubri and another one at Jawai in Meghalaya, yet, the number of BSF battalions remains the same.

Dhubri Char Islands itself require one additional BSF Battalion. Similarly, the Garo sector having Mankachar, Mahenderganj, Dolu and Porakhasia do need one extra battalion. BSF also has to provide one battalion extra for Karimganj, Cachar Sector, one for Jaintia and one for Khasi borders keeping sufficient reserves, as these are the only areas facilitating migration from Bangladesh. Border-deployed battalions should not be shifted for internal security duties or counter insurgency operations. Prohibitory order has been issued by district magistrate, Cachar, of Assam on 3rd Nov, 2012 in five kms belt of Indo-Bangladesh border as there was an information about extremist elements entering Karimganj from Bangladesh to cause disturbances. The district magistrate has also stopped movement of any boat in river Surma from 8 PM to 5 AM.[7] It is again in Khasi and Jaintia border that 23 illegal migrants were apprehended by BSF at Shillong border as stated by Inspector General BSF, Shillong. On 12th November, Hangeria BOP of Shillong frontier BSF from Jaintia hills apprehended four Bangladeshi Muslim migrants. Same day they also apprehended three Bangladeshi Muslims by their Umkiang BOP while entering into India. In both the cases, the Bangladeshi tout Sukur Ali managed to escape to Bangladesh. It so happens that, immigrants are always coming through the unfenced area and the gaps.

There should be sensor and camera system including UAVs to monitor these riverine gaps 24 hours as these will never be fenced. We have various rivers in Indo-Bangladesh border like that of Ichhamati, Mahananda, and small tributaries of river Barak where the mid-stream is the boundary line. These are areas where very strict watch has to be kept over plying of Indian boats, so as also of Bangladesh boats and fishermen, from both the sides. Out of four All Terrain Vehicles (ATVs) procured for Sir Creek in Gujarat border, two of them are not functioning and lying idle since long. All these floating vehicles and middle crafts must function round the-clock and all the speedboats must have night vision devices fitted into them along with GP system with naval commandos operating them.

Brahmaputra has very typical boats used by villagers for ferrying. They are called 'fat-fatties'. They have speed and work on diesel Kirloskar generator engine and the engine can be fitted inside the boat, the pipe is hardly one foot inside water due to which it is never stuck during winter anywhere. The BSF crafts and boats cannot be used in Brahmaputra in all its channels in winter and summer, as the streams get dried up.

Even though these 'fat-fatties' are available with BSF on rent basis, yet, as they have proved more water worthy in Brahmaputra, they can be adopted by BSF as already BSF is adopting tractors in Rajasthan in lieu of camels.

The use of multi-purpose photo identity cards for all border population and updating of national register of citizen is in vogue since long but the register for entering the names, addresses, photos of illegal migrants as stateless citizens are incomplete. Any such migrant, if leaves that area, his relations are duty-bound to report about his presence in India to the local police station and district authorities. In Bangladesh, the Grameen Bank has made a lot of progress in giving service to a number of women and girls who have opened their accounts in large numbers. The women training schools for computer have come up in Chittagong, which will automatically empower the girl children in Bangladesh to come up. India can help Bangladesh in organising and management of various fields like fishery, agriculture, piggery, cotton industries, jute mills and technological up-gradation so that Bangladesh can become self-sufficient in times to come, and only when the economical disparity between both the countries will end, the migration will come to a halt. During the visit of Ms Hina Rabbani Khar, Foreign Minister of Pakistan to Bangladesh in first week of November, 2012, Mr. Deepu Moni, the Foreign Minister of Bangladesh, expected an apology from Pakistan for the genocide carried out by their troops in Bangladesh in 1971. Islamabad since 1974, is avoiding expressing regret over the issue, however, Ms Hina Khar avoided the question replying that "it is now time to proceed forward burying the past". It is a positive sign of our Awami League government to have taken up such issues with Pakistan ('Times of India', 10th November, 2012).

Various state police personnel from Maharashtra, Kerala, Rajasthan, J&K and Punjab bring apprehended Bangladeshi migrants and request BSF at the borders to push them back. BGB's refusal to accept them poses serious administrative difficulties to these police officers.

Earlier also, on several occasions, the Bangladeshi press has accused India as a Hindu fundamentalist government trying to push Indian Muslims to Bangladesh thus inciting Hindu-Muslim riots all over the country.

Now, we are not capable to identify these 20 million Bangladeshis in India and to deport them back to Bangladesh and certainly it is not a practical solution. In future, whoever is caught at the border can be dealt under 'Foreigner's Act, 1946' and be pushed back at the earliest by the border guarding forces.

The suggestions earlier given by retired governor of Assam, Gen. S K Sinha were proper, and government, even though, implemented few of these recommendations, it must also go ahead implementing other points taking them seriously.

Bangladeshi leader of opposition, Ms Khaleda Zia, has signalled a shift in her stance regarding relations with India. Winding her weeklong India tour, Zia emphasised a fresh beginning in bilateral ties based on mutual respect. With election in Bangladesh slated for December 2013, Zia's accent on bilateral co-operation is significant. In an effort to make good India- Bangladesh ties irreversible, New Delhi has done well to reach out to different political formation in Dacca ('Times of India' of 3rd November, 2012).

Bangladesh should learn from the help rendered by three Delhites in paying fine of three lakhs to court for the release of Bangladeshi sculptor Rashid Ahmed and his daughter-in- law Noor Nahar Lovely, who were languishing in Tihar jail for the last eight years for bringing fake currency. They were released just before the Eid and were provided the air tickets to go back to Bangladesh. The sculptor had no money to pay for the fine imposed against him by the court (TOI of 23rd Oct, 2012 and 27th Oct, 2012).

Similarly, the training of local police—of not only those deployed in border areas, but also of border states and the border guarding forces—has to be given more importance. Border guarding force should invariably be not shifted and its reserves must be available for border training, field crafts, arms training, shooting skills, gathering of intelligence and various other techniques of border management. The issues of poor training standard, lack of motivation, discipline, and good behaviour on and off duty, professionalism, impartiality, tactfulness, inquisitive skills, lack of willpower and the corruption with border guarding forces must be redressed. Its infrastructure improvement, knowledge of background of the local people, knowledge of local terrain, local habits, religion, knowledge of local language, mutual interaction with other CPMFs, local police, civil administration, the army and the judiciary has to be planned properly. They must remain aware of political, social, religious, and economic issues of the border population. Prior intelligence and proper vigilance at the border can reduce infiltration significantly. There should be no ego problem between government security agencies placed at the border like that of BSF, CRPF, Police, Army, Customs, Excise, IB, State intelligence and R and AW. Local police plays an important role in providing intelligence inputs to the border guarding forces. Proper communication should be maintained with field commanders of BSF with local police stations. Similarly, the local police must be trained about manning of check posts, first aid, weapon training, shooting skills, maintaining close relation with local people without emotional or dishonest attachment, flexibility in approach to problems, surveillance of border area, helping attitude, identification of various drugs and explosives, respecting village heads and women and identification of new faces in border areas. Role of police in community development, detection of migrants, helping ethnic border people, stopping spread of communal violence/ riots and check on people, rendering help to Bangladeshi migrants, and giving them shelter in border areas, have to be taken care of.

As the local police know the people and the area better than anybody else does, they will be able to provide advance information of any activities in the border. The migrants at the time of entry always depend upon their contacts in

Indian side. The guides and vehicles are always made available to them properly planned and mostly positioned on border road head points, from where bus service starts for interior areas. One should not forget the basic psychology of the border population. Whatever has been lost from 1971 in the borders can be gained slowly and slowly with patience if the lower level commander behaves properly with the border population and helps them displaying provincialism and impartiality. There are always reports that the gates in the fencing are opened during night for the migrants to cross after bribing border guarding forces. This has to be avoided by the troops. As the border guarding forces are unknown to the local people and they change after every 3 years, the new lots coming must know the background of the people, the area, their culture, language, habits, religion, characteristics of smugglers, of militants and of migrants the observation posts, the patrolling area, the requirement of technical equipment as a force multiplier and the environment prevailing in the border area. All BOPs should be the first aid posts of the border people. Giving proper respect to the village heads, women and helping them in medical cases in emergency, evacuation of civil patients to nearby hospitals in government vehicles after providing first aid will be an effective heart-wining exercise for the troops.

Both the border people and the border guarding force, if they maintain a cordial relations, then by their combined efforts they can help in stopping migration. Manning of checkposts round-the-clock, proper surveillance of low-lying areas, helping tribals in border areas of Meghalaya, Mizoram and Tripura, avoiding tendency of falling a prey to corruption, stopping the drug menace in north-east border, strengthening of criminal justice system in the lower courts, strengthening community actions, co-ordinating enlightening programmes, and teaching drug treatment methods to the locals will definitely tilt the mind of ethnic locals in favour of the government agencies.

Development of border area is directly proportional to the level of awareness of local population. It is quite a pitiable condition in the north-east border that, neither the central government nor the state governments have taken interest for infrastructural development. There should be a change of mindset of the central government towards north-east at the earliest if the geographical, historical, social and political condition of the region has to be upgraded. People in the hinterland and the border areas are always the same. The economic prosperity of border regions must be taken into account with utmost priority, otherwise, there may be a secession of these seven states from that of India very soon, if not after 2014 election, then may be after 2019 election and, it will be the Assam first which will raise its voice of dissent and take the lead. Discussion with all the Indian insurgent groups, particularly that of ATTF, NLFT, MPLF, PLA, and UNLF needs to be carried out like that of Kuki groups, the NSCN-IM, the ULFA, the NDFB, the KLNLF and DHDJ groups.

The tribals' societies in border areas are self-governing. The central leaders must understand the border people, their aspirations, and their mood. Just because of fear of insurgents, central leaders and state leaders must not feel shy of visiting border areas. Even if our insurgent groups, like that of NSCN-IM, do not agree to give up their arms, yet, they should be called for discussion and be allowed to retain their arms until they are satisfied about their future. In order to overcome this continuous flow of migration from Bangladesh, a comprehensive master plan for development of all border districts towards Bangladesh be planned and implemented by the district administrations with participation of the local people. This will indirectly give service to the border youths.

Climate Change and Conflict in Migration from Bangladesh to India

Climate change alters habitats such that the land can no longer maintain the local population. Bangladesh gets this change often which forces locals to migrate to resource-rich locations.

Bangladesh possesses the Ganges-Jamuna-Meghna delta, one of the greatest river deltas of the world. Floods are common here but their severity and timing are becoming increasingly unpredictable. Recent floods have affected more than two-thirds of the total area of Bangladesh, causing extensive damage to crops, houses, roads, embankments, cattle, poultry, fishery and all other types of economic infrastructure. This phenomenon is worsened by the construction of massive dams and irrigation systems in Indian side which may be a cause for major natural disasters in Bangladesh. The combination of economic, social, institutional and political factors, as well as consecutive onslaughts of natural disasters forces environmental refugees to migrate to urban slums or outside the Bangladesh.

One of the migration sites, in particular, is the Assam region of India where, there had been many clashes between the indigenous (mostly Hindus) population and the Bangladeshi migrants (mainly Muslims). The indigenous people fear the loss of culture and identity in their homeland, resulting in severe violence between the groups. Some extremist groups, such as the National Democratic Front of the Bodoland (NDFB), have threated the complete ethnic cleansing of all migrants threatening their way of life in Assam, particularly in Bodoland. The Indian government is attempting to secure its borders to avoid future clashes.

Violent conflict in Assam between indigenous groups and Bangladeshi migrants began in 1979 when the presence of 70,000 immigrants was discovered in one constituency. When the government did nothing to mitigate this influx of outsiders, the local groups got polarised and organised themselves. The result was at least 4,700 deaths that year. From then on, an unstable government has endured constant civil disobedience campaigns and excessive ethnic violence.

Climate change is increasing instances and levels of major floods in Bangladesh. The effects are magnified by the construction of dams along major waterways. Most Bangladeshis live along rivers or adopt livelihoods that depend upon them. Flooding is destroying their homes and livelihoods forcing them to leave their homes in search of viable living conditions. Bangladeshi environmental refugees are relocating to various nearby regions, in particular, the Assam, where there have been violent clashes with indigenous population (Swain, 1996).

The intrusion of the massive Bangladeshi population added to the already existent strained relations between ethnic Bodos affiliated with the NDFB, and the government of Assam. The group's most vital goal was to separate completely from Assam and create their own state of Bodoland, located in the north-west region of Assam (World Bank, 2008). The United Liberation Front of Assam (ULFA) is a second insurgent group with the primary goal of maintaining Assamese societies and traditions against the encroaching Bengalis. This group is also centered in the Assam state. The ULFA has been engaged in violent clashes for the longest period in Assam. It is also the most deadly, having inflicted at least 25,000 casualties over time. The Dima Halam Daogah/Black Widow faction (DHD-BW) is the most recent radical group to arise against Bangladeshi settlers. DHD-BW operates in north-east Assam in the Dimaraji territory and is comprised of the Dimasa tribal group (World Bank, 2008).

Support for radicalism increases with added strain on jobs and resources. Bangladeshi environmental refugees are searching for sustainable livelihoods in Assam, but the state government cannot fight the migration keeping various local communities integrated.

Silting has increased alarmingly in all the Bangladesh's rivers due to increased amount of it carried by river water from countries, which are higher to Bangladesh. The Farakka dam also dries up riverbeds during six or seven months of the year, reducing the dry-season flow of the river system to southern Bangladesh. The dam disrupts the entire ecology of the delta which disrupts fishing and navigation and inundates nutrient-rich soil with salt deposits, effecting Bangladesh's agricultural and industrial production (Swain, 1996).

Erosion is also a major issue in Bangladesh due to its loose soil. This increases with more severe flooding associated with climate change. Habitable, cultivable land, and consequently livelihoods are increasingly snatched away from Bangladeshis due to massive erosion coupled with population growth. Bangladesh is quite disaster-prone, mainly a riverine country, comprised of more than 700 rivers, about 3,000 tributaries and canals. Strong currents during the summer and rainy seasons, combined with the zig-zag courses and the alluvial nature of the soil in the delta regions cause serious erosion of riverbanks. Low categories of land are waterlogged for most parts of the year. Even the medium-low categories of land suffer from waterlogging after the rainy season, especially after the floods and tidal surges.

More than half of Bangladesh lies less than 5 m above sea level, drastically multiplying the dangerous affects of flooding and sea level rise. Some forecasts predict that sea level will rise one meter by 2050 and three meters by 2100. The same predictions speak of a 100 per cent increase in population by 2050 as well, adding grievously to the already perilous situation.

India offers a higher standard of living for the environmental refugees. Because Bangladesh and West Bengal share a common ethnicity, border security tends to be less strict in the south-west and the citizens do not understand the concept of the nation-State exactly. Most consider the entire Ganges-Brahmaputra region "greater Bengal," instilling in them a sense of rightful claim to those lands (Homer-Dixon, 1994). Some Bangladeshi refugees decided to settle in nearby West Bengal, but the area is also experiencing some of the same type of degradations as their homelands, so they preferred to go to Assam. While under British colonialism, outsider Hindus from Calcutta ruled Assam, which was not liked by the locals. Britain also deemed Bengali the official language of Assam at that time. These scars make the Assamese especially cautious of losing the political and cultural control of their state (Homer-Dixon,1994).

Indo-Bangladesh relations worsened in March, 1972 after adoption of the politically controversial Indo-Bangladesh Trade Pact. They continued to grow stronger over the maritime belt dispute, Indian support for the pro-Mujib guerrillas, the sharing of Ganges waters and control of disputed land borders. Bangladeshis feel that India exploits it in an effort to dominate as when India constructed the Farakka Dam in West Bengal merely 11 miles east of the Bangladesh border. As discussed above, this dam magnifies the damaging effects of climate change and is perceived as stealing resources from Bangladesh (Hossain, 1981).

In Bangladesh, as climate change intensifies, it causes an increase in flooding along the rivers in Bangladesh. Flooding forces people, that previously lived along rivers, to find a new place to live, hence population decreases. Flooding also causes salinisation of the land, making it more difficult for carrying out agriculture and irrigation. Being a riverine country, citizens' livelihoods rely on agriculture around rivers; therefore, less cultivable land means less income. If people cannot make a living in the area, they must move, hence the decrease in population. Flooding also destroys planned and standing infrastructure, forcing people to move to areas that can provide the services they need. The increase in population also decreases the amount of resources available per capita. Inevitably, as more people are vying for the same resources, there will be conflict. In addition, the increase in population is due to a group of environmental refugees that are of a completely different culture, heritage, and religion than the indigenous population. From perspective of the people, an increase in diversity threatens the strength of the identity of both groups, which increases conflict as they fight to maintain their culture. Government officials keen upon getting the extra votes of migrants overlook the massive migration and do not pursue deportation. Now, the strain of population growth is being felt throughout India, forcing officials to secure borders (Swain, 1996).

As we have seen with the cyclone 'Aila', the effects of such disasters can last a long time, with the victims of 'Aila' still living on embankments in makeshift shelters. The impact and aftermath of cyclone Aila are reminders of the kind of challenges Bangladesh is likely to face in the future. The cyclone struck on 25th May, 2009, affected 3.9 million people and breached 1,742 kilometres of embankments. One year on, large areas remain flooded and around 1,00,000 people are still living on embankments, roads and other available elevations of land.

Climate change is expected to affect the movement of people in at least four ways: (1) the intensification of natural disasters – both, sudden and slow onset—leading to increased displacement and migration, (2) The adverse consequences of increased warming, climate variability and of other effects of climate change concerning livelihoods, public health, food security and water availability, (3) Rising sea levels that made coastal areas uninhabitable, (4) Competition over scarce natural resources potentially leading to growing tensions and even conflict and, in turn, displacement.

The consequences of climate change in Bangladesh will be most severe for India. More than 60 million people still live in poverty in Bangladesh and many of these occupy remote and ecologically fragile parts of the country, such as flood plains and river islands (chars), or the coastal zones where cyclones are a major threat. Cross-border migration to the neighbouring states in India is an important phenomenon for these displaced people. The coastal zones of Bangladesh are a highly dynamic environment and there will always be areas under threat from erosion and land loss. Over recent decades, rising sea levels have been incrementally adding too many of Bangladesh's environmental vulnerabilities in the coastal zone – such as saline water, floods and storm – and will continue to do so. Throughout the 21st century, there will be more coastal erosion, sea level rise, salt-water penetration, rising of temperature and changing of rainfall patterns. People chose to undertake long-term or permanent migration to various cities in India and were bound to cross the international border.

8

Security: Militancy, Organised Crime, ISI Linkage

Perhaps in the beginning of 1971, Hindu migrants coming from Bangladesh fleeing persecution from Muslims and fundamentalists were allowed to be settled in West Bengal and mixed with the people and there was no reaction against such penetration. Around same time, five to six lakhs of Bihari Muslims crossed over to India from Bangladesh camps and were settled between Purnia to Islampur around Katihar and Kishanganj, nearer to Bangladesh border. This belt of Bihari Muslims' resettlement area has pro-Pak elements and they give shelter to Pak ISI extremists. MoS Shri Mullapally Ramachandran had given a statement in 2010 that 1.4 million Bangladeshi immigrants have entered India in last 10 years, which has created a big problem for the country. They have posed threat to the economy and identity of few states. The lots, which came after 1975 until now, are involved in criminal activity and terrorism. They find their entry in very difficult routes particularly in the Sunderbans, Tripura border, Char Islands, Tura border, Dawki border, and the border at Salmara, Jhawkutty and Satrasal. These borders are having various gaps in the barbed wire fencing. Either, fencing has not yet been made in that area or erection of fencing was not feasible or had been washed away. Even though they came for their better future, but they are akin to the tentacles of all insurgent and fundamental groups of Pakistan and Bangladesh operating all over India in the hinterland, causing disturbances as it happened in Bombay, Pune, and Hyderabad and Bangalore. Even now, more or less, every day about 50 Bangladeshi nationals are crossing over to India through riverine and unfenced border and such crossings are very dangerous. It was also reported that those coming from Bangladesh with travel documents do not go back and every year about 20 or 25 thousand Bangladeshi nationals coming to India with valid permit are reported to be missing.

The border between India and Bangladesh cannot be sealed. This 'sealing' word is prevalent only with government and political leaders who have no idea that the border cannot be sealed at all. Even after another 100 years, India will not be able to seal the border. The migration will continue because of typical nature of border, its terrain and weather. The fencing and floodlighting will only stop migration by 90 per cent. The modern gadgets and technical equipments by another five per cent including patrolling by boats and lighting and keeping watch on riverbanks. The contributory factors facilitating infiltration from Bangladesh are ethnic, linguistic, religious commonality between migrants and our people at the border, and the willingness of the locals to give shelter to them. It is difficult to detect Bangladeshi migrants in the whole of Indo-Bangladesh border.

Problem will again arise for maintenance of this fencing and floodlighting, as every year, after monsoon, the border roads, the fencing and floodlights will require repair. In Dhubri district and Murshidabad border during every monsoon, kilometres-after-kilometres of fencing are washed away. Erection of fencing and its repair/maintenance in a big belt is not that easy matter. This author has seen the fencing in a permanent char island within river Brahmaputra when it was made. The planning was done

one year in advance and heavy equipments, stones, concrete, cement, bricks, excavators, bulldozers, vehicles, tractors were ferried by number of boats tied together in river Brahmaputra when it was in spate and offloaded in the char island as during winter and other seasons heavy stores cannot go by boat to the chars. The work started after the water receded during winter. The weather permits only three months for fencing work in such char islands. Similar is the case in a segment of river Padma and the Mizoram border. Problem in Mizoram border for fencing is that there is no border road or border track. There are no border outposts close to the international boundary. The posts are somewhere 10 to 20 kilometres from the IB and the distance between the BOPs are somewhere 20 while somewhere 40 kilometres. Here also the work is pending because heavy equipments can be taken only during winter and the work will continue for only five months in a year.

Similarly, technical equipments like censors, HHTI and Lorrooss are not that effective in mountainous and forest border including the riverine border. They have their limitations. Only modernising of border guarding forces and modernising the technical equipments will never solve migration problem from Bangladesh until and unless there is a will of the local people to stop them.

It was in Punjab that the locals own against militants but not the guns. If you start from 24 Parganas border, the Sundarbans has its own problem of river Ichhamati and various islands with full of forest and numerous channels of rivers meeting with Bay of Bengal. There is every possibility of one getting lost. One cannot find boundary pillars in the Sunderbans. To some extent from Haldiaganj, the middle mainstream of the river Ichhamati is the international boundary. There are numerous boats both belonging to Indian villagers and Bangladesh villagers plying in this river. However, Indian boats are numbered and they are being told to use Indian flags, yet it is difficult to recognise from a distance in such a vast riverine area whether the boats are from Bangladesh or from India.

All the BOPs of Bangladesh border guards are on the bundh of river Ichhamati and the BSF BOPs are also on the bundhs of India's side of this river. Yet, after traversing by ships and boats for 30 to 40 kilometres, you come across various islands and it is difficult then to know whether you have entered into Bangladesh or going through sea or you are in Indian territory. These islands are having mangrooves; full of big trees and one can find the Sundarban's royal Bengal tiger in these islands. You get down from the boat and your feet will go two to three feet deep into the mud while climbing up to the embankment. The constructions of outposts and houses are also different in this area as the water level rises when the sea water gushes in. It depends on the tidal waves of the Bay of Bengal. Visiting these places in small boats is very dangerous, particularly in monsoon, as there is every chance of the boat losing its balance in the whirls of water. The rooms are made above 15 feet of ground level as in this forest, water level rises. If the rooms are made on the ground level, it will be totally submerged. The movement in Sundarbans is always through boats. There are few uninhabited islands in Sundarbans where administratively it is difficult to maintain yourself. It is also difficult to find out whether few of such small islands belong to Bangladesh or India, and in one case it so happened in 1974, that the Bangladesh Rifles along with some smugglers with weapons occupied one of such Indian island and they had to be removed.

The government has seven floating BOPs in the Sundarbans, which can accommodate a platoon's strength of force with heavy weaponry. These floating BOPs keep on moving in the Sundarbans and it has four to five speedboats attached. Troops avail these speedboats from floating vessels to go and patrol the riverine border. Even there is a danger to the floating vessels while going very close to the sea. These areas are very marshy; there is a danger of contracting waterborne diseases, both Malaria and PF Malaria. Evacuation to a proper hospital for treatment is impossible. Similarly, you need number of shoes, as they get wet every time you go out. These are the places where the militants try to cross from Bangladesh to India.

There is a possibility of paradropping extremists by enemy countries through Bangladesh and through Bay of Bengal in Indian islands, and thus, they can get into the hinterland. This is the border through which the militants crossover from Bangladesh to India and find their way to Nepal.

If we cross 24 Parganas, we reach Nadia district border, again both riverine and land border, which provides easy access to the migrants to cross from Khulna, Rajsahi and avail rail facility from extreme border of Gede, Banpur and Hatkhola. The train goes from border direct to Sealdah railway station in Kolkata and this was the main attraction for the migrants to easily reach Kolkata and they could get down at any railway station in between, may be at Ranaghat, Krishnanagar, Chakdah, Barrackpur, Kalyani, Haringhata, Kachrapara, wherever they liked, without being checked. Next comes Murshidabad border having river Padma and lot of islands inside it; here the crossing of migrants takes place always by boat during night and it was a free-for-all situation that time. At present, those boats that were bringing migrants are being used in carrying and smuggling cattle to Bangladesh. A big open boat or a few boats tied can carry 100 to 150 cattle from Indian side to Bangladesh, and each cow costs about 10,000 takas in Bangladesh. Bangladesh government is earning 500 takas per cattle from thc smugglers at these cattle corridore. Thus, their economy is thriving in cattle smuggling, and consequently, the price of bullocks and cows in India has gone up because of outflow of cattle to Bangladesh. If we further go to north at Farakka in Malda border, the Farakka barrage during construction and just after construction, gave a nightmare to India.

On 16th May 1976, Maulana Bhashani tried to make a long march to Farakka with millions of Bangladeshis to demolish this Barrage diverting the water of Ganges by Government of India, which was going to cause disastrous ecological effect in Khulna and Rajshahi districts of Bangladesh. The Government of India was in doldrums in taking preventive action to stop this march of millions of Bangladeshis. Heavy deployment of border guarding forces and local police was made and the central government asked the chief of the border guarding force Shri Ashwani Kumar to remain present at the Malda border to supervise the deployment. Similar situation is also arising on Tipaimukh hydroelectric project in Bishnupur district of Manipur on river Barak that will cause drying up of rivers Surma, Kushiyara, and Meghna in Sylhet district of Bangladesh. The honourable Prime Minister of India has given an assurance to Sheikh Hasina that the flow of water of river Barak will remain as usual and this project will have no effect in Bangladesh. He has also asked Bangladesh to stake a claim on this Tipaimukh project in getting electricity to Bangladesh. Even until now, various social workers and NGOs including Jamatis are planning to protest against India for constructing the dam. Jamatis are behind this and inciting the Bangladeshi people against construction of this project.

On coming more towards north, i.e., the West Dinajpur border, having both riverine and land border with Bangladesh and one train line going from India to Bangladesh—from Radhikapur, Kaliaganj to Jessore—will again start working very soon. It was also one of the biggest routes of entry of Bangladesh migrants to Raiganj, Kaliaganj, and Dalkhola from Dinajpur. In the same district, if we discuss about hilly border, it is something very strange. The train line of Bangladesh passes just over international boundary on Bangladesh side. Our side of the border of the hilly region has houses all along the railway line having *angans* towards Bangladesh in that stretch. The smugglers bring their items, particularly, electronic goods and foreign cloths, and stand near the doors of the train; as the train passes very slow, the smugglers throw these items to the Indian side, which fall inside the *angans* of houses of Indian smugglers, thus, you cannot do anything about this. There are places in hilly regions where houses are also divided between India and Bangladesh. One brother with half of the house may belong to India, and the other brother in possession of the other half may be from Bangladesh. Such is the state of affairs. So one can easily imagine how the migrants enter into India unchecked through this border of Hilly, Hamjapur, Chakram, and Raiganj areas. West Dinajpur is a district where maximum adverse possession cases of land are there, that of Bangladesh in India under adverse possession of India, and Indian land under adverse possession of Bangladesh. This too was one of the factors of easy entry of migrants.

I still remember a case when few young Bangladeshi boys were coming in between Sripur and Kukradah border to India through one of this adverse possession land. They were captured by this author, but two or three young boys started running back. They were chased for three kilometres towards border, but they entered into this adverse possession land and that was the end of the matter; nothing could be done. In the meantime, the other one, who was there in Indian side and was captured, also vanished.

The fencing has come up in Karimganj and Cachar borders, so also in Mankachar, and all over West Bengal. Yet, the cutting of the fence by smugglers and cattle smuggling to Bangladesh in numbers are reported everyday due to various gaps existing in the fencing. During monsoon, a number of border areas are inundated due to flood and the fencing is washed away. In riverine areas in the whole of north-east and West Bengal border with Bangladesh, thousands of cattle are forced into other side of the border by smugglers and because of the normal current / force of water, they all go to Bangladesh. It is impossible for any border guarding force to stop such smuggling by boat. Weapons and ammunitions, including drugs, are easily brought to India through river channels. Opium is cultivated in north-east, mostly in all char islands and in various districts afflicted by left wing extremists, i.e., those from Jharkhand, Odisha and Chhattisgarh.

This is the area where maximum incursions of Bihari Muslims were noticed as this border is very close to

Kishanganj in Bihar and there is a direct bus route from Kukradah to Kishanganj. If we go further north, we will land up at Patagora, Moragati areas where one finds riverine border of that of river Mahananda. It is a river, which when on spate, is very difficult to cross and the current is to its maximum. Here also, the international border is the mid-stream of the river. This also creates a lot of problem in fishing, boating and checking the migration effectively. I can well remember of an incident in this area, whereof a group of Bihari Muslims was crossing Mahananda river with goods in 1972 during dark night hours. When they were challenged, they fired a round in air and all of them jumped into Mahananda river. I also jumped into the river, which was in spate, with my pistol in one hand, and could cross the river in about 30 minutes, but was unsuccessful after reaching opposite side to trace the group. In between, all these Bihari Muslims vanished into Bangladesh and I had no other alternative than to again jump into river Mahananda, swim it across over to reach Indian side safely with my weapon intact. If we go further north, we will land up in river Teesta in Jalpaiguri, which was the bone of contention between Bangladesh and India, and recently Mamata Banerjee, the present Chief Minister of West Bengal, refused to accompany the Prime Minister of India to go to Bangladesh as a part of Indian delegation.

Teesta also remained a hot belt for migration of immigrants. In fact, Teesta is a blessing for Bangladesh and North Bengal suffers, as, maximum benefit of Teesta water goes to Bangladesh. Three rivers of North Bengal—Karatoya, Atrayee and Punabhaba / Mahananda— get dried up in summer (TOI, 31st October, 2012). If we go further north to Coochbehar border, we have various enclaves with some of the Indian enclaves in Bangladesh, and some of the Bangladeshi enclaves in India. At present, both the governments have agreed to exchange of these enclaves, but since long, the enclaves created a lot of security problem for the Indian side as the criminals took shelter in Bangladeshi enclaves in India where India security personnel could not penetrate.

Mostly, all Indian enclaves inside Bangladesh, had free entry for Bangladeshi personnel, Bangladeshi militants, and Bangladeshi smugglers. Those were the areas where migrants came in numbers and it was difficult to apprehend them. They came from Bangladesh side, crossed the border, entered into Bangladeshi enclaves in India and further gained entry to Coochbehar, Jalpaiguri and Siliguri. The Angerpota and Dahgrahm enclaves are few major enclaves where Bangladeshi militants used to take shelter. These were the enclaves, which were given to Bangladeshi *nawabs* by Coochbehar Maharajas in earlier times. We have 51 Bangladeshi enclaves in India having 7,110 acres of land and 111 Indian enclaves in Bangladesh with 17,158.1 acres land. There was no access of Indian security forces to visit these Indian enclaves in Bangladesh earlier. There are 52 Bangladeshi lands under adverse possession of India and 49 Indian lands under adverse possession of Bangladesh. Similarly, 6.5 kilometres length of Tripura-Bangladesh border have not yet been demarcated.

The Government of India agreed to give a free passage to Bangladeshi personnel to come to their enclaves through Teen Bigha, passing through Indian soil. After the enclaves, and before the riverine border of Brahmaputra, there were enormous routes of migrants to come to India, i.e., through Satrasaal, Jhaokutti and Sahibganj border. To considerable extent, this border was utilised not only by the migrants, but also later on, by militants to enter India with weapons. These were, more or less, the routes of entries for Hindu migrants, between 1971, until 2000. After Satrasaal and Jhaokutti, one gets the great Chars of river Brahmaputra, which has more than 2000 char islands, both temporary and permanent in nature. There are some char islands like Masalabari and Shaitanbari, where the barbed wire fencing work was made taking the stores from Dhubri by boat in river Brahmaputra. These char islands are areas, even till date free for all, be they Indians or Bangladeshis. I had the opportunity to visit and stay in various char islands like that of Bansi char, Shaitanbari, Mantrichar, Bhabanpara, Hathichar, Saalpora, Bhagdowr, Patmari, Takamari, Sialda, Gaachpora, Salpara, Old deban alga, Mahamayachar, Chowkichar, Kalaichar, and Masalbari.

Masalbari is the only char island in extreme Indo-Bangladesh border inside river Brahmaputra which had two helipads, but, both the helipads have gone down into river Brahmaputra when it was in spate about 2/3 years back. Excluding one or two char islands, mostly, all inhabitant nomads are Muslims and came from Bangladesh, particularly from Mymensingh. This was the main entry route of most of Bangladeshi Muslim migrants to Assam since 1992 and it is so even today. The temporary char islands get submerged in river Brahmaputra during monsoon, and again in winter, new chars come up. These new char islands are auctioned to various Dewans by district authority of 14 districts of Assam, and further, the Dewans auction them either to earlier dwellers, or to new Muslim migrants coming from Bangladesh and earn money accordingly. I have seen personally, after monsoon, various such new chars coming up in river Brahmaputra and they were without any houses in it, but after one month or so, I could notice that a number of thatched houses came up and few civilians arrived from somewhere and started staying in these new chars. However, while entering to Dhubri, and going out from it, all boats are being directed to go via Bansichar to ensure that Bangladeshis are not travelling in those boats but that is not the only way of checking of the entry of Bangladeshis to Char Islands

The Brahmaputra, during monsoon, is very furious, and I have seen myself a portion of Takamari char going down into river Brahmaputra and that is the time when the civilians and their cattle, including goats, are evacuated by the boats of security personnel to safer char islands. The security posts in Takamari and various temporary char islands are not made permanent, but instead, from bamboo-made tats with thatched roof. Problem is for potable water in the char islands—may be for the security forces, and may be for civilians. I can well go back to the year around 2007, when for the first time, a gypsy was taken to Mantrichar by boat and it was driven in the char island for the first time. All the little boys and girls came running just to see how a gypsy travels. I ordered my men to give free ride to those children in the gypsy. Life is very tough in the char islands, and for about 3 months during monsoon, those who are there in temporary char islands, shift their houses to boats, and manage to remain inside the boat itself. Similar is the situation of security personnel operating in Indo-Bangladesh border near river Brahmaputra during monsoon. There is every possibility that the boats can go to Bangladesh with heavy current and this has happened several times. If we take into consideration Bangladeshi Muslim migrants coming to Assam, drug smuggling to Assam, cultivation of opium, everything revolves around the char islands only.

Brahmaputra is a river in which floating BOPs as available in the Sundarbans and Sir Creek cannot be placed as during winter the water level goes down. Out of five mainstreams, only one stream of Brahmaputra is fit for navigation, but, that will accomodate only middle craft and not a heavy ship like a floating BOP. During the migration period, proper water wing of the border guarding force, which is now available at Dhubri, was not sanctioned and that was the reason for such huge number of migrants coming to India from Bangladesh. Both Assam and Meghalaya, have seen various clashes after Independence between both the border guarding forces. It was from April 16 to 19 of the year 2001 that the Bangladesh Rifles surrounded its adverse possession land at Pridwa in Dowkie border of Meghalaya. The BSF was constructing one hundred meters long path to Pridwa from the Army Post and they were taken offguard when BDR surrounded them.

In retaliation, the Border Security Force wanted to take revenge at Boraibari in Assam–Mankachar border, in the adverse possession land of India in Bangladesh. The BDR and Bangladeshi civilians encircled and killed 16 soldiers of BSF after torturing them. This was not the end of conflict of adverse possession cases. In 2005 also, in Cachar, Karimganj border, the BSF and BDR came face to face and used medium machine guns when Bangladeshi villagers entered and tried to cultivate the land of Indian farmers opposite to river Surma towards Bangladesh's side. Towards north, the Meghalaya border remained the main route for Bangladeshi Muslims to penetrate into India from Sylhet through Dowkie border and through the borders of Tura,

Garo Hills and Mahendraganj. Mahendraganj is a place of Tura border in Garo Hills, which is dominated by Muslim fundamentalists. Mahendraganj itself has seen three Hindu-Muslim riots so far. There is Dargah of Hazrat Shah Kamal Baba located on the border and the Imams in Mahendraganj Dargah are having link with Jamatis and ISI in Pakistan through Bangladesh. Until now, if somebody goes to Mahendraganj, they get a feeling as if this pocket is not a part of India. When the fencing was erected in Indo-Bangladesh border at Mahendraganj, the BDR never agreed to construct the fence in front of Dargah at Mahendraganj, which is just on the border. The BDR wanted the fencing in the rear of it leaving it open to Bangladeshis for their visit. However, with a lot of persuasion, only single line fencing was allowed by BDR to be erected in front of this Masjid and fundamentalists are still playing a bigger role here inciting the local muslims for violence. The border of Mizoram with Bangladesh is now being fenced. Posts like Dimagiri, Parwa, and Longtalai are all very far from the border because of tough terrain. Posts are air maintained, difficult to climb and troops are not present on the international border for administrative difficulty. However, this belt is having its own problem due to the presence of Chakmas and because it is nearer to Cox's Bazaar which is the main arms market in Bangladesh. Militants find it easy to bring arms through this border but migration was minimal from Bangladesh to Mizoram. If we go further to Tripura border, the state is having Bengali speaking people and is very close to Chittagong Port where the road goes from Udaipur border of Tripura. The ethnic tribals in Tripura, who were earlier in majority, have gone into minority because of the infiltration of a number of Hindu migrants from Bangladesh who all came from Chittagong area. Thus, came up various young armed Indian outfits like ATTF and NLFT of Tripura led by Shri Bishwamohan Deverma whereas ATTF was led by Shri Ranjeet Deverma. Tripura has hilly terrain and porous border with Bangladesh. It has ethnic similarity across the border. It gave more patronage to Bengalis, neglected the tribals, even the state was neglected by the Centre. There was a lack of communication with the state, many land alienation cases occurred due to large scale Bengali migration, and the state treated the Bengali and tribals in a different way. Here is a state where the Bangladeshi Hindu settlers became very powerful and the tribals lost their land to new settlers. Tripura also is having 6.5 kilometres of international border with Bangladesh not demarcated even until now. They are at Dahikhata, Muhuri River, Belonia, and Dumabari. This patch is the cause of disagreement between two border guarding forces and both the governments. Recently, in the meeting of both Prime Ministers held at Dacca in first week of September 2012, it was decided to demarcate this boundary.

The Chittagong port is only 75 kilometres from Tripura. As this state is located geographically at a remote corner of country, it depended mostly on Chittagong and in the beginning; the state was not inclined to get the fencing done, as their movement to Bangladeshi market could get hampered. However, after the NLFT, ATTF and other tribal groups started giving problem to the state and had their camps in Bangladesh, particularly in Chittagong Hill tract, the state came forward to fence the border. By now, migrants from Bangladesh have already achieved their aim and the Tripurites will remain in minority in their state. Along with the terrain of Indo-Bangladesh border, a word can be given about the Bangladesh Rifles, which is the oldest border guarding force of Bangladesh having headquarter at Pilkhana, Dhaka and is financially very strong. Pak Army Officers who followed the American System of training commanded this force. Earlier, the weapons of BDR were from Pakistan Army. They never behaved friendly with Indian border guards; even after 1971, the BDR remained more or less pro-Pakistan. The middle level officers remained in contact with ISI. Even though BDR had no role in the assassination of Sheikh Majibur Rehman in 1975 but the force never reacted against the killing of the Bangabandhu and remained just a spectator. They kept the border open from 1971 until now for any sort of migration from

Bangladesh to India and never tried to stop it under any regime. The mutiny of BDR against pro-Sheikh Hasina commanders in their force including their Chief, Major General Shakil Ahmed at Pilkhana, Dhaka on 24th February, 2009 proved that they are breeds of Pakistanis and they will maintain their hostile policy always against India.

Major Disputed Areas Between India and Bangladesh

Sl. No.	*Disputed Land Area*	*Indian Side*	*Bangladesh Side*	*Area in Kilometres*
1.	Daikhataberubari	Cooch Behar District of West Bengal State	Niphanmari District	1.5
2.	Lathitilla Dumabari	Karimganj District of Assam State	Maulvibazar District	2.874
3.	Muhuri River Island	South Tripura District of Tripura State	Feni District	1.6/2.0
Total	Disputed Area			5.974/ 6.374

The BJP hoisted tri-colour of India on disputed land at Lathitila and Dumabari on 30th June, 2013. They have asked the local people not to agree with handing over of this disputed territory to Bangladesh. The land swap deal compromises India's sovereignty. Assam has been sacrificed to a great extent in the deal signed by both the Prime Ministers at Dacca in 2011. The BJP is asking the deal to be scraped (TOI, 1st July, 2013).

The butchering of 16 BSF personnel at Boraibari in 2001 clearly shows to what extent BDR can go. Whatever few crossings of Bangladesh Muslim migrants are taking place now in Assam and Meghalaya border, may be it is in the knowledge of the BGB, but officially, they have always been washing their hands off the issue from 1971 till today. I had an opportunity to visit Dinajpur in Bangladesh and its cantonment in 1972 just after the operation. It was then that young army officers were becoming more powerful and in one year itself, a change could be noticed in the minds of the army officers about their friendship with India and they never accepted that the independence was given to them by India and by our Muktibahinis. They were only referring to the loots from the bank, armoury and gold from Bangladesh by Indian troops, whether it was a fact, or otherwise.

They were blaming that whatever was taken out from the banks during the war should have been given back to Bangladesh, instead of being taken to India including number of small arms and motorcycles. So practically, the border terrain, the local people in Indian borders and the weak border security were the main reasons for which the migration could not be contained until 2000.

Some of the extremist groups have agreed to negotiations resulting in temporary ceasefires but the conflict continues to threaten the lives of migrants in Assam (World Bank, 2008). The levels of violence have caused the Government of India to call for increased border protection so as to stem the flow of illegal immigrants.

"As per the information received by us, one particular community telling another community that they have enough arms and ammunitions with them and they have brought these arms consignments by three boats through the Brahmaputra. One boat has already reached through Dhubri district and two boats will be reaching soon" – Shri Mrinal Hazarika, pro-talk ULFA leader ('The Sentinel' 27.7.12).

Again Sheikh Hasina on her visit to India on 1st Aug, 1998, stated that "We do not accept that there is any Bengali speaking Bangladeshi national living in India. So the question of deporting any Bangladeshi national by the Indian government does not arise".

The Jatiya Sansad in its report on 24th Nov., 1998, brought out that any move by India to deport anyone on the plea of his being a Bangladeshi national would be unacceptable. Similarly, most of the papers including 'Bangladesh Observer' have brought out that BDR had foiled various attempts of India's BSF to push back Bengali speaking Indian nationals from Dinajpur to Satkhira. This indirectly means whoever we push back as Bangladeshi national are reported to be Indian nationals and Bangladesh does not own them up and are very happy about the fact that the burden of population growth in their country is relieved to some extent by India. These large-scale migrations of Bangladeshis to Assam, West Bengal and Tripura had an impact on the political atmosphere of these states.

Bangladesh Land under Adverse Possession of India

Sl. No.	*Location*	*International Border Pillar number*	*Total area (in acres)*	*District*
1.	Palangir hat	1995/ 3-s to 1995/4-s	000.350	Tripura
2.	Chandan nagar	1904 to 1905	140.050	Dhalai
3.	Durga nagar	1963/ 8-s to 1963/ 21-s	020.000	Tripura
4.	Marandipara	1964/ 13-s to 1964/ 17-s	001.500	Tripura
5.	Belchera	1969/ 1-s to 1969/ 3-s 1968/ 6-s to 1968/ 8-s		Tripura
6.	Hari nagar	1354/ 2-s to 1355	007.000	Cachar
7.	Lyngkhat-i Lyngkhat	1264/ 4-s to 1265/ 4-s 1265/ 6-s to 1265/ 9-s	011.000	Khasi hills (east)
8.	Lyngkhat-ii	1266/ 11-s to 1267/ 2-s	011.000	Khasi hills (east)
9.	Kurinala	1267/ 6-t to 1268/ 4-s	014.000	Khasi hills (east)
10.	Pyrdwah	1270 to 1271/ 7-s	320.000	Khasi hills (west)
11.	Tamabil	1275/ 1-s to 1275/ 9-s	003.600	Jaintia hills

Sl. No.	*Location*	*International Border Pillar number*	*Total area (in acres)*	*District*
12.	Naljuri- i	1277/ 2-s to 1277/ 4-s	010.000	Jaintia hills
13.	Naljuri- ii	1277/1-s to 1279/ 3-s	007.300	Jaintia hills
14.	Naljuri-iii	1278/ 1-s to 1279/ 3-s	041.800	Jaintia hills
15.	Rongkhong	1280/ 4-s to 1282	042.900	Jaintia hills
16.	Amki	1282 to 1282/ 2-s	013.800	Jaintia hills
17.	Amjalong	1283 to 1283/ 4-s	021.100	Jaintia hills
18.	Muktapur	1284/ 1-s to 1285/ 2-t	053.300	Jaintia hills
19.	Chaklagarh	378/ 2-s to 379/m	060.000	Dinajpur
20.	Barabilla	380/ m to 382/ 2-s	016.000	Dinajpur
21.	Satvita	Near ibpn 386/ 1-s	060.000	Dinajpur
22.	Baragharia	387/ 3-s to 388/ 1-s	020.000	Dinajpur
23.	Dangapara	Near ibpn 392/ 3-s	005.000	Dinajpur
24.	Hathkhola	Near ibpn 388/ 7-s	002.000	Dinajpur
25.	Kumargach	402/ 3-s to 404/ 4-s	012.000	Dinajpur
26.	Manikganj	Near ibpn 772/ mp	074.440	Jalpaiguri
27.	Chillahati	Ibps not existing	454.440	Jalpaiguri
28.	Berubari (khudipara)	753/ 6-s to 754/ 2-s	028.930	Jalpaiguri
29.	Satukura	769/ m to 772/ m	628.900	Jalpaiguri
30.	Nonaganj	61/ 3-s to 61/ 5-s	020.000	Nadia
31.	Chandpur	81/ m to 82/ 12-r	005.600	Nadia
32.	Bijoypur/ haldarpara	80/ 12-r to 81/ m	002.150	Nadia
33.	Gede	78/ m to 80/ 12-r	021.610	Nadia
34.	Battali	242/ 20-r to 243/ m	005.730	Malda

Sl. No.	*Location*	*International Border Pillar number*	*Total area (in acres)*	*District*
35.	Sapmari	243/ 2-s to 243 8-s	001.070	Malda
36.	Laxminarayan pur	243/ 2-s to 243/ 8-s	024.190	Malda
37.	Khutadah/ battoli	240/ 9-r to 242/ 20-r	004.480	Malda
38.	Haripal	240/ 9-r to 212/ m 240/ m to 240/ 9-r	008.980	Malda
39.	Soneghat	239/ 13-r to 240/m	001.050	Malda

Total – 2173.270 Acres

Indian Land under Adverse Possession of Bangladesh

Sl. No.	*Location*	*International border*	*Total area (in acres)*	*District*
1.	Rangamura	1996/ 42 to 1996/43-s	000.170	Tripura (west)
2.	Akashmalik (nathpur)	1341/ 2-s to 1341/ 7-s	007.400	Cachar
3.	Rasulpur (pira nagar)	1345/ 2-s to 1347	009.300	Cachar
4.	Kashkhanakpur (liverpotta)	1347/11-s to 1348/5-s	017.600	Cachar
5.	Bialbill (liverpotta)	1350/ 9-t to 1351	005.500	Cachar
6.	Miagul (chandinagar)	1352/ 7-s to 1352/ 9-s	007.100	Cachar
7.	Ser alipur and uttarkul (harinagar)	1352/ 10-s to 1352/12-s 1352/16-s to 1353	110.900	Cachar
8.	Berathakuri (harinagar)	1353 to 1354 1354/m to 1354/7-s	019.600	Cachar

Sl. No.	Location	International border	Total area (in acres)	District
9.	Palathal (Madanpur)	1369 to 1372	384.510	Karimganj
10.	Boraibari	1066/3-s to 1067/5-s	191.440	Dhubri
11.	Lubhachera	1318/1-s to 1318/2-s	009.600	Cachar
12.	Balichera (lubhachera)	1315/15-s to 1316/3-s	004.400	Cachar
13.	Nutanchera (nunchera)	1316/6-s to 1316/13-s	007.400	Cachar
14.	Lahilling	1317 to 1317/7-s	016.200	Cachar
15.	Borohills	1269/40-t to 1270	000.150	Kashi hills (east)
16.	Sri pur	372/6-s to 372/7-s	093.000	Dinajpur
17.	Sonamati	382/1-s to 382/2-s	021.000	Dinajpur
18.	Belagachi	383/m to 385/m	017.000	Dinajpur
19.	Dingapara	Near ibp number 381	001.740	Dinajpur
20.	Kumargach	402/m to 402/3-s	004.500	Dinajpur
21.	Amarkhana	Ibps not available	063.150	Jalpaiguri
22.	Barashashi	Ibps not available	023.700	Jalpaiguir
23.	Narayanganj	929/9-s to929/10-s	001.500	Coochbehar
24	Kharija haridas	929/10-s to 930/m	01.bigha	Coochbehar
25.	Haridas kumar	930/1-s to 3 ss	02.bigha	Coochbehar
26.	Karimpur charland (madhuguri)	154/5-s to 157/1-s	01376.800	Nadia
27.	Narsharipara	152/2-s to 153/1-s	384.000	Nadia
28.	Baliashisha	150/4-s to 151/1-s	001.100	Nadia

Sl. No.	*Location*	*International border*	*Total area (in acres)*	*District*
29.	New sikarpur	149/3-s to 150/m	033.000	Nadia
30.	New sikarpur	147/5-s to 147/6-s	017.360	Nadia
31.	Charboraipur	147/7-s to 148/m	018.300	Nadia
32.	Khutadah	242/7-r to 242/10-r	001.000	Nadia

Total- 2846.350 Acres+3 Bighas.

It was at Harinagar that the land which was under adverse possession of India wase not cultivated by Indian farmers and such land was opposite to that of river Surma and during monsoon it was difficult to go to that plot because of non availability of boats in that area. It was on 28th June, 2005 that Bangladesh villagers tried to enter this Indian piece of land forcibly and started cultivating. When protested by the Indian side, the BDR intervened and there was firing between the BSF and BDR for the whole day using both light machine guns and medium machine guns and the situation remained tense. These types of firing incidents have occurred nearest to the adverse possession areas at Pridwa, Boraibari, Harinagar, Dawki, and Murshidabad border.

Since 1990, the Bangladeshi think tanks, particularly in Dhaka University, were speaking about the theory of Lebensraum, which is a German word, meaning the 'living space'. The policy makers and the educated personnel in Bangladesh argued for borderless competitive trade of commodities voicing that it can serve the consumer interests in a better way. Bangladesh should dictate about borderless competitive trade of labour. Labour is very cheap in Bangladesh, particularly the skilled one, which is one-third of the price in general market anywhere in India; may be in West Bengal, or north-east, or in Delhi and in the metro cities, it is as less as 25 per cent. They have vouched various reasons in these aspects that Bangladesh can outwit any other country because of unbridled population growth, which is beyond the control of the government of Bangladesh.

The population expansion is also related to the religious sentiment, which cannot be curtailed. The runaway population growth in Bangladesh had resulted in large density of population in a territorially small country, which presents a nightmarish picture. **130 Million** population in an area of barely 55,000 sq miles (which is also being lessened year-by-year due to the climatic change in the world and with small islands of Bangladesh getting submerged in the Bay of Bengal, the density of population has risen up to **1230 per sq mile**). Not only that Bangladesh population is growing approximately three per cent a year, but also, it is facing devastating floods every year in Sylhet, Khulna, Chittagong and various other districts. Millions of poor civilians have to leave their houses and get displaced. All these scores of people, who are displaced every year due to floods, are below poverty line. The explosion of population will have affect, adjacent to its periphery, as it cannot go towards Bay of Bengal in the south; they have a place for their adjustment in an environment similar to theirs and close to that border, and thus, the whole of north-east of India has to bear the brunt. The penetration into north-eastern states of India is mostly to Coochbehar, Dhubri, Cachar and Karimganj districts. There are number of factors including the terrain, the weak border guards, the political patronage, similar language, the ethnic similarity, hiding places for shelter, requirement of cheap labour in these areas, health, education and a hope to start a new life in new environment giving security to the children for their upbringing. This trend of displacement of over-growing population and their adjustment outside the Bangladesh in north-east states of India cannot be curtailed at any cost. Whatever efforts, the Government of India makes in securing the border, will fail to fully restrict entry of migrants for various reasons elaborated above. So long as the pace of population expansion there is not controlled and the economy of Bangladesh does not develop, such influx of migrants in numbers will continue towards Indian border and no barbed wire fencing, no wall, no border fence and security technical gadgets will be of any use.

This is well known to the Pakistani Inter Services Intelligence for the last 10 years or more and they will keep taking advantage of these penetrations of Bangladesh Muslim migrants to the north-east, of their presence and various shelters all over the states, and all along the border districts of India. The north-east insurgent groups, which are operating since a long time, also take the side of ISI as both DGFI and ISI are enemy of Indian security forces while Indian security forces are enemy of these militant groups of north-east. Migration was linked indirectly to Pakistan earlier through Bangladesh but now directly as ISI has already found its shelter in all the north-east states of our country. The ISI of Pakistan nurtured the seed once sowed by A Z Fizo, the leader of Naga insurgents in the beginning. During 1971 operation, Mr. Fizo's groups in Nagaland tried to resist the Indian Forces.

Bangladesh had no land for its expansion and Assam has abundant reserve forests, mineral resources, coal, petroleum, char islands, and its neighbouring state, that is, Meghalaya had also much less density of population both in Tura, Garo and Jaintia-Khasi belts with enough vacant lands in its hilly terrain. The lebensraum policy propounded by Bangladesh think tanks was successful in finding their access to penetrate. Mr. Sadiq Khan, a former diplomat of Bangladesh, clearly mentioned in the 'Holiday' of 18th October, 1991, that in the first decade of 21st century, Bangladesh will face a crisis of lebensraum. Bangladesh must avoid critical demographic pressure in pockets of high concentration. Barbed wire fencing and border patrol measures cannot restrain a natural overflow of Bangladesh population's pressure. The overflow of population of Bangladesh will automatically be transferred to sparsely populated lands in the south-east in the Arakan side or in the north-east, in the seven sisters side of the Indian subcontinent. Mr. Abdul Momin, former Foreign Secretary of Bangladesh also stated that ours is a small country, we are suffocating because of density of population, and we must find a place for lebensraum to adjust our extra population. He further added that Bangladesh is the only country which can provide maximum trade of labour and we must ingratiate ourselves with hill tribes adjacent to our borders, particularly that of Assam, Meghalaya, Nagaland, Manipur and Mizoram, and our bulging population must get a welcome hand of our neighbour who are always very kind to us and have given us our freedom. May be for the time being, that is, during the present regime of Sheikh Hasina, on account of fear and instructions, the Bangladesh border guards and the government missionaries there may be trying to check outflow of population from that country but it will not last long after the coming elections are over. There is every possibility that if Begum Zia comes to power, the same lebensraum policy will continue at a larger scale and with that, like that of Pakistan, a small Hindu population, now present in Bangladesh, will try to migrate to West Bengal and Tripura. Borders are quite easy to cross because of char islands in river Padma, the riverine border, adverse possession cases, the Sunderbans, and various islands having dense forests, and the same language spoken at both sides of the border. There is another policy of achieving a Greater Bangladesh, to achieve which large-scale illegal migration from Bangladesh to north-east continues even today. It may also be a fact that the illegal migration is actively encouraged by large number of political groups in Bangladesh and mostly Jamatis, including few government missionaries, to convert large parts of India's north-east states particularly Assam and West Bengal into Muslim majority areas, which they have more or less attained. Later, they will seek to separate from India and join Muslim majority of Bangladesh. Pakistan is using the same policy to annexe Kashmir to itself. It is not only to the theory of lebensraum involved in this migration but a more sinister motive of carving out a Greater Bangladesh which is in the agenda of both ISI and Bangladesh. The ISI is behind it from the day they lost the war in 1971 and Bangladesh was created. The revenge of Nelli massacre of 1983 was planned tactfully. Kokrajhar's effect was felt all over India in various states. Both Bangladesh and Pakistan want that

Indian people or Indian security forces should kill few of these migrants, which will further flare up violence and cause riots all over the country as a result of which the Indian security forces will remain preoccupied with internal security disturbances thereby affecting the economy of the country badly.

The exact figure of Bangladeshi migrants in India cannot be corroborated from figures and datas available with various states and central government agencies. Earlier, when the ICPs were not connected through electronic devices / computers, i.e., before the year 2000, the Bangladeshi people were coming with proper visas and necessary documents, but no one knows whether they returned or otherwise. Even after computerisation in all the ICPs, officially, 60,000 Bangladeshis go on missing every year and are not traceable as they get millions of houses and shelters all over India from spread from Srinagar to Goa to hide and to start their new lives as most of their relations are now already available in various parts of India. Percentage of rainfall is more all over Bangladesh, West Bengal, and in all the north-eastern states. Indirectly, it spells that maximum maintenance has to be made of the border fencing, and every year, 25 per cent of fencing will require a major repair for which funds have to be garnered and another border fencing engineering services will have to be integrated with the border guarding forces. The recent Kokrajhar incident involving Bodos and Bangladeshi migrants have imparted another dimension to anti-Muslim agenda spread by Muslim fundamentalists organisations in not only north-east but also Hyderabad, Pune, Bombay and other interior areas of our country. The differences of opinion between Indians and the people of north-east was propagated by the ISI, thus maximum exodus of north-east people from southern parts of India was reported. Its disastrous effect was felt in Parliament as the warning shot was fired by an honourable Member of Parliament. As Pakistan will never give up its nefarious desire to snatch Kashmir away from India, similarly, Bangladesh will never curb its evil designs of annexing, at least Assam, to it, *willy nilly*. After Assam, it will be the turn of Meghalaya as the Bangladeshis and ISIs are very close to the border in Tura and Garo Hills, particularly, in Mahendraganj and Mankachar belt. They have also succeeded in opening a Muslim fundamentalist organisation PULF in Manipur in the areas of Lillong, Thoubal, Kwakta and Moreh.

The policy of settling ex-Bangladesh Army, ex-Bangladesh Rifles and Jamatis all along Bangladesh border and mushrooming of various mosques and madrassas all along Indian border towards Bangladesh help the lebensraum policy of Bangladesh to settle their excess population in India. The present lebensraum effect will be mostly observed from Coochbehar to Cachar border where the Muslim migrants will try to penetrate through Siliguri corridor, Assam and Meghalaya. Even though Mizoram-Bangladesh border is quite free to cross, yet the terrain is very difficult, the language differs; the areas to traverse will be on foot. Locals there, who are more Christians, may not welcome them like that in one of the districts in Assam viz. Shivsagar where socially, politically, and culturally, the locals are against Bangladesh migrants. The lebensraum policies will continue in Changrabandha, Panchdhwaji, Gital-Daah border (where one train line was going to Bangladesh earlier), Karela, Chowdhurihat, Sahebganj, Dinhata, Jalpaiguri, Teesta border, Jhaokutti, Satrasal, and then all char islands (about 2,000 of them, both permanent, and temporary) of 14 districts of Assam, Suttarkandi, Karimganj, border of Cachar district, Jaintia and Khasi belt of Meghalaya, particularly the coal mines areas and limestone mining areas of Jaintia border, the riverine border of Dawki (where earlier, the Pridwa incident happened in the year 2001), Mankachar, Tura, Garo Hills, Boraibari, Dalu, Mahendraganj, Baghmara, Garobandha, Ghasuapara (it has got one ICP sanctioned now), Jawai, Mausyuram and Pynursula. These areas are likely to remain as entry routes for all Bangladeshi Muslim migrants to north-east only. Whatever Muslim migrants have already penetrated to 24 Parganas, Nadia, Murshidabad, Malda, North Dinajpur, Jalpaiguri, and Coochbehar border districts, to some extent, these areas can be controlled largely after fencing, excluding that of Murshidabad and the Sundarbans due to riverine border. The fundamentalists and militants/ extremists will make use of these areas to enter with weapons. The whole of Tripura and West Bengal, most probably, would see Hindu migrants facing persecution and being oppresed in Bangladesh in future. The Muslim migrants, so entered through Meghalaya and Assam border, will further move to Manipur, and then to Nagaland, after both Assam and Meghalaya get saturated. The migrants after crossing kaziranga belt of Assam, have reached the plain areas of Dimapur, already, poisoned the Dimapur belt of Nagaland and a number of Bangladeshi migrant girls have married to young Naga boys settled in Dimapur under the pretext of being Assamese. Their slogan is 'Jai Bangla' and hope, they do not utter 'Jai Pakistan' in future.

Even as the controversy over infiltration into India via the Bangladesh border rages on, the Director General (DG) of the Border Security Force (BSF) said he was not confident that there was "zero entrance" of Bangladeshis into India.

"We have pushed back 15,000 Bangladeshis this year. The border is a complex one and I cannot say with confidence that there is zero entrance from the Bangladesh border," BSF DG, U.K. Bansal said. "We are keeping a strict vigil at the Bangladesh border. It has its own character and problems. It is a human issue and it cannot be completely sealed as people have relatives on both sides".

Bangladesh-India Border not Strict, Admits BSF Chief IANS, Jalandhar, August 29, 2012

Exchange of Enclaves between India and Bangladesh

The enclaves were used as stakes in card or chess games, centuries ago, between two regional kings, the Raja of Cooch Behar and the Maharaja of Rangpur. The little territories were the result of a confused outcome of a treaty between the Kingdom of Cooch Behar and the Mughal Empire.

After the partition of India in 1947, Cooch Behar district was merged with India and Rangpur went to the East

Pakistan, which became Bangladesh in 1971. In 1974, both countries agreed either to exchange the enclaves or at least to provide easy access to the enclaves, but little materialised. Talks between the two countries on the issue resumed in 2001, but the lack of a concrete period relegated the issue to the backburner.

The residents of the enclaves live in abysmal conditions, lacking water, roads, electricity, schools and medicines to name a few. Crime also is rampant, as complaining would mean crossing the international boundary due to the lack of law enforcement resources. Residents of the enclaves may go to their respective countries only on the production of an identity card, after seeking permission from the border guards, causing much resentment. Recently the countries have moved towards an agreement to absorb the enclaves, but the resulting nationality of the current residents remains an impediment as it could have implications for border disputes in other parts of the region.

In September 2011, the Governments of India and Bangladesh announced an intention to resolve the issue by means of swapping 162 enclaves, giving residents a choice of nationality. The Tin-Bigha Corridor, a strip of Indian territory separating the Dehgram–Angalpota enclaves from the mainland, was leased indefinitely to Bangladesh for access to the enclave. Giving this Tin Bigha corridor and free access to Bangladeshis to Dahgram and Angarpota enclaves is one of the greatest blunders committed by our government just to please government of Bangladesh. One must go to the timing of opening of the gate of entry of this road through Indian land and can see number of persons coming to Bangladesh enclaves in India. They may be criminals, smugglers, drug mafias, arm smugglers, extremists, and may be, even Pak ISI agents. Once they reach Dahgram and Angarpota they are free to mix with Indian crowd and easily get entry to Cooch Behar, Jalpaiguri, Siliguri, Guwahati, and later on to their destination in the hinterland in India or in north-east. There is no boundary of these Bangladeshi enclaves inside India and the border guarding forces fail to exactly indicate the terrain and the boundaries of these Bangladesh enclaves as they change after every three years. A new person coming will take time to know the location of all these enclaves. I still remember an incident of 1977 and 1978 during my deployment in Cooch Behar border. I came across few Bangladesh personnel entering into India from a distance through the international border. Being challenged, all 7 to 10 of them entered into one of these Bangladesh enclaves and that was the end of it, as I could not penetrate into that enclave inside our country to apprehend these Bangladeshis coming with headloads. Even though the Indians in our enclaves in Bangladesh will be asked to volunteer to come to India or to remain in Bangladesh during exchange of these enclaves, but few may like to come to India and few, may like to remain in Bangladesh. Yet, if equal land is not exchanged between both the countries, it will lead to complications and there will be political protest in various districts and state capitals of West Bengal and Assam against this exchange of enclaves.

Muslim United Liberation Tigers of Assam (MULTA) is an Islamist extremist organisation founded around 1996 in the eastern Indian state of Assam. The South Asia Terrorism Portal (Satp. Org) describes it as part of the All Muslim United Liberation Forum of Assam (AMULFA), and that Muslim United Liberation Front of Assam (MULFA) is a sister organisation under the AMULFA umbrella. It is alleged that MULTA is supported by the Pakistani Inter-Services Intelligence (ISI) Agency.

Take these incidents in BTC areas recently: Four Bodo youths were killed in front of a police inspector and no harsh measures could be taken against the attackers. What more can be said? There is a permanent solution i.e. to throw out illegal immigrants. They should be pushed out and action should be taken against them. It is a threat to the country's entire north–eastern region. It has to be taken seriously by all parties concerned. Hangrama said, "I have been demanding a complete sealing of the international border with Bangladesh and action against Badruddin Ajmal (AIUDF leader and Dhubri MP). He is behind all this, as he is facilitating the entry of illegal Bangaldeshi infiltrators into India. However, the helpless BTC officials could do nothing, as they do not have essential powers to deal with these cases and prevent them. There are no other radical groups playing mischief here apart from HUJI, Muslim United Liberation Tigers of Assam and United Muslim National Army. They are bent upon creating problems not just here but throughout the country" (TOI, August 25, 2012).

The President of All Bodo Students Union, Shri Pramod Boro had called for sealing of border with Bangaldesh. All India Assam Students Union and Pramod Bodo demanded that the centre must implement the Assam accord *in toto* and state government should cancel counterfeit ration cards and voter ids. ('Sahara Time', August 25, 2012).

It was not a Bodo-Muslim conflict: - It was propagated as a Bodo vs Muslim conflict. However, in reality, it was a war in between the natives of Assam and the Bangladeshi Muslim infiltrators. That all other communities may be Bengali Hindu, Adivasi (tea garden labour), Bihari, Rajbongshi, Garo or any body else, if they are non- Muslims, it was enough for migrants to target them, kill them and loot their properties and burn down their houses. It was spree for occupying land, and ultimately to convert it into a Muslim majority region.

The Lok Sabha MP Sansuma Khunggur Biswamuthiary said, "It was not only the Bodo and indigenous Muslims who are affected from the settlement of illegal Muslims. The Rajbongshi, Garos and other Tribes too had been targeted. At Naopara in Bijni, over 50 houses belonging to Rajongshis were torched" ('The Seven Sisters Post', 2.8.2012).

Shri H.S. Bhrama wrote, "Since 1971, it has been noticed that, to a large extent, government land in char areas and lands, earmarked as grazing grounds, has been systematically appropriated by illegal migrants, in collusion with the district and local administrations." ('The Indian Express', 28.7.2012). Khampa Borgoyari, Deputy Chief of the BTC says, "We are sure that over 35 per cent of government vacated khas land has been encroached upon by illegal settlers." ('The Sunday Express', July 29, 2012).

According to BTC officials, so far, 39,276 Bangladeshis occupied 2,22,042 bighas of land illegally. The district-wise data is as follows:-

Sl. No.	*District*	*No of encroachers*	*Land in Bighas*
1.	Kokrajhar	20, 423	1,30,269
2.	Chirang	5,570	66,987
3.	Baksa	7, 562	8,252
4.	Udalguri	5,721	16,534
	Total	39,276	2,22,042

The Bangladeshi infiltrators who occupied the river islands, forest land and grazing field started acting as a springboard to accelerate the infiltration from Bangladesh. The char areas of Brahmaputra river, which are occupied by them, caused security problems (It is to be noted that BTAD is a Sixth Schedule area where non-tribals are not allowed to purchase land). Besides, they engaged themselves in perpetrating the following acts:

1. Smuggling cattle to Bangladesh.
2. Huge circulation of fake currency.
3. Occupying jobs of the native people.
4. Smuggling arms and ammunition from Bangladesh.
5. Engaging in criminal activities.
6. Affecting the election results by enrolling their names in the voter list, etc.

All these have created social unrest and economical and political imbalance in the BTAD area.

The names of Muslim fundamental organisations in north-east in various states are given as under:

Assam

1. Muslim Uunited Liberation Front of Assam (MULFA)
2. Muslim Liberation Tigers of Assam (MULTA)
3. Islamic Liberation Army of Assam (ILAA)

4. Islamic Liberation Force (ILF)
5. Islamic Revolutionary Force (IRF)
6. United Muslim liberation Front of Assam (UMLFA)
7. United Reformation Protest of Assam (URPA)
8. People's United Liberation Front (PULF)
9. Muslim National Volunteer Force (MNVF)
10. Adam Sena (AS)
11. Muslim United Liberation Army (MULA)
12. Student Islamic Movement of India (SIMI)
13. Islamic Revolution Army (IRA)
14. Muslim Liberation Tiger's Force (MLTF)
15. Assam Minority Liberation Army (AMLA)
16. Islamic Sevak Sangha (ISS)
17. Harkat-Ul-Muzahideen (HUM)
18. Harkat-Ul-Jihaad Islami(HUJI)

Manipur

1. People's United Liberation Front (PULF)
2. United Islamic Liberation Army (UILA)
3. North Eastern Minority Front (NEMF)

Some of the other small militant groups, which are in league with above, are given below:

1. Jamiat-ul-Ulama-e-Hind
2. Jamat-e-Islami
3. Tabligh-Jamaat
4. Aval-e-Sunnat-vat-Jamaat
5. Cachar Muslim Unnayan Parishad–Barak Valley Group
6. Anjuman-Talmiva-e-Sunnia–Barak Valley Group
7. Anjuman-e-Tarakhi–Barak Valley Group.

Indian Militant Groups which had training camps in Bangladesh helped by ISI and DGFI

According to Indian Intelligence Agencies, terrorist

training camps in Bangladesh are training north-east insurgents, and get patronage and protection from both Bangladesh Army and the Bangladesh border guards. Most of the important camps are in Dhaka, Chittagong, Sylhet, Habibganj, Mymensingh, Rangamati, Khagrachari, Bandarbun, Sherpur, Moulovibazaar, Netrokona and Sunamganj. Cox's bazar in Chittagong district is being used for the transhipment of weapons and explosives. Earlier, Indian security agencies put the figure of terrorist training camp in Bangladesh to about 100 approximately (43 of them were from the National Liberation Front of Tripura-NLFT). There are several joint camps that involve the NSCNIM, NSCN Khaplang, ULFA, NDFB, NLFT, ATTF, PLA, and UNLF. For example, ATTF and ULFA cadres were operating from camps in Khagrachari and Saatchari in Habibganj district. NDFB and NSCNIM training centres existed at Aliqa dam in Bandarbun district. ULFA had 24 camps mostly in Dhaka, Sylhet, Khagrachari, Moulovibazar and the Chittagong Hill Tracts. The NLFT's were located mostly in Chittagong Hill Tracts and Khagrachari. The ATTF is active in Moulovibazar, Habibganj and Comilla (these evidences are based on electronic and technical intelligence).

1. NSCN- IM/ K: National Socialist Council of Nagaland (Isac-Muivah)/Khaplang–Nagaland

   (At Sylhet, Chittagong, Moulovibazar, Haluaghat, Alikadam, New market Dacca, Khagrachari, Bandarban, Rangamati)

2. ANVC - Achick National Volunteer Council – Meghalaya

   (Netrakona, Mymensingh, Sherkut, Dhaka)

3. HNLC - Hymniewtrep National Liberation Council – Meghalaya

   (Chittagong, Sylhet, Moulovibazar)

4. ATTF - All Tripura Tiger Force – Tripura

   (Habibganj, Moulovibazar, Comilla, Khagrachari, Saatchari)

5. NLFT - National Liberation front of Tripura

   (Khagrachari, Habibganj, Bandarbun, Rangamati, Moulovibazar, Chittagong Hill Tracts)

6. ULFA - United Liberation Front of Assam

   (Dhaka, Sylhet, Khagrachari, Moulovibazar, Chittagong Hill Tracts, Rangamati, Sonamganj, Mymansingh, Sherpur, Bandarbun, Tangrail, Kurigram, Cox's Bazar)

7. NDFB - National Development Front of Bodoland

   (Cox's bazar, Alikadam)

8. PLA - People's Liberation Army–Manipur

   (Sylhet, Chittagong Hill Tracts, Khagrachari, Moulavi Bazar, Bandarbun, Hobibganj, Sherpur, Cox's Bazar)

Excluding that, Bangladesh provided its soil for organising training camps and recruiting camps for ISI at Cox's Bazar, Jessore, Chittagong, Bandarbun, Sylhet, Rangamati and Sundarganj.

Jamat-e-Islami had their camps at Mymensingh, Sylhet, Sunamganj and Moulovi Bazar.

The ICS also had their training camps in various madrassas at Chittagong and Lalmanirhat.

The Al-Queda continued their training camps mainly at Nilphamari in various mosques and madrassas. The Harkat-ul-Jihad had also located their training camps at various mmosques and madrassas of Nilphamari and Cox's Bazar.

Almost all other splinter/minor terrorist outfits either took shelter or were based in Bangladesh independently.

Shri Ajay Raj Sharma, the then Director General, BSF handed over a list of 99 terrorist training camps operating in Bangladesh to his BDR counterpart in 2002. Shri A K Mitra, again Ex-DG, BSF, added that guerilla outfits from north-east were using Bangladesh as a safe haven which was confirmed later on.

Indian Militant Groups operating in north-east are involved in getting support from either Bangladesh,

Pakistan or fundamental organisations, and are operating against national interest, thus posing threat to National Security.

Assam

1.	Assam Tiger Force	ATF
2.	Bodo Liberation Tiger Force	BLTF
3.	Dima Halam Daoga	DHD
4.	National Development Front of Bodoland	NDFB
5.	Rabha National Security Force	RNSF
6.	United Liberation Front of Assam	ULFA
7.	Bodo Volunteer Force	BVF
8.	Kamatapur Liberation Army	KLA
9.	Kamatapur Liberation Organisation	KLO
10.	Karbi National Volunteers	KNV
11.	Karbi Long National Liberation Front	KLNLF
12.	Koch Rajbongshi Security Force	KRSF
13.	North Eastern Guerilla Army	NEGA
14.	United Bodo National Liberation Front	UBNLF
15.	United Peoples Democratic Solidarity	UPDS
16.	Adivasi Cobra Force of Assam	ACFA
17.	Adivasi Suraksha Sena	ADISS
18.	Adivasi United Liberation Front of Assam	Adi-ULFA
19.	Birsa Commando Force	BCF
20.	Assam Minority Liberation Army	AMLA
21.	Islamic Liberation Front	ILF
22.	Islamic Revolutionary Army	IRA
23.	Islamic Revolution Force	IRF
24.	Islamic United Liberation Army	IULA
25.	Muslim Liberation Front of Assam	MLFA
26.	Muslim Liberation Tiger Force	MLTF
27.	Mulsim Liberation Tigers of Assam	MULTA
28.	Muslim National Volunteer Force	MNVF

29. Muslim United Liberation Army — MULA
30. Muslim United Liberation Front of Assam — MULFA
31. Students Islamic Movement of India — SIMI

Meghalaya

1. Achik National Volunteers Council — ANVC
2. Hynniewtrep National Liberation Council — HNLC
3. Meghalaya Peoples Liberation Council — MPLC
4. Garo National Liberation Army — GNLA

Tripura

1. All Tripura Bengali National Police — ATBNP
2. All Tripura Tiger Force — ATTF
3. Bru National Liberation Front — BNLF
4. National Bengali Volunteer Force — NBVF
5. National Liberation Front of Tripura — NLFT
6. Tripura National Volunteers — TNV
7. United Bengali Liberation Force — UBLF

Arunachal Pradesh

1. All Liberation Tigers of Arunachal Pradesh — ALTAP
2. Arunachal Dragon Force — ADF
3. National Liberation Front of Arunachal — NLFA
4. National Socialist Council of Nagaland (Khaplang) — NSCN(K)
5. Patriotic Revolutionary Army of Arunachal — PRAA
6. Peoples Liberation Army of Arunachal — PLAA
7. United Liberation Army of Arunachal — ULAA
8. United Liberation Movement of Arunachal — ULMA
9. United Liberation Tigers of Assam — ULTA
10. United Peoples Volunteers of Arunachal — UPVA

Manipur

1. Chin - Kuki Revolutionary Front — CKRF
2. Hmar Peoples Convention Democracy — HPC-D
3. Hmar Revolutionary Front — HRF
4. Ireibak Khnna LUp — IKL

5. Kanglei Yawol Khnnalup KYKL
6. Kangleipak Community party KCP
7. Kangleipak Liberation Organisation KLO
8. Kuki Defence Force KDF
9. Kuki National Army KNA
10. Kuki National Front KNF
11. Kuki National Organisation KNO
12. Kuki Security Force KSF
13. Manipur Peoples Liberation Front MPLF
14. Meitei State Army MSA
15. National Socialist Council of Nagaland (Isac Muivah) NSCN(IM)
16. National Socialist Council of Nagaland (Khaplang) NSCN(K)
17. North Eastern Minority Front NEMF
18. Peoples Liberation Army PLA
19. Peoples Republican Army PRA
20. Peoples Revolutionary Party of Kangleipak PREPAK
21. Peoples United Liberation Front PULF (Muslim)
22. Revolutionary Peoples Front - Kangleipak RPF(K)
23. Revolutionary peoples Front (Political Front of PLA) RPF
24. Special Sacrifice Force (Kuki) SSF
25. Thangajil Hill Area Defence Coucil THADC
26. United Islamic Liberation Army UILA
27. United National Liberation Front UNLF
28. Vaiphei National Organisation VNO
29. Zomi Reunification Organisation ZRO
30. Zomi Revolutionary Army (Armed Wing of ZRO) ZRA
31. North Eastern Council Army NECA

Nagaland

1. National Socialist Council of Nagaland (Isac-Muivah) NSCN(IM)
2. National Socialist Council of Nagaland (Khaplang) NSCN(K)
3. Naga National Council NNC
4. Naga Federal Government/Naga Federal Army NFG/NFA

Mizoram

1. Bru National Liberation Front BNLF

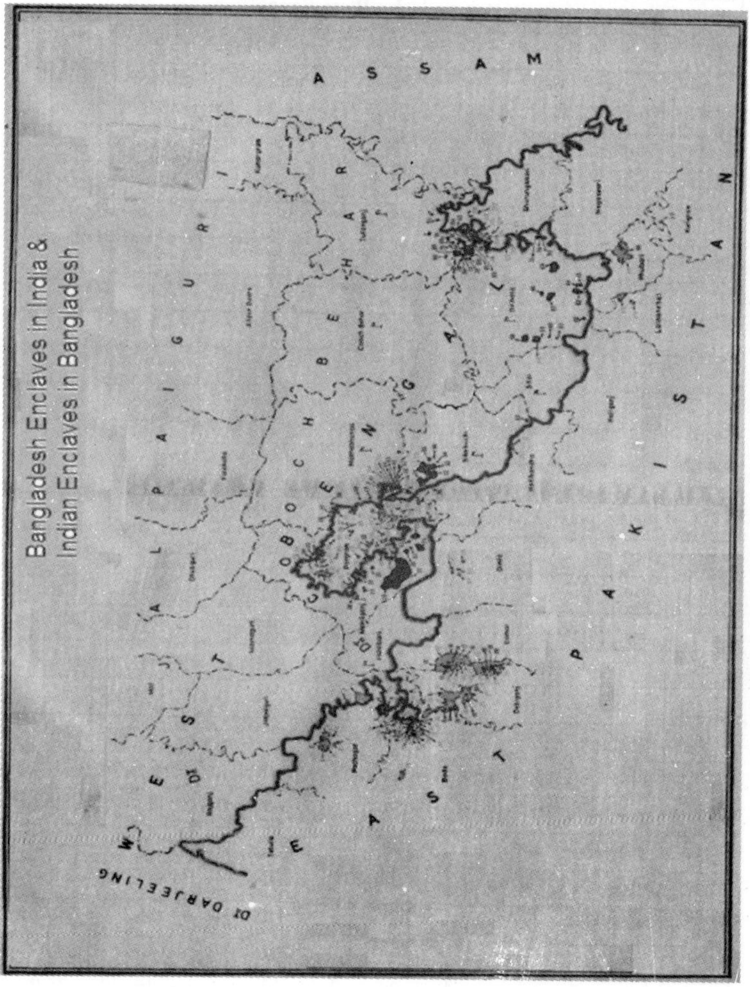
Bangladesh Enclaves in India &
Indian Enclaves in Bangladesh
ASSAM
EAST PAKISTAN
WEST BENGAL
JALPAIGURI
COOCH BEHAR
DT DARJEELING

Exchangeable Indian Enclaves in Bangladesh with Area

Enclaves with independent chhits

Sl. No.	*Name of chhits*	*Chhit No.*	*Lying within police station*		*Areas in acres*
Bangladesh - West Bengal					
1	2	3	4	5	6
1.	Garati	75	Pochagar	Haldi bari	58.23
2.	-do-	76	-do-	-do-	0.79
3.	-do-	77	-do-	-do-	18.00
4.	-do-	78	-do-	-do-	958.66
5.	-do-	79	-do-	-do-	1.74
6.	-do-	80	-do-	-do-	73.75
7.	Singimari Part-I	73	-do-	-do-	6.07
8.	Nazirganja	41	Boda	-do-	58.32
9.	-do-	42	-do	-do-	434.29
10	-do-	44	-do-	-do-	53.47
11.	-do-	45	-do-	-do-	1.07
12.	-do-	46	-do-	-do-	17.95
13.	-do-	47	-do-	-do-	3.89
14.	-do-	48	-do-	-do-	73.27
15.	-do-	49	-do-	-do-	49.05
16.	-do-	50	-do-	-do-	5.05
17.	-do-	51	-do-	-do-	0.77
18.	-do-	52	-do-	-do-	1.04
19.	-do-	53	-do-	-do-	1.02
20.	-do-	54	-do-	-do-	3.87
21.	-do-	55	-do-	-do-	12.18
22.	-do-	56	-do-	-do-	54.04
23.	-do-	57	-do-	-do-	8.27
24.	-do-	58	-do-	-do-	14.22
25.	-do-	60	-do-	-do-	0.52
26.	Putimari	59	-do-	-do-	122.80
27.	Daikhata Chhat	38	-do-	-do-	499.21
28.	Salbari	37	-do-	-do	1188.93
29.	Kajal Dighi	36	-do-	-do-	771.44

Sl. No.	*Name of chhits*	*Chhit No.*	*Lying within police station*		*Areas in acres*
Bangladesh - West Bengal					
1	2	3	4	5	6
30.	Nataktoka	32	-do-	-do-	162.26
31	-do-	33	-do-	-do-	0.26
32.	Beuladange Chhat	35	-do-	-do-	0.83
33.	Balapara Khagrabari	38	Dobiganj	-do-	1752.44
34.	Bara Khankikharija Gitoldeha	30	Dimlo	-do-	7.71
35.	-do-	29	-do-	-do-	36.83
36.	Bara khangir	28	-do	-do-	30.53
37.	Hagarjikabari	31	-do-	-do-	33.41
38.	Kuchlibari	26	Patgam	Mekli-ganj	05.78
39.	Kuchlibari	27	Patgam	Mekli-ganj	2.04
40.	Bara Kuchlibari	Fragment of J.D. 107 of P.S. Mekliganj	Patgam	Mekli-ganj	4.35
41.	Jamaldaha Balapukhari	-do-	-do-	-do-	5.24
42.	Uponchowki	115/2	-do-	-do-	0.32
	Kuchlibari				
43.	-do-	7	-do-	-do-	44.04
44.	Bhotbari	4	-do-	-do-	36.83
45.	Balapukhari	5	-do-	-do-	55.91
46.	Barakhangir	4	-do-	Mekli-ganj	50.51
47.	-do-	9	-do-	-do-	87.42
48.	Chhat Bagdogra	10	-do-	-do-	41.70
49.	Ratanpur	11	-do-	-do-	58.91
50.	Bagdogra	12	-do-	-do-	25.49
51.	Pulkar Dabri	Frag-ment of J.L.101 of P.S. Mekliganj	-do-	-do-	0.88

Sl. No.	*Name of chhits*	*Chhit No.*	*Lying within police station*		*Areas in acres*
Bangladesh - West Bengal					
1	2	3	4	5	6
52.	Kharkharia	15	-do-	-do-	60.74
53.	-do-	13	-do-	-do-	51.62
54.	Lotamari	14	-do	-do-	110.92
55.	Bhot bari	16	-do-	-do-	205.46
56.	Kamat Changrabandha 16A	-do-	-do-	42.80	
57.	-do-	17A	-do-	-do-	16.01
58.	Panisala	17	-do-	-do-	137.66
59.	Dwarikomari Khasbagh	18	-do-	-do-	36.50
60.	Panisala	153/P	-do-	-do-	0.27
61.	-do-	153/O	-do-	-do-	18.01
62.	-do-	19	-do-	-do-	64.63
63.	-do-	21	-do-	-do-	51.40
64.	Lotamari	20	-do-	-do-	283.53
65.	-do-	22	-do-	-do-	98.85
66.	Dwarikamari	23	-do-	-do-	39.052
67.	-do-	25	-do-	-do-	45.73
68.	Chhat Bhothat	24	-do-	-do-	56.11]
69.	Baokata	131	-do-	Betha-bhonga	22.35
70.	-do-	132	-do-	-do-	11.96
71.	-do-	130	-do-	-do-	20.48
72.	Bhogrampuri	133	-do-	-do-	1.44
73.	Chenakata	134	-do-	Mekli-ganj	7.81
74.	Banskata	119	-do-	Hatha-bhanga	413.81
75.	-do-	120	-do-	-do-	30.75
76.	-do-	121	-do-	-do-	12.15
77.	-do-	113	-do-	-do-	57.86
78.	-do-	112	-do-	-do-	315.04
79.	-do-	114	-do-	-do-	0.77
80.	-do-	115	-do-	-do-	29.20
81.	-do-	122	-do-	-do-	33.22

Sl. No.	*Name of chhits*	*Chhit No.*	*Lying within police station*		*Areas in acres*
Bangladesh - West Bengal					
1	2	3	4	5	6
82.	-do-	127	-do-	-do-	12.72
83.	-do-	128	-do-	-do-	2.33
84.	-do-	117	-do-	-do-	2.55
85.	-do-	118	-do-	-do-	30.95
86.	-do-	125	-do-	-do-	.61
87.	-do-	126	-do-	-do-	1.39
88.	-do-	129	-do-	-do-	1.37
89.	-do-	116	-do-	-do-	16.96
90.	-do-	123	-do-	-do-	24.37
91.	-do-	124	-do-	-do-	0.21
92.	Gotamari Chhit	135	Hatibanda	Sital Kuchi	126.51
93.	-do-	136	-do-	-do-	20.02
94.	Banspachai	151	Lalmon-irhat	Din-hota	217.2
95.	Banspachi	152	-do-	-do-	81.7
	Bhitorkuthi				
96.	Dasiar Chhora	150	Palbari	-do-	1643.44
97.	Dakurhat	156	Kurigram	-do-	14.27
	Dakinirkuthi				
98.	Kalamati	141	Bhungan-amari Dinhata	21.21	
99.	Shahebganj	153	-do-	-do-	31.58
100.	Seotikurba	142	-do-	-do-	45.63
101.	BaraGoachulka	143	-do-	-do-	39.00
102.	Goachulka - II	147	-do-	-do-	0.90
103.	Goachulka-I	146	-do-	-do-	8.92
104.	Dighaltari –II	145	-do-	-do-	8.81
105.	Dighaltari-II	144	-do-	-do-	12.31
106.	Chhota Garal Jhora-II	149	-do-	-do-	17.85
107.	Chota Garal Jhora-I	148	-do-	-do-	35.74

Sl. No.	*Name of chhits*	*Cchhit No.*	*Lying within police station*		*Areas in acres*
Bangladesh - West Bengal					
1	2	3	4	5	6
108.	1 Chhit Without name and JL No. at the southern end of JL No.38 and Southwestern End at JL No. 39		Patgram	Mekl-iganj	1.00
Enclaves with fragmented chhits					
109.	(i) Bewladanga	34	Handibari	Boda	
	(ii) Bewladanga	Frag-ment	-do-	Debi-ganj	
110.	(i) Kotbhajni	2	-do-	Debi-ganj	
	(ii) Kotbhajni	Frag-ment	-do-	-do-	
	(iii) Kotbhajni	-do-	-do-	-do-	
	(iv) Kotbhajni	-do-	-do-	-do-	
111.	(i) Dahala	Khag-rabari	-do-	-do-	
	(ii) -do-	Frag-ment	-do-	-do-	
	(iii) -do-	-do-	-do-	-do-	
	(iv) -do-	-do-	-do-‘	-do-	
	(v) -do-	-do-	-do-	-do-	
	(vi) -do-	-do-	-do-	-do-	
Total Area 17,158.13					

Exchangeable Bangladesh Enclaves in India with Area

SNo	*Names of Chhits*	*Lying within Police Station*		*DL No*	*Areas in acres*
W. Bengal/Bangladesh					
1	2	3	4	5	6
1.	Chhit Kuchlibari	Mekliganj	Patgram	22	370.64
2.	Chhit land of Kuchlibari	-do-	-do-	24	1.83
3.	Balapukhari	-do-	-do-	21	331.64

SNo	*Names of Chhits*	*Lying within Police Station*		*DL No*	*Areas in acres*
W. Bengal/Bangladesh					
1	2	3	4	5	6
4	Chhit land of Panbari No.2	-do-	-do-	20	1.13
5	Chhit Panbari	-do-	-do-	18	108.59
6	Dhabalsati Mirgipur	-do-	-do-	15	173.88
7	Bamandal	-do-	-do-	11	2.24
8	Chhit Dhabalsati	-do-	-do-	14	66.58
9	Dhabalsati	-do-	-do-	13	60.45
10	Srirampur	-do-	-do-	8	1.05
11	Jotto Nijjama	-do-	-do-	3	87.54
12	Chhit Land of Jagatbar No. 3	Mathab-hanga	-do-	37	69.84
13	-do- No. 1	-do-	-do-	35	30.66
14	-do- No. 2	-do-	-do-	36	27.09
15	Chhit Kokoabari	-do-	-do-	47	29.49
16	Chhit Bhanderdeha	-do-	-do-	67	39.96
17	Dhabalguri	-do-	-do-	52	2.50
18	Chhit Dhabalguri	-do-	-do-	53	22.31
19	Chhit Land of Dhabalguri No. 3	-do-	-do-	70	1.33
20	-do- No. 4	-do-	-do-	71	4.55
21	-do- No. 5	-do-	-do-	72	4.12
22	-do- No. 1	-do-	-do-	68	26.83
23	-do- No. 2	-do-	-do-	69	13.95
24	Mahishmari	Sitalkuchi	-do-	54	22.77
25	Bura Saradubi	do	Hatiba-ndha	13	34.96
26	Palanpur	-do-	Patgam	64	506.56
27	Amjhol	-do-	Hatibandha	57	1.25
28	Kistmat Batrigachh	Dinhata	Kaliganj	82	209.95
29	Durgapur	-do-	-do-	83	20.96
30	Bansua Khamar Gitaldaha	-do	Lalmon-irhat	1	24.54
31	Poaturkuthi	-do-	-do-	37	589.94

SNo	*Names of Chhits*	*Lying within Police Station*		*DL No*	*Areas in acres*
W. Bengal/Bangladesh					
1	2	3	4	5	6
32	Paschim Bakalir Chhara	-do-	Bhurug-amari	38	151.98
33	Madhya Bakalir Chhara	-do-	-do-	39	32.72
34	Purba Bakalir Chhara	-do-	-do-	40	12.23
35	Madhya Masaldanga	-do-	-do-	3	136.66
36	Madhya Chhit Masaldanga	-do-	-do-	8	11.87
37	Paschim Chhit Masaldanga	-do-	-do-	7	7.60
38	Uttar Masaldanga	-do-	-do-	2	27.29
39	Kachua	-do-	-do-	5	119.74
40	Uttar Bansjani	-do-	-do-	1	47.17
41	Chhat Tilai	-do-	-do-	17	81.56
42	(i) Nilgram	Sitalkuchi	Patgram	65	
	(ii) -do-	-do-	-do-	65	97.34
	(iii) -do-	-do-	-do-	65	
43	(i) Chhit Nalgram	-do-	-do-	66	
	(ii) -do- (Fragment)	-do-	-do-	66	49.50
44	(i) Batrigachh	Dinhata	Kaliganj	81	
	(ii) -do- (Fragment)	-do-	-do-	81	577.37
45	(i) Karala	-do-	Phulbari	9	
	(ii) -do- (Fragment)	-do-	-do-	9	
	(iii) -do- (Fragment)	-do-	-do-	9	269.91
46	(i) Sibprasad Mustati	-do-	-do-	8	
	(ii) -do- (Fragment)	-do-	-do-	8	373.20
47	(i) Dakshin Masaldanga	-do-	Bhurun-gamari	6	
	(ii) -do- (Fragment)	-do-	-do-	6	57.38
	(iii) -do-	-do-	-do-	6	
	(iv) -do-	-do-	-do-	-do-	6
	(v) -do-	-do-	-do-	-do-	6
	(vi) -do-	-do-	-do-	-do-	6

Sl. No.	*Names of Chhits*	*Lying within Police Station*		*DL No*	*Areas in acres*
W. Bengal/Bangladesh					
1	2	3	4	5	6
48.	(i) Pashim Masaladanga	-do-	-do-	4	
	(ii) -do- (Fragment)	-do-	-do-	4	29.49
49.	(i) Purba Chhit Masaldanga	-do-	-do-	10	
	(ii) -do- (Fragment)	-do-	-do-	10	35.01
50.	(i) Purba Masaldanga	-do-	-do-	11	
	(ii) -do- (Fragment)	-do-	-do-	11	153.89
51.	(i) - Uttar Dhalganga	-do-	-do-	14	
	(ii) -do- (Fragment)	-do-	-do-	14	24.98
	(iii) -do-	-do-	-do-	-do-	14

Terror Network and ISI Activities

Bangladesh has emerged as the new hub of terrorist activities from the day of assassination of Sheikh Mujibur Rehman. A number of terrorist training centres did emerge after BNP government came into power with the fundamentalist parties of Jamaat-e-Islami (JEI) and Islamic Oikay Jote having the only anti-Indian agenda. Earlier, the ISI was sponsoring about 127 training camps all over Bangladesh under patronage of JEI, Harkut-ul-jamait-e-Islami (HUJI) and Islamic Morcha. Maulana Abdul Raut was the main kingpin who coordinated with Lakshar-e-Toiba, Jayesh-e-Mohammad and Al-Queda. A number of militants apprehended in Indo-Bangladesh border by BSF and by State Border Police Organisation confirmed presence of large number of such fundamentalist groups training north-east Indian insurgent groups and recruiting their own cadres. These insurgent groups used to target railway tracks, bridges, trunk roots, power stations and telephone exchanges. Bangladeshi migrants gave them safe havens in India. Indian insurgent groups starting with NSCN-IM and ULFA, from 1992 onwards, used Bangladesh soil. Pakistan-sponsored ISI activities emerged after 2001 only. This became known when West Bengal police arrested few ISI agents at Calcutta who crossed from Bangladesh in

2002. Mr. Jaswant Sinha, the then Minister of External Affairs gave a statement in our Parliament that Pakistani High Commission in Dhaka has became the hub of ISI activities for terrorism in India. He confirmed that Indian insurgent groups had established training camps in different parts of Bangladesh and a large number of madrassas have sprung up along the Indo-Bangladesh border.

Dhaka's Directorate General of Forces Intelligence (DGFI) gave all out support to the operations of ISI. The report goes that earlier the ISI and DGFI were running 17 camps in Dhaka. The disclosure made by arrested ISI agents gave the following intelligence inputs:

1. ISI was planning to train large number of Muslims to wage holy war to liberate north-east.
2. To foment violence and terrorism in all parts of India where they get shelter.
3. Promoting indiscriminate violence in India by supporting local militant outfits, like Indian Muzahideen. Making use of ULFA and other militant outfits like PLA and UNLF for creating large-scale disturbances.
4. To create new fundamental militant outfits along communal and ethnic lines by instigating religious and ethnic groups in north-east and border districts.
5. Make use of ULFA and north-east militant fundamental outfits for destroying oil pipelines, refineries, industries, train lines and other public properties.
6. Supplying explosives and sophisticated arms and ammunitions to various terrorist organisations in India like NSCN-IM, PLA, UNLF, Prepak, PULF and Indian Muzahideens.
7. Launching economic warfare against India to siphon off money by underground elements of Pakistan and other countries and to print and pump large quantity of fake Indian currency into north-east.
8. Causing sabotage of communication lines and roads.

9. Increase communal trouble in north-east by inciting both the Muslim migrants and local Muslims by creating misunderstanding and hatred against non-Muslim population, as it has happened in Kokrajhar against Bodos.
10. Promoting fundamentalism, creating fundamentalist groups and raising militancy among local Muslims in north-east and along border of India with Bangladesh. Misleading border youth Muslims in the name of Jihad.
11. Propagating communal trouble in north-east and creating tension between Hindu and Muslim citizens by way of false and highly inflammatory propaganda.

Bangladesh foreign minister Deepu Moni visited Delhi on 25 July, 2013 towards the end of the tenure of both the governments. She came to speed-track the Teesta river water and the land-boundary / exchange of enclaves agreements and laid the ground work for Bangladesh prime minister Sheikh Hasina's visit in September 2013. She may announce election in Bangladesh just after her visit to India. India has assured help to Bangladesh in the field of education, power and healthcare.

Dipu Moni has mustered support from opposition leaders of India for empowering the Congress which lacks political support. She met Arun Jaitley, leader of opposition in Rajya Sabha where a constitution amendment bill was supposed to be introduced. It is necessary because of exchange of enclaves and territory. She also met her counterpart Salman Khursid. Both, the BJP and AGP opposed introduction of this bill for ratification by two-thirds of the members present in the Parliament and taking part in voting. On 26th July 2013, she warned India that not moving ahead on the land boundary issue and Teesta water agreement could influence the outcome of the result in Bangladesh election to be held in January, 2013. She further added in Delhi that the delay in the bills ratification by Indian Parliament will hit Hasina's poll prospect. She asked India that as Sheikh Hasina has co-operated with India in all security matters, so India must help Hasina in early ratification of the land bill. The Bangladesh foreign minister met the Prime Minister and attended the Iftar party with Shri Salman Khursid and held discussions with Shri Arun Jaitley to be positive, even though the leader of opposition was non-committal and replied to take up with his party colleagues.

It is a wake-up call for Hasina to win the election. The Awami League desperately wants India to clear Teesta river and land boundary pacts so. India is concerned that the defeat of Hasina will dramatically change the security scenario in the border region if an Islamist regime with the JEI in the coalition with Begum Zia assumes power. Militant organisation like Bangla Bhai, in a Taliban-like activities will further kill intellectuals, judges, journalists and foreign diplomats particularly that of India and USA. It was perhaps a mistake of Hasina to forcibly stop the Shahabag demonstrators which disillusioned her huge secularist vote bank even as the Islamic right was on a counteroffensive. There was comprehensive defeat of Awami League candidates in five city corporation polls in June and July, 2013. It shows a trend of change of regime in Bangladesh. Yet, India should refrain from interfering in the poll process of Bangladesh. We also could not gain anything in giving support to Ang Sue Ki of Myanmar and going against the military rule there earlier. Similarly, the security forces take immediate field decisions at the Indo-Pak border in any skirmish. We know it very well that Pak is a devil and its policy towards us. No political discussion with Pakistan will ever yield any result. So, known devil is better than unknown inner threats from Bangladesh. We have suffered more from Bangladesh than from Pakistan. Even if Begum Khalida Zia comes to power, we must be prepared for this and strengthen our border rather than become a part of their political party indirectly. Bangladesh has never found India to be a good neighbour in their relations and they are not trust worthy. Should India provide more Teesta water to Bangladesh when its own population in north-east suffers from scarcity of water in winter and summer, as the rivers Atrai and Mahananda get dry up? Can we stop China from making a barrage on river Brahmaputra and divert its water which will have tremendous effect in Arunanchal and Assam?

It is reported that Al-Queda, Rohingyas and fundamentalists in Bangladesh have formed a close nexus. A number of Al-Queda members took shelter in Bangladesh after return from Afghanistan. They were given patronage by Bangladesh's, Begum Zia government, so as also by Bangladesh Army. The CIA was aware of such Al-Queda presence in Bangladesh for which they established a base in Dhaka to keep a watch. Cox's Bazaar in Bangladesh was the main hideout of Al-Queda because of presence of Rhohingya refugees in that belt. About 22,000 Rohingya Muslims were earlier staying in various camps in Bangladesh as per report and equal numbers were staying outside in Cox's Bazar in Chittagong district. We had previously witnessed some entry of Rohingya Muslims into India in Karimganj border. Cox's Bazaar is the major transit haven for terrorists as it is one of the longest sea beaches in the world and is very close to Chittagong hill tracts and Myanmar. At present, it has become one of the biggest underground arms market in South-East Asia. The Harkut-ul-Ansar is maintaining few terrorist training camps in Cox's Bazaar. The ISI had been assisting the insurgent groups in north-east with weapons and training them for small-scale operations against Indian security forces excluding that of PLA, which is pampered by China. Pakistan ISI is now looking after all other militant groups of India including Muslim fundamentalist organisations. Even they have captured the mother of insurgent group of India operating abroad, i.e., NSCN-IM. Now added to it, is ULFA. The infight between Indian insurgent groups have gone in favour of ISI i.e. like NSCN-IM Vs NSCN-Khaplang, Kukis Vs Thangkul Nagas, NDFB Vs BLT, HNLC Vs ANVC, ATTF Vs NLFT, Bodo's Vs Santals, Arunachalis Vs Chakmas and UNLF Vs PLA. Similarly, ISI also took interest in Greater-Bangladesh issue, Muslim-Assam issue, Bodo issue, Karbi issue, Barak Valley issue and Greater Nagalim issue. The ISI wants to convert insurgent movements to low-intensity conflicts. They are aiming at taking over all sub-insurgent groups and supplying them with arms, ammunitions, communication equipments, guidance, advice, training, and shelter including funding. Instructions have been circulated by ISI to all insurgent groups in India to give up Bangladesh Muslim migrant's issue. They are trying to incite ethnic old Muslim settlers in north-east and border districts of 24 Parganas, Murshidabad, Nadia and Maldah district to raise their voice posing as if they are acting as a threat to their minority groups. Regrouping of all Muslim organisations in north-east under one umbrella is their primary task.

ISI is also propagating fillers against local people/old ethnic settlers and trying to remove them by acquiring their properties and land fraudulently, pumping drugs to north-east and to hinterland, mushrooming drug smugglers, arms couriers, supplying fake currency notes from Pakistan through Nepal, Myanmar and Bangladesh border, and printing fake Indian currency note in Chittagong area in Bangladesh. As a result, one can now find in most of the banks operating in north-east, even to some extent in SBI also, fake currency notes in various denominations. They have also forced Government of India to pour and dump more money in north-east so as to spend it for anti-insurgent operations as a result of which the economy of the country will slump.

Clear instructions have been issued to all insurgent groups in north-east to act against Indian security forces, kill them, snatch their weapons and ammunitions so that *per force*, heavy deployment of security forces will have to be made and expenditure on security will automatically go on higher side which would be harmful for the progress of the country.

To spread insurgency, the ISI is planning to cut the chicken-neck area of Siliguri, so that the complete north-east portion can be separated from the mainland. At the end, instead of fighting a war, they will force Indian insurgent groups and Indian Mujhahideen and various Muslim fundamentalist organisations to resort to Jihad. Their aim is also to keep the route clear for China in order to help it in this holy war/Jihad by supplying arms through Nepal border, Myanmar border and the border of Sikkim to Indian insurgent groups and other Muslim fundamentalist organisations.

On 10th of August 1999, the Assam Police arrested four ISI agents in Guwahati who were involved in getting explosives and arms to Assam through Karimganj and Sylhet border.

1. Qari Salim, Salim Ahmed, Abdul Aziz, son of Abdul Rashid, resident of village Mehilki, district Muzaffarnagar, UP. The profile of Qari Salim is as under:

   [He worked as a teacher in a madrassa and then as Alim in Durul Ulum Shawala madrassa, in District Kupwara in J&K. Salim went to Bangladesh with Faruque in May, 1997 through Karimganj border. On May 29, 1997, Salim travelled from Dacca to Pakistan in a PIA flight with one Qasim, a HuM activist. In Pakistan, Salim met Chief Amir HuM, who advised him to organise HuM in UP, J&K and in Assam by recruiting local Muslim youths for undergoing arms and explosive training in Pakistan. He has visited Assam several times and has stayed with many important people in Assam during such trips. He has been the main inspiring force in recruiting large numbers of Muslim youths from Goalpara, Dhubri and Barpeta districts after which he organised their trip to Pakistan via Bangladesh for imparting arms and explosive training organised by HuM through ISI operatives. During his stay in Dacca on his return from Pakistan, Salim received an explosive consignment of 34 kg of RDX, nine timer devices, 30 pieces of detonators, three time pencils and five blasting machines from an ISI operative located in Bangladesh. Salim brought the consignment to Rajshahi and handed over the same to Maulana Abdul Jabbar, an Iman of Rajshahi in Bangladesh. This consignment was intercepted near the Indo-Bangladesh border by a joint team of Assam and West

Bengal police after it was smuggled into India on August 14, 1999] (p. 205, 'North-East India' by Jaideep Saikia).

2. Maulana Hafiz Md. Akram Mallick, Musaffar Hassain, Atabulla, Bhajjan, Abdul Awal, son of Md. Abdul Aziz of village Muam Shahwali, Kupwara, Jammu and Kashmir (J&K State).
3. Md. Javed Wakhar, Md. Musaffar, Md. Mehraj, Abdul Rahman Danish, resident of Karachi, Pakistan
4. Md. Fasih Ullah Hussaini, Hamid Mahmood, Khalid Mehmood, son of Syed Habibulla, resident of Hyderabad, Sind, Pakistan.

A suspected Jaish-e-Mohammed (JeM) operative arrested in Dhaka has told Bangladeshi investigators that he arranged safe passage to India from Bangladesh for several Islamist militants who were involved in the 1999 hijack of an Indian Airlines plane. Nannu Mia alias Billal Mandal alias Billal told during interrogation that he helped in sending such 12-13 militants to India from Bangladesh. He knows one Abdur Rahman among them. ["The Daily Star" quoted an interrogator who quizzed Billal at the Task Force for Interrogation (TFI) cell]. In December 1999, militants hijacked the Delhi-bound Indian Airlines plane (flight number 814) after it took off from Kathmandu. They forced the aircraft to land in Kandahar in the then Taliban-ruled Afghanistan. Indian authorities had to release four terrorists, including Jaish founder Moulana Masood Azhar in return for safe release of all the passengers. Billal (aged 35 yrs) was arrested on March 5, 2010, along with four other suspected JeM militants, including Rezwan Ahmed, a Pakistani national who has been coordinating the Jaish activities in Bangladesh for the last five years. Billal has admitted his involvement in the 1999 plane hijack. ('Samachar' of 6th March 2010, Dhaka)

Six Harkat-ul-Mujahideen militants, who were trained in Batrasi in Pakistan, surrendered at Guwahati in March 2001, including Abu-Bakkar-Siddiqui, the General Secretary of Hizbul Mujahideen, Assam unit. Bakkar Siddiqui@

Abdulla was recruited by one Mahummad Fakruddin at Guwahati. He went to Karachi in Pakistan via Bangladesh and remained in HuM office there. Further, he was trained in Batrasi training camp under one Waqqas for two months. He returned to Rawalpindi, joined ISI training camp for explosive training of 39 days and returned to Assam in December, 1998. Later on in 2001, he surrendered to Police. He further disclosed that the Nunai madrassa at Jatrabari Dhaka was being used for ferrying Assam militants to Pakistan for weapon training. He further mentioned that the visit was arranged to Kurigram in Bangladesh from Dhubri via Maslachar by boat. (pp. 141 and 143, 'Terror Sans frontiers' by Jaideep Saikia).

The ISI was also helping in spreading of Harkut-ul-Muzaheedin in Karimganj, Dhubri and Goalpara district of Assam as they have already recruited a number of youths from these areas and dispatched them from Assam for training in Pakistan. It could be known only after the apprehension of the chief organiser of Hizbul Mujahideen in Assam namely Md. Muslimuddin (in Goalpara). It could be ascertained from him that the chief of HuM in India, Maulana Mohammad Fakruddin belongs to Goalpara Assam, and at present, he is based at Pakistan.

Mushrooming of madrassas and mosques all along Indo-Bangladesh border and their misuse by Pakistan and ISI

In 1990, West Bengal had 955 mosques and 455 madrassas. In 2008, there numbers were raised to 1,466 mosques and 810 madrassas respectively which were registered. Only Maldah consisted of as many as 172 madrasas and 55 mosques. Similarly, in Assam-Karimganj border, 193 madrassas and 10 mosques were reported. In Dhubri, 135 madrassas have mushroomed. In Tripura, 133 madrassas and 32 mosques are existing in the border districts. About 519 mosques and madrassas are now reported in Assam border areas itself. In Hailakhandi district of Assam and West Garo Hills, several madrassas have mushroomed in last five years including that of Mahenderganj. The madrassas in Bhaitabari is reported to be having very high technical facilities. 125 out of 208 registered madrassas of Cooch Behar, Jalpaiguri, Nadia, and 24 Parganas have radical elements, trained by Pakistan and it has been reported that arms also have been supplied to these madrassas and mosques and they are engaged in inciting local Muslims against India. These madrassas were earlier reported to be funded by Islamic Development Bank of Jeddah, The Habib Bank of Pakistan and Bangladesh.

It has also been reported by Bharti Jain on 21st July, 2013 that the Pakistan based Laskar-e-Toiba and Indian Mujahiddin are opening another front close to the North-Eastern region of the country, along the Bangladesh-Myanmar border. She has also quoted that RAW has confirmed that LeT and its overground organisation called JUD (Jamat-ud-Dawa) are working along Bangladesh-Myanmar border to provide help to Rohingya Muslims and also for internal imbalances in India by the IM. The JUD leaders Nadim Awan and Shaheed Rahmatullah are forging ties with Islamic organisation in Bangladesh and Myanmar. The JMBs are also trying to exploit Rohingya and opening various camps at Bandarban in Bangladesh trying to keep a link with Pakistan and Nepal and the Indian Mujahidin.

Deeptiman Tiwary on 5th August, 2013 has stated that IM has grown strong in north-east and Bangladesh. They have footprints in Sylhet region of Bangladesh and have created influence in Bangladesh-Myanmar border through LeT and are recruiting members from Rohingya Muslims.

Habib Bank of Pakistan.

Islamic Development Bank.

Jeddah Himalayan Bank of Kathmandu.

A number of Gulf nations have also helped in funding various mosques and madrassas in Indian side of the Indo-Bangladesh border. In Nadia district border, i.e., in Krishan Nagar, there are 404 mosques and 636 madrassas. Kishanganj, which is not on the border but is a part of Bihar and very close to Indo-Bangladesh border, is having number of mosques and madrassas. The teachings of madrassas in selected places are for *'jihad'*, i.e., to kill or die. These madrassas encourage the Muslim youths to be armed. They breed fundamentalist mindset. It has also been reported that a number of Saudi Arabia Muslim leaders, ISI agents and Pak officials have been visiting the Himalayan Bank, Kathmandu in Tarai regions several times. It is also reported that highly fanatic agents of ISI are penetrating madrassas to spread propaganda and to sabotage minds of local Muslims. They are spreading their tentacles and getting the help of Jamat-e-Islami members on both sides of Indo-Bangladesh border. There is one all Madrasatus Salafia dar-ul madrassa in an island in Padma river opposite to Rajsahi district which is funded by one Md. Alafuddin of Saudi Arabia. Similarly, funds for mosques in Lilong, Kwakta and Moreh in Manipur reportedly have come from Saudi Arabia. There are few more banks which are also involved in transferring of funds to fundamentalist groups. They are Islamic Bank of Bangladesh, Social Islamic Bank and Al-Rajhi Bank of Saudi Arabia. These banks are transferring funds from various extremist groups located at Mexico, Iran, Saudia Arabia and Syria. Recently, on 15th October, 2012, one ISI agent named Akhtar Hussain, who is an Afghan national, was arrested at Dhemaji in Assam. The Islamic militancy had emerged in Bangladesh since 2005. The religious fundamentalism was imported from Saudia Arabia by followers of Wahabism. It was further reported that Osama Bin Laden released 20 million takas to 427 madrassas in Bangladesh for recruitment of Talibans. Two foreign HuJI members, who were apprehended in Dhaka, gave this information. The name of one such person apprehended was Ahmed Sadiq of South Africa. The HuJI recruited about 5000 young boys from Bangladesh madrassas and 10,000 young boys from Rohingya community with help of the chairperson of Muslim Liberation Front of Myanmar. These young boys, were sent to Afghanistan for training (refer 'Telegraph' of Calcutta of 7th July, 1999). The Jamaat-e-Islami, the Al-Queda, the JMD kept direct liaison with Hek-matayar group in Afghanistan from Chittagong and Rajasahi. The Hizb-ul-towhid is the brainchild of Pak ISI Bayezid Khan Panni aka Salim, who is the founder of Pani Group that kept link with Muslim fundamentalist groups in India through ISI. The intelligence group also reported that Abdulla Khan of Indian Mujaheed, who was involved in Mumbai blast, 2011, is hiding in Bangladesh. It became known that Major Yasir, a deserter of Bangladesh Army was also involved in Delhi High Court blasts. Even, Begum Khalida Zia's son, Tarik Rehman, is the business associate of ULFA chief, Paresh Barua, and at present, Paresh Barua is hiding in China–Myanmar border. Madrassas in Bangladesh border districts are primary source of recruitment of radical Islamic outfits, besides, many of the Pakistani and Bangladeshi Jihadi outfits have gained control over few madrassas in Maldah, Dhubri, Nadia and Karimganj borders. There are two kinds of madrassas, one the Aliya madrassas and the the other Quomoi madrassas. Mostly, the Aliya Madrassas are recognised, and in the last 10 years, the Indian border with Bangladesh, has seen numerous quomoi madrassas, which have religious orientation to Deobandh curriculum. In these madrassas, the admission of girls are limited up to primary level only and there are no female teachers. Madrassa education is gaining momentum rapidly in Indo-Bangladesh border and theory of Islamic jihad is propagated in these madrassas. The continuous growth of mosques and madrassas in Indo-Bangladesh border is a matter of concern. The state and district authorities must keep a watch over opening of unauthorised madrassas and mosques funded from other countries. West Bengal-Maldah border has the highest number of mosques and madrassas, and in Assam, it is Karimganj Vs Dhubri, which are always trying to gain top position. These madrassas were, and are still being used as shelters for fundamentalists, transit point of militants, storage of arms before supply to hinterland, and as a base of ISI operatives for both infiltration and exfiltration. The Muslim fundamental groups have not only had an eye on Indian side of the border for opening of madrassas; more than it, they have opened mosques and madrassas in border districts of Chittagong, Cox's Bazaar, Rangamati, Sylhet, Braman-Baria, Manikganj,

Mymensingh, Sathkhira and Rangpur. It will be easier for them to send their representatives to madrassas on Indian side.

Recently, in September 2012, the DG BSF, U K Bansal handed over the fresh list of Indian insurgents hiding in Bangladesh to the Bangladesh border guards. It was also taken up by the DG, BSF with his counterpart to resolve 162 adverse possession land cases in Indo-Bangladesh border for which the militants easily gain access to border areas through these routes often. Recently a deserter of Meghalaya police, Dy. SP Packchara R Sangma, the chief of GNLA, who escaped earlier to Dhaka and maintained contact with ULFA, NDFB and NSCN-IM, was handed over to BSF by BGB. It has been reported that Packchara R Sangma, who created GNLA group in Garo hills, will contest the elections in 2013 from Meghalaya. Again on 5th September, 2012, the BSF apprehended a self-styled Lt. of PLA militant group, Shri A S Singh of Manipur from Dawkie border while trying to cross over to Bangladesh.

The Director General of Police of West Bengal Naparajit Mukherjee said on 18th October, 2012 that Pakistan is routing arms through north-east rebels. He had further added that the Maoists have forged a deadly alliance with the Pakistani spy agency ISI through remnants of banned outfit SIMI. Murshidabad and Maldah border districts had noticed activities that hinted at Maoists-ISI linkage. The link is believed to be helping the ultras in getting arms and ammunitions through existing network of north-east insurgents ('Times of India', 19th Oct, 2012).

The BSF arrested an ISI agent, Farooq Mian, aged 30 years, of district Sunamganj, Bangladesh, on 2nd Oct, 2010 at Betgara border of east Khasi hills.

Bangladesh's utility to Pakistan is an alternate proxy war base against India. Momin Khan, an ISI agent, who was apprehended in the first week of October at Sonamara in Agartala border, was tasked to visit Assam and Delhi to get army intelligence and he was supposed to contact other ISI agents in India. ISI is facing difficulty to enter into

India in western border, because of completion of barbed wire fencing and heavy deployment of Army, BSF and Police. They find it easier to penetrate through long gaps and unfinished fencing of Meghalaya, Assam, Tripura and Mizoram in the Bangladesh border. Another ISI agent, Abu Baker Siddique of Bangladesh was apprehended by BSF at Sabroom, Tripura border on 30th Oct, 2010. Indo-Bangladesh border has now become a safe passage for ISI, particularly north-east border. Munir Khan, another ISI agent was apprehended on 3rd July, 2010 at Agartala-Tripura border. He was a SI in Pakistan Intelligence wing. His other name was Omar Asraf. He was going to Punjab to collect intelligence on Indian Army. One more ISI agent was caught with arms and ammunitions on 4th July, 2010 at Sidhi Ashram, Agartala. On 3rd July, 2010, Nayeem Md Mamoon, an ISI agent was apprehended at Lakhmura border, Agartala. Along with Munir Khan, Abdul Rahman of Al-Queda, Daud Merchant and Sangram Ali of HUJI were also apprehended. Recently, the co-ordinator of ISI for west of India named Sirajuddin Fakir was caught at Bhuj, Jamnagar on 14th Oct, 2012. We have number of ISI agents apprehended in various parts of India as they get shelter in the houses of these Bangladeshi Muslim migrants, who are everywhere, in all corners of the country. Thus, these migrants are a security threat to the nation and it is easy to cross the border from Bangladesh in the north-east, as the border is not monitored properly.

The ISI is also involved in spreading inflammatory communal propaganda in various parts of our country, particularly, in the north-east, in mosques located close to the border. The time of mullahs of Deoband, UP is over now. They are being replaced slowly and gradually by ISI-trained extremists who are capable of giving sensitive, inflammatory and communal speeches to not only migrant Muslims but also in inciting the local Muslims in north-east border areas. What is even more disturbing is that some of our own politicians try to take advantage of the situation and sow the seeds of communal hatred. Abdul Ghani Khan Choudhury as early as in 1983 had said, “If Hindus kill one Muslim, the Muslims should realiate by killing three Hindus and the Government would support you..."

The names of few more ISI agents apprehended in north-east are as follows:

- Zakir Hussain, Md Rafiqe, s/o Md Golam Ali of Chandmari, Goalpara
- Abul Qasim, Osman, s/o Altaf Hussain of Khoridhra, Goalpara
- Muslimuddin, Muslim Ali, s/o Jonab Ali of Paikan, Goalpara
- Md Akbar Ali, s/o Md Amir Ali of Joshihatipara, Barpeta
- Kifayetullah, s/o Liakatullah of Bidyanagar, Kamrup
- Sajid, Mainuddin, s/o Hajrat Ali of Gorgari, Nalbari
- Allauddin Ahmed, Md Omar, Ashik Ahmed, s/o Md Muktarur Rahman of Purani bazaar, Dhubri
- Saiful Islam, Bulbul, s/o Md Wazed Ali Khan of Pulkipara, Barpeta
- Mainul Haque, Jamaluddin, s/o Faizuddin of Rampur, Goalpara
- Jehirul Islam, s/o late Ahed Ali, Jehirul Haque, Jahu, Saddam Hussain, Mithun of Dhumarpathar, Barpeta
- Haji Billauddin Ahmed, s/o late Haji Sahid Ali of Manugram, Karimganj
- Md Abdul Mukit Chaudhury, s/o late Motahir Choudhury of Kakri bazaar, Karimganj
- Md Tazrul Islam, Tahuddul of Bilashipara, Assam

It clearly reveals that ISI was using mostly Agartala, Meghalaya and Assam borders to cross their elements and all north-east insurgent groups, Indian Mujahiddins, local Muslims, and the Muslim migrants provided them the shelter.

Md Asgar Ali, a Pak-trained ISI militant was apprehended on 17th April, 2003 at Hyderabad along with

M.A. Rauf, who were responsible for firing and killing Haren Pandya at Ahmedabad on 26th March, 2003. Asgar Ali received arms training in Pakistan and entered India through Bangladesh. Pak ISI always used Bangladesh as their launching pad.

Naga and Mizo insurgents in Chittagong hill tracts used Bangladesh land in the beginning. The radical Islamism got an upper hand after assassination of Sheikh Mujibur Rehman and it was during Gen Zia-ur-Rehman's regime that the ISI started penetrating into both, Bangladesh and India, and established their link with ULFA. After the withdrawal of Soviets from Afghanistan, ISI was full of jihadis, which they wanted to operate in India through use of Bangladesh. The ISI could come closer to the Directorate General of Forces Intelligence (DGFI) of Bangladesh and started sending Indian insurgent groups for training in Pakistan and funding and supplying of arms and explosives to them in India.

The radicalisation of Islam in Bangladesh helped ISI largely, and thus, the Pakistan's proxy war continued against India through Bangladesh. The vast land border of Bangladesh with India and massive influx of Bangladeshi Muslim migrants to the north-east became handy for ISI network. Alongwith that of ISI, the Bangladesh intelligence unit also started following the same pattern of arranging training to Indian insurgent groups in their soil and sending weapons to Indian insurgent groups through Myanmar border; the then Home Minister Shri Inderjeet Gupta, the former Home Minister, replied this in Lok Sabha in December, 1996.

The Jamat-e-Islami became very powerful in Bangladesh, both religiously and politically, and started the Islamic movement in their strongholds at Jessore, Khulna and Satkhira border districts.

There was a big arms haul at Chittagong port where arms and ammunitions and explosive materials were seized, which were supposed to be dispatched to the north-east insurgents in India. This seizure of 2nd April, 2004, included around 150 rocket launchers, 840 rockets more than a million of ammunitions, about 2500 grenades and 1700 rifles. Bangladesh, then, was not in a position to procure these arms and to supply free to Indian insurgents. In fact, they all came from Pakistan as in Bangladesh newspapers the hint was aimed towards ISI. It is not a fact that Bangladesh intelligence forces were in dark about such arms smuggling through Chittagong port. They were supposed to be sent to north-east so that Indian insurgent groups could easily target Indian security elements.

Bangladesh gave shelter and support to Paresh Barua, the Commaner-in-Chief of ULFA, Ranjan Daimari, the President of NDFB (Now handed over to BSF at Dawkie border), Bishwamohan Dev Verma, President NLFT, and Ranjit Dev Verma, President ATTF.

Bangladesh soil was also used by ULFA to tranship their members to Pakistan where they were flown from Dhaka. A number of training camps were run by ISI and DGFI, both, very close to Tripura and Shillong borders.

The Harkut-ul-Jihad-al-Islami, Jamat-ul-Mujahideen, and Al-Queda members in Bangladesh started formation of Muslim fundamentalist groups in north-east like MULFA, MULTA, MVF, MLA, IURPI, AAMLF, MLTA, etc. The funds for raising these fundamentalist groups in Assam are what Bangladesh receives from various Muslim countries, i.e., Pakistan and Saudi Arabia.

The Pak ISI continued their links with both Muslim fundamentalist organisations in the north-east and the Islamic terrorist groups operating in Jammu & Kashmir. Pakistan organised training for various Muslim militant outfits like Hizbul Mujahideen, Tehrik-ul-Mujahideen, Muslim Mujahideen, Hakat-ul-Mujahideen, Harkat-ul-Jihad-e-Islami and Lashkar-e-Toiba operating in Jammu & Kashmir, on the soil of Bangladesh.

The Indian insurgent groups like PLA, UNLF, ULFA, Pre-Pak, NDFB, NLFT and ATTF got shelter, hideouts, safe haven and transit in Bangladesh. They also got the help for transit of their leaders to Pakistan, Myanmar and

China through Bangladesh. Our insurgent groups manipulated their bases for recruitment, motivation, infiltration and exfiltration from and to Bangladesh.

Bangladesh provided fake travel documents and fake identity cards to north-east insurgent groups. These north-east insurgent groups, with help of Bangladesh, transported their weapons through Cox's Bazaar and Chittagong ports and brought them to India through Myanmar border.

The IIGs were also trained not only by the ISI in Bangladesh but also by Talibans in Afghanistan. All these Indian insurgent groups used their bases, very close to our border as launching pad for infiltration of their trained cadres from Bangladesh along with supply of weapons to various parts of north-east.

This is proved from the apprehension of militant Quari Salim who divulged *modus operandi* of Pak ISI groups operating in Bangladesh and India and their tasks / aims.

Another group, which was raised in India by ISI was the Indian Mujahideen which was funded and raised by the help of Al-Queda, HUJI, Jamatis and the Hizbul Mujahideen group of both Pakistan and Bangladesh. It is a deadly group in India which is operating in all the hinterlands where these Bangladesh Muslim migrants are settled. They get full support and shelter from these migrants and their homes are used as safe shelters for Indian Mujahedeen group. The funds coming from abroad, particularly, from Pakistan reach to train these Indian Mujahedeen groups and provide them with weapons from these Bangladesh Muslim migrants whose presence in numbers at various corners of India help Pakistan in achieving their goal to plan subversion activities and sabotage all over India. This also will not result in raising of finger by international community towards Pakistan as it will be the Indian Mujahedeens who will be behind all such violence and actions and their direct involvement will help Pakistan indirectly in achieving their aim.

The islands in Sundarbans are also safe havens for the ISI. We have a number of such islands where penetration from Bangladesh was very easy using boats and in most of these islands, Bangladeshis are settled since ages and they give shelter to ISI agents coming to West Bengal through Sundarbans. They have expanded their network in most of the places in Rajasthan, Punjab, J&K, Bombay, Pune, Hyderabad, Madhya Pradesh and Uttar Pradesh, besides north-east. All their agents in India are keeping contact with the headquarters through Bangladesh only and instead of crossing the borders in the western side, they find it easier to cross through the Sundarbans in West Bengal or in Assam border of north-east or that of Tripura border. The ISI intends to use Sundarbans as a major route for most of their future operations. Both, Bangladesh and Indian fishermen in the Sundarbans are employed as their couriers. Tariq Aziz, the Bangladesh ISI agent is reportedly involved in using this route along with land border of Nadia.

Pakistan's proxy war against India through Bangladesh is quite visible from the following acts helping north-east insurgent groups and Islamic fundamentalist groups in the north-east:

Providing bases, shelter, arms/ammunitions to terrorist groups operating in Jammu and Kashmir and sending weapons to them through hinterland via Bangladesh.

Establishment link of Indian insurgent groups with Islamic terrorist groups in Bangladesh via Indo-Bangladesh border.

Despatching trained religious fundamental propagandists after nurturing them at Indian mosques and madrassas.

Expansion of espionage network throughout India with their trained agents already settled in the hinterland.

Inciting disgruntled elements in India, including Indian Mujahedeens for violence and sabotage activities so that the security scenario of the country always remains at tenterhooks.

The Islamisation was considerably spread in Bangladesh during Begum Khalida Zia's period. During her time, the

Pak High Commissioner in Dhaka was increasingly posting ISI agents, who kept liaison with DGFI and the Bangladesh border guards, the Bangladesh's student union groups, politicians and bureaucrats. The Pak embassy in Dhaka was directly involved in assisting Indian north-east militant groups in providing arms, ammunitions and explosives and arranging their training in selected Bangladesh madrassas. Due to the presence of migrants and mushrooming of madrassas in the border districts, the ISI found a safe haven to operate and fund Muslim fundamentalist organisations all over India. The Jamaat-e-Islami party regrouped during the regime of BNP. The Islamist group in Bangladesh have flourished with financial help from outside, particularly, from Al-Queda and Saudi Arabia. Saudi Arabia also has helped in funding Al-Queda in establishing number of madrassas in Bangladesh.

As the elections are to be held in Bangladesh in 2013, India requested BNP chairperson Khalida Zia to visit Delhi. Mr. Pankaj Sharan, our High Commissioner in Bangladesh, had met Khalida Zia at Dhaka. Her meeting with PM and President of India, and visit to Ajmer Dargah was planned keeping in view the result that may come out in the coming elections at Dhaka. Since long, BNP has shown anti-India stance. New Delhi knows it very well that BNP has kept a link with Pakistan, yet it is looking for an oppurtunity to have better relations with South Asian Countries. India has maintained a good relations with Bangladeshi government during the tenure of Sheikh Hasina led Awami League government in concluding a land boundary agreement, but it is crucial to have better relations with BNP to control the effect of ISI, both in Bangladesh and in India, and also to keep a check on Muslim fundamentalist organisations that are being funded by Pakistan. A check on north-east militants nurtured by ISI, and on pushing arms, ammunitions and explosives for causing riots and violence in hinterland of India through Indian Mujahideen groups needs to be also kept. (Refer 'Times of India'-24.10.2012). The JMJB, i.e., Jagrata Muslim Janta Bangladesh is one of the most dreaded Islamic outfits in

Bangladesh. It preaches for a puritanical way of Islamic living asking men to grow beard, women to wear burkas and to follow the Taliban way of living. Along with that, Hizbul-ul-Taheer and Islamic Chatra Shibirs are few more Islamic groups of Bangladesh having a link with Al-Queda; similarly these has been Islamic Oikya Jote's growth in spreading a global network of terror. There were reports that about 500 youths of Hyderabad were trained in operating arms in Bangladesh and Baluchistan with the help of HUJI Bangladesh, Lashkar-e-Toiba and Jayesh Mohmmad. These groups were also involved in organising a joint operation for causing a serious bomb blast in Varanasi on 7th March, 2006 along with SIMI members. These groups were also involved in Delhi blasts of 29th October, 2005, IIM Bangalore attack on 28th December 2005 and Mumbai blasts on 11th July, 2006. Bangladesh has already achieved potential to become Islamic extremist operations nerve centre. It is granted as the shelter soil of most of the fundamental groups operating in the world. The growing Islamic fundamentalist movement linked with Al-Queda and presence of Pakistan intelligence agency at Dhaka have given a thrust to all terrorist operations in India and South-East Asia. Mr. S.S. Harishang (who is a South Asia expert) in his article published on 2nd Aug, 2006 has categorically stated that ISI will keep on harassing India all along the 4000 kilometres of border with Bangladesh (as published in 'Washington Post'). The eastern sector has become too handy for ISI to operate. This border is very porous and having number of entry and exit routes in West Bengal, Assam, Meghalaya, Tripura, and Mizoram. Bangladesh is surrounding Siliguri corridor by settling of Bangladeshis within five kilometres of the border on Indian side. Presence of Muslim fundamentalist organisations, madrassas and mosques for shelter in all the border districts and lastly anti-Indian insurgent groups of the north-east coming forward to help ISI, and now the left wing extremists in the hinterland of a number of states which require funds, arms, ammunitions, explosives and training for their survival are getting inclined to Bangladesh. Islamic

NGOs are funding militancy in the name of building mosques and setting up madrassas, educational institutions, health care centres, hospitals in both sides of the border areas to promote Islamic culture and to teach for waging jihad. These NGOs are based at Rangpur, Dinajpur, Rajshahi, Khulna and Satkhira border areas, received funds from Al-haramain Islamic Foundation of Saudia Arabia, and thus, spread their tentacles in obtaining more funds from Kuwait, United Arab Emirates and from United States and United Kingdom.

The middle-east countries, for funding these madrassas and mosques reached Bangladesh for distribution, which were transacted through Bangkok and Singapore. Ravita-al alam-al-Islam, a Saudi Arabia-based NGO, is running various hospitals in Cox's Bazaar and Chittagong hills tracts including another NGO called Servants of Suffering Humanity International, funded by Taliban/Osama bin laden in these areas, which have converted it to a major arms market not only in Bangladesh but in whole of South-East Asia. Being a neighbour of Bangladesh, with its border running thousand of kilometres, India is facing Islamic fundamentalism and terrorism threat more from Bangladesh now in comparison to Pakistan.

More anti-Hindu notes, and preaching of various Mullahs guided by Pakistan and other Islamic fundamentalists in north-east are now seen particularly in Karimganj, Dhubri, Cachar, Nadia, Maldah, Kishanganj and Murshidabad districts.

All madrassas along Bangladesh's border are now the primary source of recruitment for the radical Islamic outfits and other jihadi groups like Al-Queda, SIMI, LET, HUJI-B and Harkut-ul-Ansar. Jamatis have their own madrassas and they use their own way of preaching not only to Bangladesh youths but also to various youths going from Jammu and Kashmir, West Bengal, Tripura, Assam and Sikkim. The connections are always, through these migrants with radical elements.

Bangladesh is tense on the eve of war crimes ruling. On 14th July, 2013, on the eve of the key verdicts of the trial of radical Islamist accused in 1971 liberation, Ghulam Azam (91 years), the former chief of Jamat-e-Islami, the member of international crime tribunal justice Ajm Fazle Kabil took three months to listen to all the charges and the JEI activists injured three policemen, hurled bombs and smashed vehicles on Dacca roads. The Bangladesh court on 15th July, 2013 sent top Islamist Ghulam Azam to 90 years in prison for master minding atrocities during the 1971 war. He was spared from death penalty in view of age and health. Ghulam Azam was not less than Adolf Hitler and was the mastermind behind killing three million people in Bangladesh during 1971 liberation war. He was arrested in January, 2012. However, the life term punishment gave a disappointment to the Bangladeshis. Azam was the fifth Jamat leader to be sentenced for a war crime.

The fresh violence over the conviction of JEI supremo 91 years old Ghulam Azam left four persons dead and people went on rampage enforcing a nationwide strike on 16th July, 2013 (TOI of 17th July, 2013). The Jamat activists used illegal weapons and homemade bombs in their attack with police. Bangladeshi society stands at a crucial juncture today. It is locked in a battle between liberal and regressive forces that will determine the future of Bangladesh. The Islamic movement such as the Hefazat-e-Islam would turn Bangladesh into a Taliban state. Not only would this impede Bangladesh's political and economic progress, it would also pose a huge security challenge for South Asia as a whole. It is to be seen how Bangladesh will handle the peaceful protest against war crime trial verdicts (TOI of 17th July, 2013).

Dacca Supreme Court on 17th September, 2013 sentenced a senior Islamist leader to death for mass murder which has sparked fresh violence. Abdul Quader Molla 65, the fourth biggest leader of JeI party was also given life sentence. The tribunal since January has convicted six Islamists of crimes related to the 1971 war in which pro-independence fighters were helped by local Islamist leader.

Molla's life sentence had sparked protests in the port city of Chittagong. There were about 2000 Jamat protesters who rioted, torched a police van and a car. Police fired rubber bullets and gas to disperse demonstrators. There were protests in Dacca and Bogra who injured a police inspector. Molla was convicted for murder of 350 unarmed Bengali civilians, a poet and a top journalist. He was then a student of Physics in Dacca University. He was called as butcher of Mirpur. Molla could be executed in year end unless he gets a pardon from the President (AFP Dacca of 18th September, 2013).

Pradeep Das, a Hindu student of Dacca was brutally killed by an Islamic fanatic student friend Ata-ur-Rehman in July, 2013 to get his girl friend.

In a landmark ruling Bangladesh's biggest fundamentalist party JeI was on 1st August, 2013 declared illegal by the High court which disqualified it from contesting future polls. Moazzem Hussain, the chief judge of a high court panel hearing the high profile case ruled that Jamat's character breached the secular constitution. He declared that the registration given to Jamat by the election commission was illegal and void. Jamatis protested against the verdict and called for a nationwide bundh from 12th August, 2013 for two days. Bangladesh Tariquat Federation which preaches Sufi philosophy and promotes secularism petitioned the high court against the Jamatis. It voiced that a communal outfit cannot be considered as a political party. The writ petition was filed on 25th January, 2009. Time will tell its outcome in Bangladesh.

In another blow to the JeI of Bangladesh, their supreme court on 5th August, 2013 had rejected the plea of the JeI against the verdict of the high court which has declared it to be illegal and barred it from contesting next poll. Justice AHM Shamsuddin Choudhury Manik refused to give stay on the verdict of the high court (Ref. 'Daily Star' of Bangladesh of 5th Aug., 2013.) However the judge allowed the jamats to go on appeal in a bench. It is a matter to see how the future poll of Bangladesh will be.

Bangla oppn leader gets live term for war crimes

A special Bangladeshi tribunal on 10 Oct. 2013 sentenced opposition BNP's 83-year old leader Abdul Alim to jail until death for committing large scale killings and other war crimes during the 1971 liberation war against Pakistan.

Three Killed in Bangla Strike Violence

Three people died and scores of others were injured on 4th November, 2013 as protesters set off homemade bombs and torched cars during an opposition strike demanding that Bangladesh's government step aside ahead of January elections, report said. Security was tight across the capital, Dhaka, with extra police and paramilitary guards patrolling the streets at the start of the three-day strike.

Oppn Rallies in Bangla Turn Violent, Five killed

At least five protesters were killed and over 300 injured as workers of the main opposition BNP clashed with security forces during rallies across Bangladesh demanding a neutral caretaker government to oversee the next general election.

BNP chief Khaleda Zia, addressing a massive rally here, issued an ultimatum to her archrival PM Sheikh Hasina to initiate talks on her demand. The former PM said if the demand was not accepted, the party would enforce a 60-hour nationwide strike from October 27.

Two demonstrators were killed in southeastern Cox's Bazar when security personnel fired at BNP supporters. Two more were killed in central Chandpur district when protesters clashed with security forces. One protester died in northern Jaldhaka town when Rapid Action Battalion personnel opened fire at supporters of the rightwing Jamaat-e-Islami, a key ally of the BNP. Violence also erupted in different parts of Bangladesh, including south-western Patuakhali, leaving over 300 people hurt.

Bangla Sentences Opposition MP to Death for War Crimes

A prominent law-maker of the opposition BNP was on

1st Oct 2013 sentenced to death by a special Bangladeshi tribunal for genocide during the country's 1971 liberation war against Pakistan, becoming the first MP and seventh person to be convicted of crimes against humanity.

"He (Salauddin Quader Chowdhury) will be hanged by neck till he is dead," Justice ATM Fazle Kabir, chairman of the three-member International Crimes Tribunal, announced.

Chowdhury, 65, the first member of the main opposition Bangladesh National Party (BNP) to be tried by the court, was found guilty of rape, torture, murder and genocide during the war of independence.

Despite tight security across the country, the verdict sparked violence in Chowdhury's home city of Chittagong and in the capital Dhaka, with protesters torching many of the vehicles on the streets. A driver of a van that was set afire sustained burn injuries.

The government had yesterday boosted security in anticipation of violent protests by opposition parties. Paramilitary Border Guards were deployed in Chittagong, while police in riot gear patrolled the streets in the capital and other cities.

Sitting on a Powder Keg

Bangladesh is in a violent phase and India must do all it can to see a friendly regime return to power

Bangladesh is headed for a political crisis that might impact Asia's regional balance. When Prime Minister Manmohan Singh was in China signing the border defence agreement and addressing future ideologues at the Chinese Communist Party school, Indian diplomats in Dhaka were desperately trying to get the two leading ladies – Prime Minister Sheikh Hasina Wajed and opposition leader Khaleda Zia – to speak to each other and start a dialogue to ensure peaceful and inclusive elections to ensure a democratic transition in Bangladesh.

Hasina finally broke the ice and offered an all-party interim cabinet comprising ruling and opposition coalitions to conduct the upcoming parliament polls. She quickly followed it up by speaking to Khaleda over telephone and extending her a dinner invite. Khaleda refused the invitation and instead decided to go ahead with a 60-hour nationwide strike that turned very violent. The 37-minute conversation was reduced to a squabble involving past actions and Khaleda's out-of-order special telephone and did little to inspire the nation's confidence.

The BNP chief stuck to her demand for restoration of a neutral non-party caretaker Hasina insisted that was not possible after the 15th constitution amendment had scrapped it and kept offering the all-party interim cabinet instead. But the BNP chief stuck to her guns, dashing the hopes of a political reconciliation. As the conversation went viral on internet and was broadcast over Dhaka-based TV stations, Bangladesh wondered what lay in store in the days ahead.

The main show had a sideshow to it – one involving the US and Indian ambassadors. Local media reports have been agog with rumours of a no-holds barred spat between the two diplomats during a breakfast meeting, following which the US envoy Dan Mozena, flew to Delhi for consultations with Indian officials. On his return to Dhaka, media reports quoting US embassy sources suggested, "India and the US were on the same page in Bangladesh." Upset with these reports, the Indian high commission and the ministry of external affairs reacted furiously. Quoting unnamed Indian diplomats, the local media reported that India and the US were "not on the same page".

Privately, Indian diplomats told journalists that Mozena was "behaving like a standing committee member of the BNP". They say he is "doing everything to bring back the BNP to power" and Khaleda is ever so determined to bring down the Hasina government through violent street protests increasingly orchestrated by the radical Jamaat-e-Islami with US encouragement.

And when media reports surfaced over India and the US being on the same page, Indian diplomats saw it as an American move to drive a wedge between India and its best friend in Dhaka, the Awami League, whose government has delivered on India's security and connectivity concerns like no government in Dhaka has ever done. India has good reasons to feel beholden to the Hasina government, though the diplomats are not oblivious to the anti-incumbency she faces. But if Washington has a choice in Dhaka, how can it deny India having a right to its own choice of a friend?

The US feels a BNP-led government will serve its strategic interests and may help it stop Chinese inroads into the country. India has reservations about the BNP after trying to unsuccessfully court it during Khaleda's 2001-06 tenure. For Delhi, the real worry is Jamaat-e-Islami and Hefazat-e-Islam.

Delhi has good reasons to fear such a dispensation as likely to be inimical to its security. India feels the US is overlooking the spectre of a revival of Islamic radicalism Bangladesh experienced when Khaleda was last in power and thus weakening the focus of the war against terror.

But the most important element in the US-India spat in Dhaka was an unnamed Indian diplomat describing the Chinese stand on the emerging political crisis in Bangladesh as "constructive". Chinese ambassador Li Jun has been more vocal than any of his predecessors. In recent weeks, he has thrice issued statements on Bangladesh's political crisis, asking "wisdom to prevail over violence" and even suggesting China was trying to mediate in the crisis through "our friends in both the parties".

China is keen to go ahead with its plans to build a deep sea port in Sonadia off the Chittagong coast. For the first time, Indian diplomats are not worried about another 'pearl in the string'. They believe Sonadia can help India access its northeast better and the whole project can fit into the Bangladesh-China-India-Myanmar plan to develop connectivity for increased trade, investment and commerce.

As Bangladesh slides into a violent imbroglio, India appears nervous over the future of its east and northeast which are afflicted by violent statehood movements and insurgencies. It cannot afford a hostile government in

Dhaka. This, in a way, revives the pre-1971 scenario where a similar situation forced India to back the Bengali insurrection and militarily intervene in East Pakistan, braving threats of a US naval intervention.

The only difference now is that befriending China to balance off the US and vice versa is a realistic option for India. Delhi appears keen to demonstrate it is nobody's surrogate and retains the option to balance off the US with China by what it does in Bangladesh in the days ahead.

Different choices for India, US in Bangla polls?

While New Delhi is more Aligned with Hasina's Party, Washington Seems to Favour BNP-Jamaat Combine

New Delhi: Publicly, India and the United States may appear to be on the same page regarding the situation in Bangladesh. But in reality, India is increasingly uncomfortable with the US' position and believes it can have negative implications for Bangladesh and the region.

Last week, US ambassador to Dhaka, Dan Mozena, visited South Block and spent long hours meeting foreign secretary Sujatha Singh and other senior officials. As hartals and street violence take over domestic politics in Bangladesh, India and the US have shared concerns regarding its stability.

Sources said Sheikh Hasina had invited her rival Begum Khaleda Zia for a meeting and dinner to end the impasse over the caretaker government. But the main opposition, Bangladesh Nationalist Party (BNP), is unwilling to end the violence and insisting on a neutral dispensation.

But India remains more concerned about the colour of politics being pursued by BNP. This is where Indian and the US positions diverge.

The US appears much more comfortable with the BNP-Jamaat combine, who have made no secret of their radicalised politics. India believes if this succeeds, Bangladesh would be very different as a nation. The politics of BNP and Jamaat have become more radicalised in the past couple of years. Indian intelligence has detected influences of both Pakistan-based Lashkar-e-Taiba (LeT) and Al-Qaeda. There is a lot of funding available to these groups from West Asian countries, and some from Pakistan.

The US is less comfortable with Sheikh Hasina's government, especially after the PM's confrontation with Mohammed Yunus of Grameen Bank — the fracas over funding for the Padma bridge project — and also the war crimes tribunal. There appears to be a part of official thinking in the US that believes, according to sources here, BNP-Jamaat have better free market credentials, and that they would move away from radical Islam once they are in power. "They are too far away to have a realistic view of the street," they said.

India is haunted by the 2001 Pyrdiwah massacre, when 15 BSF personnel were massacred by BDR troops in an ugly confrontation. BNP had explained Jamaat's place in government thus: it would be better to have them in than out. But once in government, Jamaat occupied the ministries crucial to furthering their radical agenda.

Those years saw the flowering of Jamaatul Mujahideen Bangladesh (JMB) and other terror groups like HuJI. India is opposed to a return to those days.

An added regional vulnerability is the Rohingya problem in Myanmar. With heightened communal tensions in Myanmar along with considerable Rohingya population in Bangladesh, New Delhi believes that the situation is ripe for disaster.

The implications of increased radicalised politics in Bangladesh would have terrible implications for Myanmar's stability. Again, reports of LeT and Al-Qaida infiltration among Rohingyas are popping up frequently. The instability as a result of radical politics could spread to India's north-east and even China's Yunnan province.

Four killed on last day of strike in Bangla

At least four persons were killed as fresh violence erupted on Tuesday across Bangladesh on the final day of a 60-hour opposition strike demanding a caretaker regime to oversee the next general election, taking the overall death toll in the political unrest to 20.

A youth leader of the ruling Awami League was hacked to death by unidentified persons in Chittagong, police said. Reports from Cox's Bazar district said two workers of the right-wing Jamaat-e-Islami, a key ally of the main opposition BNP, died when police fired on protesters.

Witnesses said a BNP cadre was killed in clashes between police and protesters in western Magura district. An injured worker of the Awami League died overnight in northern Kishorganj, officials said. The BNP-led 18-party opposition alliance called the shutdown to press for the restoration of the neutral caretaker government system to oversee the next election. The polls are to be held by January 25, 2014.

Supporters of BNP and Jamaat torched a bus in Manikganj and vandalised at least eight vehicles in Gazipur. Opposition activists earlier exploded crude bombs in front of Awami League leaders houses in Dhaka.

Oppn strike starts in poll-bound Bangla, Five killed

At least five persons were killed, over 100 injured, trains and a Hindu temple were attacked as opposition parties on Sunday enforced a 60-hour strike across Bangladesh demanding a neutral caretaker government to oversee the next election.

Supporters of the main opposition Bangladesh Nationalist Party (BNP) and its right-wing ally Jamaat-e-Islami set afire vehicles and exploded crude bombs in the capital city Dhaka as the strike got under way early on Sunday morning.

The incidents of clashes, arson, vandalism and homemade bomb blasts were reported from other parts of the country, including port city Chittagong, Rajshahi, Natore and Bogra.

In Rajshahi, demonstrators attacked a Hindu temple and vandalised several shops, Bdnews 24 reported. In Chittagong, the report said picketers stopped an autorickshaw carrying a pregnant woman to a hospital and set it afire.

Police recovered gunpowder and 17 handmade bombs from a house in the Dhaka University staff quarters. Opposition supporters tried to set fire to the record room of Dhaka chief metropolitan magistrate's court using petrol. Officials said the blaze damaged some documents.

In northwestern Joÿpurhat, the opposition members set two trains afire, injuring nearly 70 passengers.

Demonstrators torched the two trains— Rupsha Express and Rocket Mail—within a short span of time at Joypurhat, a railway spokesman said. The trains were bound for southwestern Khulna, he added.

Authorities overnight deployed thousands of additional police and paramilitary personnel countrywide to prevent any untoward incident.

Unrest in Dhaka

Failure to conduct peaceful polls in Bangladesh will affect regional security

The ongoing pre-election political turmoil in Bangladesh not only bodes ill for democracy in that country but also threatens peace and prosperity in the subcontinent. The current 60-hour hartal called by the opposition BNP-led 18 party alliance to force the issue of a non-political poll-time government does little to bolster the prospect of a smooth transition of power. With the ruling Awami League and its allies announcing counter demonstrations, political violence in the run-up to the polls could worsen.

There are several reasons why the next - yet to be announced - election Bangladesh is crucial. It'll be the first since the enactment of the 15th amendment to the Bangladeshi Constitution that restored some of the basic feature of the 1972 secular charter that had been subsequently amended by military regimes. The 15th Amendment also does away with the caretaker government system that had been envisaged as a temporary mechanism to oversee elections. This system's pitfalls were exposed when the 2007 election was deferred by almost two years thanks to a military-backed caretaker government that suspended democratic norms and proclaimed emergency rules.

Yet the distrust plaguing Bangladeshi polity prevents the two main parties - Awami Leagu and BNP—from agreeing to a poll-time formula. Add to this the trials and convictions of severa opposition leaders - including the entire top leadership of Jamaat-e-Islami - for war crimes committed during Bangladesh's 1971 liberation struggle, and it's easy to see why the BNP-led alliance is in desperation mode. However, for Bangladeshi democracy to deepen, smooth conduct of elections is a non-negotiable imperative. Both Awami and BNP must end the culture of destructive street agitations and allow a constitutionally empowered election commission to conduct peaceful polls.

Failure to do so would weaken democratic institutions and roll back any economic gains that Dhaka has hitherto made - the World Bank has alread: brought down Bangladesh's projected growth to 5.7 per cent from 6.2 per cent. Should the political crisis endure it would also allow nefarious elements to fish in trouble waters. While the Awami regime has done a commendable job of cracking down on terror groups, the looming US withdrawal from Afghanistan would embolden extremists to step up their activities in Bangladesh. This in turn will have a ripple effect on regional security; linking up security issues from Kabul to Naypyidaw. Hence, all stakeholders in Bangladeshi polity must come to the talking table and ensure smooth polls ahead.

Unofficial/Illegal Trade

One of the oldest challenges India is facing in the east pertains to illegal trade and smuggling, which were facilitated due to these migrants. The informal trading centres on Indo-Bangladesh border are Fuckhetgram, Mankachar, Karimganj, Litchubari, Dawkie, Tlangbong, Kalaisahar, Agartala, Sunamara, Belonia, Sabrong, Petrapole, Bagda, Majdia, Lalgola, Mohedpur, Radhikapur, Kaliaganj and Hilly. Large markets, and railways, are available very close to these trading centres near the border, which lure the smugglers to continue with their trade. Illegal traders coming on foot from Bangladesh, carrying headloads by cycles, vans and boats are easily received by these migrants on Indian side and also by various touts and Indian smugglers.

Seizures made by BSF give an indication of the extent of smuggling and illegal trade on the Indo-Bangladesh border. Since neither the smuggling transactions can be monitored, particularly the cattle smuggling, nor it can be stopped, the actual amount may be more than thrice which has been reported by BSF. This is because of evasion of tariff differences in the rates, high demand nature of border terrain, habitation of population and connivance of officials on both sides of the border.

A number of commodities of public distribution system of border states of India mostly find their way to Bangladesh excluding that of rice and jute, and nowadays cotton/ fabrics. The biggest item on the agenda of smugglers is cattle. There are about 500 cattle corridors all along the border inside Bangladesh and the cattle are transported by trucks even without being checked through all the national highway check posts from Punjab, Rajasthan, UP, MP, and Bihar. This has resulted in rise of price of cattle all over India, as there is a huge demand of cattle in Bangladesh. Due to religious sentiments, India is not able to have a trade of cattle with Bangladesh as they all will be taken for slaughter in Bangladesh. Practically, this is going on unofficially through the border day and night with tens of thousands of cattle transported to Bangladesh; not to speak about riverine border, but also about land border, that also, in cutting the fence and destroying the fence. There are clear instructions for the border guarding force, BSF, not to fire on anyone crossing the border.

About two to three millions of cattle are illegally exported to Bangladesh from India every year. These cattle are brought up to Mandis of the border districts in the Indian side out of BSF's reach, i.e., 15 kilometres away from the border. In small cattle herds, they are guided by one/two persons to different points of the border and they find their way to Bangladesh through not only unfenced border, but also by smashing the fenced border at night. I have personally seen more than thousands of cattle being pushed into river Brahmaputra in its various channels going to Bangladesh from Dhrubri district and these cattle easily reach Bangladesh as it is just impossible to catch cattle inside a river and one cannot kill them also. Even though 10 per cent of the cattle die in water, still, that also gives enough profit to the smugglers on both the sides as even the skin of the dead cattle is of use to Bangladesh smugglers.

However, the government of Bangladesh collects 500 takas from each such cattle landing in their areas from India and gets a lot of revenue. Similarly, the leather market of Bangladesh has prospered tremendously because of flow of cattle from India and Bangladesh is exporting beef to other countries and getting foreign exchange. The worst fact is that the leather that is processed in Bangladesh by making use of the Indian cattle comes later on to Indian market.

There was considerable decline in the illegal migration since work on the barbed wire fencing had started but there is every possibility of it getting resumed again once BNP government comes to power next year, which is almost certain.

Madhav Godbole, who headed a task force on border management, in his report submitted to government in Aug., 2000, stated the figure of his estimate of the migrants to be of 1.5 crores, adding further that three lakhs Bangladeshi nationals illegally enter India every year.

In a landmark ruling Bangladesh's biggest fundamentalist party JeI was on 1st August, 2013 declared illegal by the high court which disqualified it from contesting future polls. Moazzem Hussain, the chief judge of a high court panel hearing the high profile case ruled that Jamat's character breached the secular constitution. He declared that the registration given to Jamat by the election commission was illegal and void. Jamatis protested against the verdict and called for a nationwide bundh from 12th August, 2013 for two days. Bangladesh Tariquat Federation which preaches Sufi philosophy and promotes secularism petitioned in the high court against the Jamatis. It voiced that a communal outfit cannot be considered as a political party. The writ petition was filed on 25th January, 2009. Time will tell its outcome in Bangladesh.

In another blow to the JeI of Bangladesh, their supreme court on 5th August, 2013 had rejected the plea of the JeI against the verdict of the high court which has declared it to be illegal and barred it in contesting in next poll. Justice AHM Shamsuddin Choudhury Manik refused to give stay on the verdict of the high court. (Ref. 'Daily Star of Bangladesh of 5th August, 2013'). However the judge allowed the jamats to go on appeal in a bench. It is a matter to see how the future poll of Bangladesh will be.

Challenges to Border Management

The Bengal boundary commission, chaired by Sir Cyril Radcliffe, drew the India-Bangladesh border. While mapping the India - East Bengal boundary, Radcliffe noted that the province of Bengal provided very few natural boundaries. The border was thus drawn based on old district maps. The boundary became zigzag and instead of following natural barriers passed through villages, agricultural lands and rivers rendering the border extremely porous with many disputed pockets. The undemarcrated streches, existent chhit-mohols and adverse possession have caused constant friction between the border guarding forces of both the countrics. Because of the nature of the boundary, some old disputes persisted and new disputes arose leading to tensions between India and Pakistan. This was because of Hilly, Berubari, 24 Parganas, Jessore boundary, Bholaganj in Meghalaya, Piyain, Feni and Surma rivers and Coochbehar enclaves. To address boundary disputes and to reduce tensions, first Nehru-Noon Agreement on India-East Pakistan border was signed in Delhi on 10th September, 1958. As it could not settle the disputes, Indira Gandhi and Sheikh Mujibur Rehman made another agreement in 1972 showing methods for demarcating various disputed stretches of Indo-Bangladesh boundary in which southeren half of south Berubari enclave was retained by India and Bangladeh retained Dahgram and Angarpota enclaves. It was here, where India promised to lease three Bigha (178 Metres × 85 metres corridor) to connect these two enclaves. It was decided to exchange all the adverse possesion areas. India is not having any access to its enclaves in Bangladesh. It has not provided any facility of police stations, courts, schools, roads, hospitals, banks or markets in our enclaves inside Bangladesh. Neither these persons are taken in consideration any census. During the September, 2012 Manmohan Singh and Sheikh Hasina agreement, again, it has been decided to exchange all enclaves and all adverse possession lands but Indian Parliament's ratification is still pending. Thus, the border remains porous. We had a number of push factors from Bangladesh for migrants to come out from that country and a number of pull factors in India which attract the influx of Bangladeshis. The porosity of the border also allowed Indian insurgents to cross over to Bangladesh and other neighbouring countries for asylum. They also created their own bases in Bangladesh. The laxity in vigilance contributed escalation of trans-border crimes including illegal immigration, cattle smuggling and smuggling of drugs. Government of India is losing about 10 to 15 thousand crores to cattle smugglers every year. The cattle smuggling is accompanied with human trafficking, narcotic trafficking and inflow of counterfeit Indian currency. The BSF is guarding Indo-Bangladesh border with 75 numbers of battalions. The distances between BOPs along Mizoram border and Tura border are far greater than the recommended 2.5 kilometres as per GoM. Government has already sanctioned 383 additional BOPs for Indo-Bangladesh border which are being raised and the water wing of BSF is being strengthened. At present, nine floating BOPs are available in Indo-Bangladesh border. They function as mothership from where speedboats are sent for regular patrolling of Sunderbans and Padma areas. Brahmaputra is covered by boats only. A number of technical upgradation and force multipliers for greater

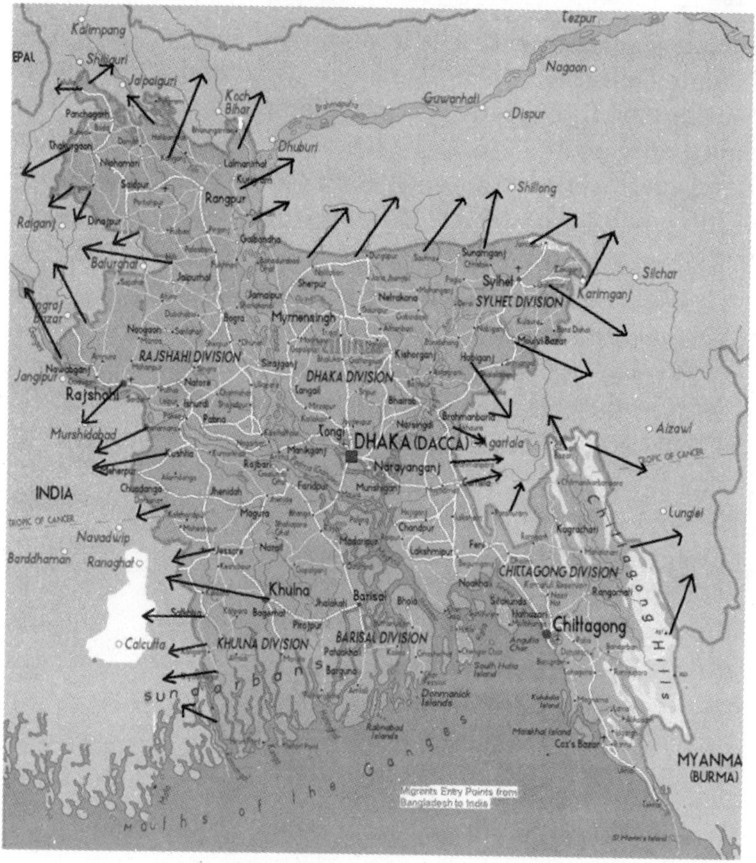

Exit route map of migrants from Bangladesh to India.

surviellience of BSF are in hand ('India's Border Management' by Pushpita Das, pp. 2, 3, 4 and 5).

Finally, it would be pertinent to mention the role played by some international organisations in voicing against India's north-east. One such instance is mentioned below.

The Islamic Cultural Centre, based in London has been taking active role against the interest of India and Assam, in particular. The Director of the Centre has taken some specific programmes for inclusion of a major portion of Assam, specially covering oil fields to Bangladesh with aid and help from a specific country and from the organisations of London. The 'Arab Times' (January, 1990) said, "Kuwait will assist in a programme to provide aid for Muslims in

Indian sub-continent. The programme sponsored by the Islamic Cultural Centre in London is to assist millons of Muslims of India with special reference to Assam". The paper also said, "Bedawi suggested a plan to attract Bangladeshi Muslims, which then could take the number of Indian Muslisms to 200 millions so as to give them more protection".

9

Counter Measures

To stop the migration and to develop border areas, the central government has initiated various programmes; they mainly focus on social, economic, and political development of border areas. The group of ministers has stressed in their report that the border management must be interpreted in its widest sense and the border management should be a coordinated affair of political leaders, administrators, diplomats, security experts, intelligence agencies, legal experts, judiciary, regulatory and economic agencies of the country to secure our borders in the best interest of the country.

Recommendations of Group of Ministers, February 2001

[This chapter on border management in the Group of Ministers' report states that proper border management is vital for national security and it should be viewed in its widest sense implying coordination and concerted action by political, administrative, diplomatic, security, intelligence, legal, regularity, and economic agencies of the country to secure the borders. It shows the problems of border management, which include, undefined borders (both maritime and land border), porosity, multiplicity of border guarding forces on the same border, repeated withdrawl of large number of BGF for internal security, counter insurgency and other duties, lack of institutional arrangement for intelligence sharing, illegal migration, smuggling and vulnearability of coastal areas.

The GoM recommended that the government should resolve all outstanding border problems and demarcate all land and maritime boundaries. They also recommended the establishment of a Border Management Department under the Ministry of Home Affairs' Home Secretary. The principle of 'one border one force' may be adopted. Thus, BSF was entrusted with the whole of Indo-Bangladesh border. The border guarding force needs to be differentiated from Central Paramilitary Forces and Central Police Organisations as they have distinct functions. The BGF should not be withdrawn from the borders except under exceptional circumstances. The BGF also should be entrusted with the responsibility of preventing illegal migration, smuggling, infiltration and collection of intelligence for the effective execution of these tasks. The BGF may be conferred with the powers under the Customs Act and Indian Criminal Procedure Code. The GoM recommended the demarcation of the border should be completed for prevention of smuggling along the Indo-Bangladesh border. It recommended joint operations conducted by the State Police, Customs, and BSF and formalising cross-border trade. The guidelines for setting up of joint check posts between BSF and Bangladesh Rifles should be established.

For the identification of illegal immigrants, the GoM recommended the issuance of multi-purpose national identity cards and the launching of Prevention of Infiltration of Foreigners Scheme. For development of the border areas, the GoM recommended that a composite plan should be formulated for border area development activities. The outlay for BADP should be enhanced to 2000 crores in the Tenth Five Year Plan. Atleast, 15 per cent of the total outlay under BADP should be entitled to the BGF for undertaking security-related works. Participation of people in the border areas should be encouraged for keeping vigil of the borders and reporting any illegal activities. For this, a village volunteer force may be created.

The GoM also has recommended in Para 5 (8) that since many of our borders are man-made artificial boundaries and not based on natural features such as rivers, water shades, etc., they are extremely porous and easy to cross. Border guarding forces need to be distinguished from Central Police Organisations. Being more akin to the Army and different from Central Police Organisations, which are called in aid of civil power from time to time, they need to be appropriately strengthened, both in terms of equipment and manpower. The repeated withdrawal, in large numbers, of paramilitary forces from border guarding duties for internal security and counter insurgency duties has led to a neglect of the borders. These forces have also been unable to perform optimally due to cannibalisation of battalions and even companies. Illegal migration from across our borders has continued unabated for over five decades. We have yet to fully wake up to the implications of the unchecked immigration for the national security. Today, we have about 15 million Bangladeshis. Demographic changes have been brought about in the border belts of West Bengal, several districts in Bihar, Assam, Tripura and Meghalaya because of large-scale illegal migration. Unfortunately, illegal immigration assumes communal overtones with political parties taking positions to suit the interst of their vote banks. The massive illegal immigration poses a grave danger to our security, social harmony and economic well-being. Smuggling of different consumer and intermediate goods, trafficking in drugs, etc., flourish through large parts of our border. For clandestine cross-border transit, communities of professional couriers have come up in the villages and towns close to our land borders and maritime coasts. The Pak ISI is also reportedly involved in encouraging these activities. Drug couriers are allowed passage on condition of collecting and reporting trans-border intelligence. Trained saboteurs and terrorists are prevailed upon to carry drugs for sustenance and operational expenses from the sale proceeds. Passage to couriers of [illegible] is often conditional to carrying and delivering of arms and ammunition. Smugglers are given assistance and facilities, in exchange of services for landing of explosives, arms and ammunition. A smuggler, drug trafficker - militant nexus engaged in anti-national activities has emerged.] ('Indian Border Management' by Pushpita Das, pp. 257, 262, 263, and 264).

Camps in Pakistan that train the north-east Indian militants–ethnic and Islamist—must be destroyed. International monitoring of the destruction is suggested/ required.

Pakistan must be pressured by the international community into desisting from mounting operations in the region (especially north-east India) by way of its intelligence-security agencies such as the ISI.

A close watch must be kept on the growth and activities of the madrassas in the region.

The illegal immigration into Assam from neighbouring Bangladesh must be stopped forthwith. The government of Bangladesh must accept this as a reality and take active steps for the return of its citizens who are illegally settled in India.

The sensitive areas along border have to be identified and number of border posts in these areas must be increased. The strength of the border guarding personnel in sensitive border outposts requires augmentation.

The training of border guarding forces should not face problem of availability of companies / battalions for rotational annual training and reserve battalions must replace border battalions regularly for training purpose. Modern gadgets and better weapons like that of removing INSAS rifle be taken into consideration. Better alarm system and sensor system, including all weather CCTV cameras for providing better response and to detect breach of fence, have to be catered for.

More number of observation posts in the gaps have to be made and adequate availability of manpower to plug all permanent gaps and riverine gaps, and gaps of nullahs and rivulets, must be planned. The working and living conditions of the border guarding personnel have to be improved to boost their morale. Proper housing facilities, education of the children, availability of seats in graduate, post graduate and technical institutions for their wards and proper health care to all family members must be the top priority.

Better coordination among all agencies involved in border management, such as, border guarding forces, the border police, the state police, the excise, the customs, the intelligence agencies, the administrative agencies, the law enforcing agencies, the health care agencies, the principals of various educational institutions at the border, the CPWD, the PWD and all such central and state agencies must be maintained. They must coordinate their action and share not only the intelligence but also work towards the upliftment of border areas.

The border population living within five kms belt of border have to be sensitised and encouraged to work as eyes and ears of the border guarding forces and under no circumstances there should be a difference of opinion between border population and the border guarding force. All, willing, educated and fit youths of the border areas be recruited in all such border guarding forces as they know the terrain and the language.

Even though alarm system has been installed to detect breach of fencing, yet the response should be the quickest. The human habitation or cultivation very close to the fencing where the sensors are put has to be avoided. The line of vision from the fencing towards the IB has to be clear and villages within IB and border fencing have to be shifted back.

All trades with Bangladesh have to be legalised with all essential items including cattle. Open haats and markets near the border where the people can buy and sell goods without paying any duties have to be arranged like that of Meghalaya border at Dowki, which was opened by the North-East Council (NEC).

We have to take seriously the issue of multi-purpose identity cards to the people residing along the borders, which have not been implemented since long to distinguish between our citizens and the illegal immigrants.

Border areas remain inaccessible and underdeveloped due to difficult terrain and lack of facilities like proper roads, educational institutions and hospitals. Lack of economic opportunities make the border population more susceptible to smuggling and human trafficking. We must provide adequate social and economic infrastructure. Promotion of participation of border people themselves in the development will eliminate the sense of alienation and instil a sense of security among the border people. We must work towards all-round development of the entire border of Bangaldesh including riverine gaps. With that, attempts should be made to deny the border people from illegal activities as well as to remove the feeling of alienation in them. Border development programmes have to be planned for effective and greater participation of the border people, which can develop their skills, particularly, that of the women and the girl child.

We also have to strengthen bilateral mechanisms by frequently convening meetings of concerned officers to ease tensions as well as to resolve border disputes.

Proper strength of the BGF has to be maintained at borders including reserves. The border management section of MHA must release maximum funds towards BADP, Civic Action Programme and various border projects submitted by borders states. Fishermen found violating the international boundary in rivers Padma, Brahmaputra, Ichhamati, Jinjiram, Surma, Barak, Mahananda, Teesta, Kushiara, Atrai and various rivers in Indo–Bangladesh border be fined and their boats impounded. They have to be numbered, they must use Indian flag, and boats must have the same colour as authorised to them.

The difficult terrain and complex socio-economic and political conditions along the border coupled with unhealthy attitude of neighbours, effective management of Indo-Bangladesh international border is quite a challenging task.

Problems like smuggling, drug trafficking, human trafficking, illegal movement of people, goods, insurgents, criminals and tensions between the border guarding forces of both the countries have given a nightmarish challenge to the country. These issues have made the border areas insecure and are the basic reasons for creating friction between the two countries. However, we have constraints like lack of political will, vested interests and lack of coordination between the centre and the border state governments, which have made the problem solving a considerable timetaking task. We must start with smaller issues and ask the border guarding forces, the local border people, and other security and administrative agencies at the border to work freely to handle these situations properly taking the help of border people in tackling these difficulties (Reference pp. 23, 31, 32, and 33 of 'India's Border Management' by Pushpita Das).

Adequate protection must be provided to the indigenous Indian Muslims in the border areas and they should not be harassed. The Indian Muslims need to be taken into confidence to fight against the menace of Islamic militancy and illegal immigration from Bangladesh and under no circumstances any non-Muslim ethnic group should be allowed to harass genuine Indian Muslims. The work permit idea for migrants of Bangladesh, all over in the border states including West Bengal, have to be reviewed showing them as Stateless citizens as is permitted by Government of Meghalaya in both Khasi and Jaintia.

Any abnormal growth of madrassas in the entire border areas, which are being exploited by the fundamentalists have to be checked and the validity of appointment of imams and moulabis in various mosques in border areas, have to be investigated in depth by intelligence agencies and their credentials have to be checked about their genuinity of being Indian nationals.

We call ourselves a big power; we pride ourselves on our national strength. Yet we do not have the national will to act firmly and decisively against the Bangaldeshi-origin illegal migrants who are slowly corroding our internal security. The only solution of stoping illegal immigration is through border fencing, identifying and throwing out who have come in with no question of their illegality being regularised (B. Raman, on 29th July, 2012, in 'Eurasia Review').

Border Fencing

Minister of State for Home, Shri Jitender Singh, has said the porous areas along Indo-Bangladesh border in Assam state will be sealed soon. He said it on 31st May, 2012 at BSF frontier head quartered at Silchar. He himself has seen the erosion of Barak river, the collapse of barbed wire fence and border roads in Cherulbhag and Jabainpur villages of Karimganj district. (1st June, 2012, 'Times of India' Guwahati edition).

The illegal cross-border movement from Bangladesh can be curtailed to 90 per cent by erecting a well-lit border fencing so that the movement of personnel can be channelised and watched. Besides fencing, the exchange of intelligence between all border security agencies by a lead security agency at both, state level, and border guarding force level are also taken up regularly. The border surveillance is to be augmented by providing night vision devices and other technical equipments to the border patrolling groups. The border roads are being repaired and maintained, connecting all border outposts and bridges on them, that are being constructed.

The fencing is complete in the Indo-Bangladesh border up to 90 per cent and only few portions are left behind in Tripura, Meghalaya and Mizoram. However, the progress of border floodlighting is slightly slow. Another 101 kilometres border length in West Bengal Indo-Bangladesh border fencing is pending for land acquisition. This was stated by Murapalli Ramachandran in the Rajya Sabha on 12th December, 2012. Bangladesh has also recently allowed fencing work to be completed at nine places along the Indo-Tripura border.

The progress of such border roads, and border fencing and border floodlighting jobs entrusted to CPWD, NBCC,

NPCC, and the Assam PWD, etc. by the border management group of the Ministry of Home Affairs is given in pages below.

Fencing and Flood Lighting of Borders

Fencing and flood lighting of the border are important constituents of maintaining vigilance along the borders. In order to curb infiltration, smuggling and other anti-national activities from across Indo-Pakistan and the Indo-Bangladesh borders, the government has undertaken the work of construction of fencing, flood lighting and roads along these borders.

The Indian side of the Indo-Bangladesh border passes through West Bengal (2,216.7 km), Assam (263 km), Meghalaya (443 km), Tripura (856 km) and Mizoram (318 km). The entire stretch consists of plains, riverine belts, hills and jungles. The area is heavily populated and cultivated right up to the border.

Name of State	*Phase I*		*Phase II*		*Total (I + II)*	
	Sancti-oned	*Completed*	*Sanct-ioned*	*Compl-eted*	*Sancti-oned*	*Comp-leted*
West Bengal	507.00	507.00	1021	715.00	1528.00	1222.00
Assam	152.31	149.29	77.72	72.27	230.03	221.56
Meghalaya	198.06	198.06	272.17	182.00	470.23	380.06
Tripura	-	-	856.00	730.50	856.00	730.50
Mizoram		-	352.33	206.00	352.33	206.00
Total	857.37	854.35	2579.22	1905.77	3436.59	2760.12

Border Roads (Length in km.)						
Name of State	*Phase I*		*Phase II*		*Total (I + II)*	
	Sanct-ioned	*Com-pleted*	*Sanct-ioned*	*Com-pleted*	*Sanct-ioned*	*Com-pleted*
West Bengal	1770.00	1616.57	0.00	0.00	1770.00	1616.57
Assam	186.33	176.50	102.42	85.42	288.75	261.92
Meghalaya	211.29	211.29	328.00	210.85	539.29	422.14
Tripura	545.37	480.51	645.00	466.00	1190.37	946.51
Mizoram	153.40	153.06	484.30	205.00	637.70	358.06
Total	2866.39	2637.93	1559.72	967.27	4426.11	3605.20

The Indo-Bangladesh border is marked by a high degree of porosity and checking illegal cross-border activities has been a major challenge. The main problem is of illegal migration from Bangladesh into India. In order to prevent illegal immigration and other anti-national activities from across the border, the Government of India had sanctioned the construction of border roads and fencing in two phases. The total length of the Indo-Bangladesh border approved for fencing is 3,436.59 km, out of which about 2,760.12 km of fencing has been completed.

Fencing : Length in kms so far been completed. There have been some problems in construction of fencing in certain stretches on this border due to riverine/low-lying areas, population within 150 yards of the border, pending land acquisition cases and protests by border population, which has led to delay in completion of the project.

In addition, 3,605.20 km of border patrol roads have also been constructed out of sanctioned length of about 4,426.11 km The phase-wise progress of fencing and roads is shown above.

277 km of floodlighting has been completed in West Bengal as a pilot project. The government has decided to

undertake floodlighting in the states of West Bengal, Meghalaya, Assam, Mizoram and Tripura in 2,840 km along Indo-Bangladesh border at an estimated cost of Rs 1,327 crore. The work has been assigned to CPWD, Engineering Project India Limited (EPIL) and National Project Construction Corporation (NPCC). The work of floodlighting in new border areas for a length of 775 km (West Bengal - 345 km and Tripura - 430 km) has been completed, of which 750 km has been energised. Additionally, in about 600 km work of erection of poles, laying of cables and fitting of fixtures is under progress.

Floodlighting along the Indo-Bangladesh Border in West Bengal

Phase-III - Replacement of Fencing

Constructed under Phase-I

Much of the fencing constructed under Phase-I in the states of West Bengal, Assam and Meghalaya has been damaged due to adverse climatic conditions, repeated submergence, etc. The Government of India has sanctioned a project (Phase-III) for erection of 861 km of fencing replacing the entire fencing constructed under Phase-I at an estimated cost of Rs 884 crore. The work has been assigned to CPWD, National Buildings Construction Corporation (NBCC) and NPCC. So far, 790 km of fencing has been replaced.

However, the latest progress of border fencing with floodlights and border roads received from the Border Security Force is mentioned below (*Source*: Annual report Ministry of Home Affairs for 2011-2012, Government of India).

Border Guarding Force

Summary of Deployed BNS Along Indo-BD Border

State	*IB Bn*
West Bengal	39
Assam	06
Meghalaya	09
Tripura	18
Mizoram	03
Total	**75**

Details of Border Fence, BFL, Border Roads and Composite BOPS (Status as on 10th Oct, 2012)

Works	*Sanctioned*	*Completed*	*Balance*	*Work in progress*	*Name of agency*
Border Fence	3436.590	2520.610	915.982	316.142	CPWD/NBCC/ NPCC/BRO/ EPIL/PWD
BFL	3117.001	1179.088	1937.913	807.698	CPWD/ NPCC/ EPIL
Border Roads	4326.240	3029.291	1296.949	517.620	CPWD/NBCC/ NPCC/ BRO/EPIL/PWD
Composite BOPs	383	-	383	71	CPWD/NPCC/ EPIL

However, it was known that till October 2013, 2784 km of border fencing, 1535 km of BFL and 3585 km of border roads had been completed.

The use of non-lethal weapons like pump-action guns and stun grenades by Border Security Force (BSF) personnel along the Indo-Bangladesh border may have resulted in fewer deaths of Bangladeshi nationals but the attacks by criminals from across the international border on India's border guarding force has gone up. Senior BSF officials brought up this matter with their counterparts, the Border Guard Bangladesh (BGB), during the recently concluded five-day DG level Border Co-ordination Conference between the two forces in Dhaka, in September, 2012. "Criminals in Bangladesh have come to know that BSF personnel are carrying non-lethal weapons".

They are attacking BSF personnel with lethal weapons. We have brought this matter to the notice of the BGB and they have assured increased surveillance along the border. Till date, 2008 co-ordinated patrols of the BSF and BGB have been conducted along the international border. Telephone numbers have been exchanged at all levels and officers are in direct communication with each other to diffuse any tension along the border," B D Sharma, Additional Director General, East, BSF, said in Kolkata on 30th Sep., 2012 (ref. TOI of 1st Oct, 2012). According to him, there has been a decline in the number of deaths along the international border since 2009. This has happened due to the issuance of non-lethal weapons and sensitisation of troops. The number of deaths in 2009 was 93. In 2010, the figure dropped to 55. In 2011, 17 people were killed along the border and in 2012, the casualty figure was 16. These figures were presented to BGB officials in Dhaka when they brought up the issue of deaths of Bangladeshi nationals along the border.

State	*Distance (in km)*
West Bengal	4.2
Assam	2.8
Meghalaya	3.7
Tripura	3.6
Mizoram	12.2

***Note** - After completion of 383 Composite BOPs along Indo-BD Border, the *inter se* distance between BOPs will then be 3.5 km.

The BSF is looking after all the borders of WB 2217 km, Assam 262 km, Meghalaya 443 km, Tripura 856 km, Mizoram 318 kms and 75 Bns man the border with 987 BOPs.

The average distance between BOPs comes to 5.5 kms.

Sanctioned BOPs	1185
Temporary BOPs	185
Permanent BOPs	802
Total No. of BOPs	987

There are 115 gaps having length of 1017.266 kms existing in the fencing due to BGB objection, low-lying area, riverine belts, adverse possession, objection raised by locals and other miscellaneous reasons. These all will take time to get sort-out; excluding the riverine border and low-lying areas, these gaps have to be covered by deploying modern security technical gadgets, sensors, LORROS, CCTV with night vision devices, battlefield surveillance radars, speedboats, thermal imagers, UAVs, direction finders, all terrain vehicles and extra force deployment. The objections raised by Meghalaya border villagers to construct the fencing on the borderline are justified as mostly Meghalaya is in the hills. Only plain land available to them is the stretch of 150/200 feet from the IB upto the fencing. Border villagers will not be able to part with this land, which is the only source of their income.

Out of 987 total BOPs at present, 86 BOPs are vulnerable to crossing over by migrants and militants. They are those BOPs in West Bengal, Assam, Meghalaya and Tripura mostly in front of whom, gaps are existing in the fencing.

OPS PROFILE, INDO - BANGLADESH BORDER OF BSF

State-wise Summary of Existing Permanent BOPs

1.	West Bengal	-	410
2.	Assam	-	85
3.	Meghalaya	-	108
4.	Mizoram	-	18
5.	Tripura	-	181
	Total	-	802

State-wise Composite Bops Sanctioned in Indo-Bangladesh Border (Total - 383)

West Bengal			
	24 Parganas	-	29
	Nadia	-	22
	Murshidabad	-	10
	Malda	-	16
	South Dinajpur	-	22
	North Dinajpur	-	31
	Darjeeling	-	5
	Jalpaiguri	-	23
	Cooch Behar	-	65
	Total	-	223
Assam			
	Dhubri	-	5
	Cachar	-	1
	Total	-	6
Meghalaya			
	South Garo Hills	-	10
	West Garo Hills	-	3
	Jaintia	-	1
	East Khasi Hills	-	2
	West Khasi Hills	-	1
	Total	-	17
Mizoram			
	Mamit	-	29
	Lunglei	-	21
	Lawng Tlai	-	23
	Total	-	73
Tripura			
	Tripura North	-	10
	Tirpura South	-	26
	Tripura West	-	17
	Dhalai	-	11
	Total	-	64

Modernisation of the border guarding force deployed in the Indo-Bangladesh border is in full swing, both in expansion of battalions and acquiring technical gadgets, floating BOPs, medium crafts, speedboats, all terrain vehicles, anti mine vehicles, battle field surveillance radars, hand-held thermal imagers, long range reconnaissance observation system, direction finders, effective night vision devices, various sensors, 9 mm Barreeta Italian carbine machineguns, hovercrafts, first attack crafts, medium crafts and floating platforms.

Similarly, the intelligence gathering and coordination among various security agencies operating in the borders is quite important and as per the report of the Group of the Ministers on reforming the national security system, it has been recommended that the intelligence wing of the principal border guarding force deployed in the border, should be the Lead Intelligence Agency for that Border. The LIA is responsible for coordinating activities of all such agencies operating in a particular border segment and sharing actionable intelligence without losing anytime.

Border Area Development Programmes

The Ministry of Home Affairs has taken up many programmes has a special cell for border management to meet the challenges with effective coordination of various border area development programmes.

The Ministry of Home Affairs has taken up many programmes for development of border areas. Until 1970, a number of common border haats were available in the extreme border areas where the border villagers of both the side used to find a market for selling their home products, including cattle.

The central paramilitary organisations, the central government, the state governments and various voluntary agencies located at the border areas are the executive agencies to implement these projects.

The Department of Border Management of the Ministry of Home Affairs has been implementing a Border Area

Development Programme (BADP) through the state governments as a part of comprehensive approach to border management with the aim to provide balanced development of border areas through growth and improvement of infrastructure and promotion of a sense of security and well being among the border population. The programme covers 362 border blocks in 94 border districts of 17 states located along the international land border. The programme is a 100 per cent centrally-sponsored scheme. Funds are provided to the states as a non-lapsable Special Central Assistance (SCA) for execution of projects relating to infrastructure, livelihood, education, health, agriculture, allied sectors and culture of border population.

The Border Area Development Programme (BADP) is being implemented under the guidelines framed by the Planning Commission. The funds are allocated by the Planning Commission annually which are re-allocated to the border states taking into consideration (i) length of international border (km); (ii) Population of the border block, and (iii) Area of the border block (sq km). Weightage of 15 per cent, over and above the total allocation, is also given to states having hilly/desert/kutchh areas. The funds are an additive to normal central assistance and are allocated for redressing the special problems faced by the people of the border areas. Funds are released to the states in two installments. First installment comprises of 90 per cent of total allocation for the state and second installment comprises of the balance 10 per cent.

The schemes under this programme are prepared by the state government and approved by the State Level Screeening Committee headed by the Chief Secretary of the State. It is executed by the agencies of the state government. Security-related schemes can be taken up under BADP but the expenditure on such schemes should not exceed 10 per cent of the total allocation in a particular year. The funds under BADP are to be used for schemes in the identified border blocks only.

In accordance with the recommendations of the Task Force, guidelines of BADP were revised in May, 2008. In order to ensure more qualitative implementation of BADP and to ensure implementation of schemes in those villages, which are located closer to the border, guidelines of BADP have been further revised on February 19, 2009 and communicated to the state governments.

The emphasis is now on specific socio-economic and infrastructure development of villages located between 0 to 10 km', from the border. The villages have been arranged in an order from the zero line to 10 km The village development profile of each village is being prepared. All the major development infrastructure facilities like pucca road connectivity, electricity, safe drinking water, telephone facilities, primary school building, PDS shop, and community centres are being developed in a planned way. Village plan and block plan of each village are being prepared. After saturating the villages falling between 0 to 10 km from the border, the next set of villages falling between 10-15 km and 15-20 km will be taken up for implementing the schemes under the BADP. The state governments have been directed that *ad hoc* projects should not be taken at all. The village plan should be integrated with district plan for the proper and sustainable development of the remote villages. The selection of the project is, therefore, expected to be more organised and responsive to area needs.

According to the revised guidelines, BADP schemes should be designed to take care of the special needs of the border people with emphasis on remote areas. The state government is required to devise an Annual Plan that accords priority to villages near the international border. All centrally-sponsored schemes and BADP should converge for filling critical gaps in infrastructure and providing livelihood. State government should earmark resources for border area planning, and surveys should be conducted to ascertain the gaps in physical infrastructure. Greater participation of grassroot institutions and local population in formulating the scheme should be ensured.

State governments should prepare village and block level plans, which would form part of the District plan. Major points, such as, development of basic as well as social infrastructure, attraction of investments, ensuring economies of scale and value addition to local produce, and increase in the stake of the state governments in development of border areas should be kept in mind while formulating plans. Further, smaller projects as well as maintainence of infrastructure would be funded by the state government whereas large projects would be funded under BADP. An empowered committee under the chairmanship of Secretary (border management) would formulate policies regarding BADP. The Screening Committee headed by the state's Chief Secretary would clear individual schemes for each state.

Both the Central and State governments along with paramilitary forces, voluntary agencies and Panchayati Raj Institutions/District Councils/Territorial councils can execute the schemes under the BADP. The State governments will closely monitor the schemes taken up under the BADP and send them to the Ministry of Home Affaris on a quarterly basis. 'Management Information System (MIS)', with village as a basic unit, will be developed for generating reports for policy decisions (Reference pp. 61, 62, 63, 129, and 130 of 'India's Border Management' by Pushpita Das).

This also indirectly helps in keeping a better relation between the border population and the border security agencies and the border administrative networks. The neglected villages and the suffering of poor villages get mitigated to a considerable level by these border development programmes. There has been an increase in the budget of BADP in the year 2011-12.

The funds released by the Ministry of Home Affairs through Border Area Development Programme to all the 5 states having border with Bangladesh for the last three years is given below:

States	*2009-10 (in lakhs)*	*2010-11 (in lakhs)*	*2011-12 (in lakhs)*
Assam	2395.62	4000	3161
Meghalaya	1647.19	1247	2000
Mizoram	2494.42	2506	3702
Tripura	3005.89	3579	4126
West Bengal	6222.16	10961	11818.27
Total budget for all	635 crores	691 crores	900 crores

Border states (Inc. Pak, China and Myanmar border) 990 crores had been sanctioned by the MHA towards BADP in the year 2012/2013 for all border states.

On 24th August, 2013, BSF seized FICN worth 9 lakhs from Baishnav Nagar Maldah BOP Churiantapur which was thrown from Bangladesh above the fence. They were all in the denominations of 1000 and 500 notes.

Similarly on 11th August, 2013, BSF BOP Churiantapur of 125 Bn also seized one lakh FICN of 1000 and 500 denomination. They were thrown in a plastic packet by BD smugglers above the fence.

On 5th August, 2013, BSF seized Phensidyl of worth 19,00,700 Rs from east Barjara from the house of a smuggler near Tripura-Bangladesh border.

On 5th August, 2013, BSF BOP Dhalai in Mizoram seized 4504 WY tablets worth 585,520 Rs from Champai, bordering Bangladesh.

Legal Mechanism

Laws in India and their Implementation against Illegal Immigrants

1. An illegal immigrant in India is a person residing in the country without an official permission as prescribed by relevant Indian law. Those who are granted refugee status do not fall under this category.

Although no reliable numbers of illegal immigrants are currently available, Bangladeshis form the largest group of migrants in India.

The Bombay High Court in March, 2013 came down heavily on the union and the state governments for having no policy in place to deal with illegal migrants and failing to deport them to their own countries. "This is a matter with wide ramifications on national security", the division bench of Justice AM Khanwilkar and Justice AR Joshi said, adding, "How can the state authorities allow a person to remain in India by simply registering a bailable offence. By not deporting the person, you are giving him a licence to stay here and mix with the citizens".

The Judges directed Advocate General of the state to appear in the matter on the next date of hearing on 6th August to apprise them about the state policy for dealing with cases of illegal immigrants.

The court was hearing a petition by a Pakistani national Siraj Khan, resident of Pakistan-occupied-Kashmir (PoK) seeking quashing of the FIR registered against him under various sections of the Passport Act and Foreigners Act and direction to the authorities to deport him to his native place Manesara in PoK along with his family.

We have various laws in our country to deal with illegal immigrants. The laws applicable, various Pacts and Treaties related to this are enumerated below.

2. Indian Passport Act, 1920

Any persons entering to India by land, air or water routes must require a passport issued by the central government or offices prescribed by the central govt as per rules of this Act.

The Central Government had made rules requiring that persons while entering India shall be in possession of their passports. Such rules may:

(a) Prohibit the entry into India, or any part thereof, of any person who has not in his possession a passport issued to him.

(b) Prescribe the authorities by whom passports must have been issued or renewed, and the conditions with which they must comply, for the purposes of this Act.

(c) Provide for the exemption, either absolutely or on any condition, of any person or class of persons from any provision of such rules.

Any contravention thereof, or of any order issued under the authority of any such rule, shall be punishable with imprisonment for a term which may extend to three months, or with fine or with both.

3. Foreigners Act, 1946

The Foreigners Act is a law by which one can check the illegitimate entry of foreigners into our country. The

Foreigners Act always has a provision that whenever the State feels a person has entered the country illegally; the onus of proof is on this person to show that he is a legitimate resident or a citizen. Therefore, the Foreigners Act worked very well since it was framed. Every time the government of India feels that somebody, whether it is from any friendly or unfriendly State, has wrongfully entered into India or overstayed, the Foreigners Act notice is given.

It was enacted on 23rd November, 1946 and determines the rules of citizenship and matters relating to naturalisation, etc. in India. The term 'foreigner' according to the definition given in the Foreigners Act, 1946 and the Registration of Foreigner Act, 1949 means a person who is not a citizen of India. According to this definition, a person, who is not a citizen of India as defined in the Citizenship Act, 1955 and who had not acquired Indian citizenship under the naturalisation Act 1926, as amended up-to-date, including a person who had acquired citizenship under the Pakistan Citizenship Act, 1957, is a foreigner.

This is an Act to confer upon the central government certain powers in respect of foreigners. As per this Act, the central government is exercising certain powers in respect of the entry of foreigners into India, their presence therein and their departure therefrom. It extends to the whole of India.

The central government may by order make provision, either generally, or with respect to all foreigners, or with respect to any particular foreigner, or any prescribed class or description of foreigner, for prohibiting, regulating or restricting the entry of foreigners into India or their departure therefrom or their presence or continued presence therein.

Orders made under this section may provide that the foreigner shall not enter India or shall enter India only at such times and by such route and at such port or place and subject to the observance of such conditions on arrival as may be prescribed; shall not depart from India, or

Shall depart only at such times and by such route and from such port or place and subject to the observance of such conditions on departure as may be prescribed;

Shall not remain in India or in any prescribed area therein ; shall, if he has been required by order under this section not to remain in India, meet from any resources at his disposal the cost of his removal from India and of his maintenance therein pending such removal;

Shall remove himself to and remain in such area in India as may be prescribed;

Shall comply with such conditions, as may be prescribed or specified, requiring him to reside in a particular place; imposing any restrictions on his movements; requiring him to furnish such proof of his identity and to report such particulars to such authority in such manner and at such time and place as may be prescribed or specified ;

Requiring him to allow his photograph and finger impressions to be taken and to furnish specimens of his handwriting and signature to such authority and at such time and place as may be prescribed or specified,

Requiring him to submit himself to such medical examination by such authority and at such time and place as may be prescribed or specified;

Prohibiting him from association with persons of a prescribed or specified description;

Prohibiting him from engaging in activities of a prescribed or specified description;

Prohibiting him from using or possessing prescribed or specified articles ; otherwise regulating his conduct in any such particular as may be prescribed or specified ;

Shall enter into a bond, with or without sureties, for the due observance of, or as an alternative to the enforcement of, any or all prescribed or specified restrictions or conditions shall be arrested and detained or confined;

In addition, may make provision for any matter, which is to be, or may be prescribed and for such incidental and supplementary matters as may, in the opinion of the Central

Government, be expedient or necessary for giving effect to this Act.

Any authority prescribed in this behalf may with respect to any particular foreigner make orders under clauses shown above.

The central government may, by order, declare that all or any of the provisions of this Act or of any order made there under shall not apply, or shall apply only in such circumstances or with such exceptions or modifications or subject to such conditions as may be specified in the order, to or in relation to the citizen's of any such Commonwealth country as may be so specified; or any other individual foreigner or class or description of foreigner.

A copy of every order made under these provisions shall be placed on the table of both Houses of Parliament as soon as, may be after, it is made.

Any foreigner in respect of whom there is in force any order directing that he be detained or confined, shall be detained or confined in such place and manner and subject to such conditions as to maintenance, discipline and the punishment of offences and breaches of discipline as the Central Government may from time to time by order determine. Any foreigner, in respect of whom there is in force an order requiring him to reside at a place set apart for the residence under supervision of a number of foreigners, shall while residing therein is subject to such conditions as prescribed.

No person shall knowingly assist an internee or a person on parole to escape from custody or to place him in part for his residence, or knowingly harbour an escaped internee or person on parole, or

(b) Give an escaped internee or person on paroles any assistance with intent thereby to prevent, hinder or interfere with the apprehension of the internee or the person on parole.

The central government may, by order, provide for regulating access to, and the conduct of persons in places in India where internees or persons on parole are detained or restricted, as the case may be, and for prohibiting or regulating the dispatch or conveyance from outside such places to or for internees or persons on parole therein of such articles as may be prescribed.

4. Delhi Pact, also called Nehru-Liaquat Pact

This pact was made on April 8, 1950, following the escalation of tension between India and Pakistan and East Pakistan (now Bangladesh) after economic relations between the two countries had been severed in December, 1949. An estimated one million people—Hindus from East Pakistan and Muslims from West Bengal—crossed the borders during 1950.

In spite of the opposition of his colleague Vallab Bhai Patel, Jawaharlal Nehru, prime minister of India, concluded a pact with Liaqat Ali Khan, prime minister of Pakistan, whereby refugees were allowed to return unmolested to dispose of their property, abducted women and looted property were to be returned, forced conversions were unrecognised, and minority rights were confirmed. Minority commissions were established to implement these terms, and confidence was, in fact restored for a time; however, in the months following the pact, more than a million additional refugees migrated to West Bengal.

The deportation of people during independence movement in 1947 caused much antipathy in Pakistan. It led to a conciliatory gesture from India in the form of Nehru-Liaquat Ali Khan Agreement on 8th April, 1950. The Agreement allowed return of those people to India who had been deported until December 31, 1950. However, this Agreement has no bearing to the problem of illegal immigrants.

5. Immigration Expulsion of Assam Act of 1st March, 1950

This Act was made to provide power for the expulsion of certain immigrants from Assam. It extends to the whole of India. If the central government is of opinion that any person or class of persons, having been ordinarily resident in any place outside India, has or have, before or after the commencement of this Act, come into Assam and that the stay of such person or class of persons in Assam is detrimental to the interests of the general public of India or of any section thereof or of any Scheduled Tribe in Assam, the central government may by order direct such person or class of persons to remove himself or themselves from India or Assam within such time and by such route as may be specified in the order.

Central government can give further directions in regard to his or their removal from India or Assam as it may consider necessary or expedient; provided that nothing in this section shall apply to any person who on account of civil disturbances or the fear of such disturbances in any area, now forming part of Pakistan, has been displaced from or has left his place of residence in such area and who has been subsequently residing in Assam.

The central government may, by notification in the Official Gazette, direct that the powers and duties conferred or imposed on it can be exercised or discharged also by any officer subordinate to the central government; the Government of Assam, Meghalaya or Nagaland or any officer subordinate to that government.

Any person who contravenes or attempts to contravene or abets the contravention of any order or fails to comply with any direction given by any such order, or harbours any person who has contravened any order, or has failed to comply with any direction given by any such order, shall be punishable with imprisonment which may extend to three years and shall also be liable to fine.

No suit, prosecution or other legal proceeding shall lie against any person for anything which in good faith done or intended to be done under this Act. In this Act, references to Assam shall be construed as including also a reference to the states of Meghalaya, Nagaland, the Union Territories of Arunachal Pradesh and Mizoram.

6. Indian Citizenship Act, 1957

At the commencement of the Constitution, every person, who has his domicile in the territory of India and

(a) Who is born in the territory of India, or

(b) Either of his parents was born in the territory of India, or

(c) Who has been ordinarily resident in the territory of India for not less than 5 years, immediately preceding such commencement of the Constitution, shall be a citizen of India.

The person who has migrated to the territory of India from the territory now included in Pakistan, shall be a citizen of India at the commencement of this Constitution if:

(a) He or either of his parents or any of his grandparents was born in India as defined in Government of India Act, 1935.

(b) In the case where such person has so migrated before the 19th day of July 1948, he has been ordinarily resident in the territory of India since the date of his migration, and

In the case, where such person has so migrated on or after the 19th day of July 1948 has been registered as citizen of India.

Article 6 of the Constitution clearly defines citizenship in case of persons who migrated to India from Pakistan as follows (the persons who migrated from East Pakistan, now Bangladesh, before 24 March 1971 can only be deemed to have migrated from "Pakistan", because that was their legal status before 24th March, 1971):

Article 6: Rights of citizenship of certain persons who have migrated to India from Pakistan. Notwithstanding anything in article 5, a person, who has migrated to the territory of India from the territory now included in Pakistan, shall be deemed to be a citizen of India at the commencement of this Constitution if—

(a) he or either of his parents or any of his grandparents was born in India as defined in the Government of India Act, 1935 (as originally enacted); and

(b) (i) In the case where such person has so migrated before the nineteenth day of July, 1948, he has been ordinarily resident in the territory of India since the date of his migration, or

(ii) In the case where such person has so migrated on or after the nineteenth day of July, 1948, he has been registered as a citizen of India by an officer appointed in that behalf by the Government of the Dominion of India on an application made by him, therefore, to such officer before the commencement of this Constitution in the form and manner prescribed by that government: Provided that no person shall be so registered unless he has been resident in the territory of.

(i) Citizenship by birth

Any person born in India, on or after 26th January, 1950, but prior to the commencement of the 1986 Act on 1st July, 1987, is a citizen of India by birth. A person born in India on or after 1st July, 1987 is a citizen of India if either parent was a citizen of India at the time of the birth. Those born in India on or after 3rd December, 2004 are considered citizens of India only if both of their parents are citizens of India or if one parent is a citizen of India and the other is not an illegal migrant at the time of their birth.

Our politicians take it differently in supporting the cause of the immigrants. When a team of Janajati Faith and Culture Protection Forum met Hon'ble Governor of Assam to narrate the gravity of BTAD, he opined as, “people who came from Bangladesh just after 1971 have become old and infirm while their off springs became natural citizens of India. So, it is a very complex issue to deal with”.

In many countries there are similar laws—if a child takes birth there, he or she will be taken as its natural citizen. Therefore, when a country issues a visa, it sees whether the travelling woman is pregnant or not.

Everything goes according to legal procedure. However, the question arise here that, what type of legal formalities has been followed when those Bangladeshi Muslims intruded into our land. Mr Badruddin Ajmal said that they are living here even before the birth of Hangrama Mohilari, but even our progeny have the right to say them foreigners. The sons and daughters of illegal infiltrators cannot be legalised at any point of time, even no court of law, mentioned this point in their judgement. Of course, it is a ploy of politicians or they are not thorough in this legal matter.

(ii) Citizenship by Descent

A person born outside of India on or after 26th January, 1950 shall be a citizen of India by descent, if his father is a citizen of India at the time of birth.

Person born outside India on or after 10th December, 1992 are considered as citizens of India if either of their parents is a citizen of India at the time of their birth.

From 3rd December, 2004 onwards, persons born outside of India shall not be considered citizens of India unless their birth is registered at an Indian consulate within one year of the date of birth. In certain circumstances, it is possible to register after one year with the permission of the central government. The application for registration of the birth of a minor child must be made to an Indian consulate and must be accompanied by an undertaking in writing from the parents of such minor child that he or she does not hold the passport of another country.

(iii) Citizenship by Registration

The central government may, on an application, register as a citizen of India under section 5 of the Citizenship Act, 1955, any person (not being an illegal migrant) if he belongs to any of the following categories:

1. a person of Indian origin who is ordinarily resident in India for seven years before making application under section 5(1)(a) (throughout the period of twelve months immediately before making application and for six

years in the aggregate in the eight years preceding the twelve months);

2. a person of Indian origin who is ordinarily resident in any country or place outside undivided India;
3. a person who is married to a citizen of India and is ordinarily resident in India for seven years before making an application for registration;
4. minor children of persons who are citizens of India;
5. a person of full age and capacity whose parents are registered as citizens of India;
6. a person of full age and capacity who, or either of his parents, was earlier citizen of independent India, and has been residing in India for one year immediately before making an application for registration;
7. a person of full age and capacity who has been registered as an overseas citizen of India for five years, and who has been residing in India for one year before making an application for registration.

(iv) Citizenship by Naturalisation

The central government may, if satisfied, can issue citizenship by naturalisation under the provisions of fourth schedule of the Constitution.

A foreigner who has resided in India for twelve years can acquire citizenship of India by naturalisation. The applicant must have lived a total of 12 years in India in a period of 14 years, and must have lived in India for 12 months uninterrupted prior to applying for citizenship.

(v) Citizenship by Incorporation of Territory

If any territory becomes a part of India, the central government may by order notify in the official gazette, specify the person who shall be citizen of India by region of their connection with that territory, and those persons shall be citizens of India as from the date to be specified in the order.

(vi) Overseas Citizenship

The central government may, by notification in the official gazette, can issue overseas citizenship to selected personnel.

The Overseas Citizenship of India (OCI) Scheme was introduced by amending the Citizenship Act, 1955 in August, 2005. The Scheme was launched during the Pravasi Bharatiya Divas convention 2006 at Hyderabad.

The Scheme provides for registration as Overseas Citizen of India (OCI) of all Persons of Indian Origin (PIOs) who were citizens of India on 26th January, 1950 or thereafter or were eligible to become citizens of India on 26th January, 1950 except who is or had been a citizen of Pakistan, Bangladesh or such other country as the central government may, by notification in the official gazette, specified.

OCI is not to be misconstrued as 'dual citizenship'. OCI does not confer political rights. The registered overseas citizens of India shall not be entitled to the rights conferred on a citizen of India under article 16 of the Constitution with regard to equality of opportunity in matters of public employment.

The OCI documents consist of OCI registration booklet and a universal visa sticker. It is mandatory for registered OCIs to carry their passports, which carry the universal visa sticker for entry into/exit from India.

A registered Overseas Citizen of India is granted multiple entry, multi-purpose, life-long visa for visiting India, he/she is exempted from registration with Foreign Regional Registration Officer or Foreign Registration Officer for any length of stay in India, and is entitled to general 'parity with Non-Resident Indians in respect of all facilities available to them in economic, financial and educational fields except in matters relating to the acquisition of agricultural or plantation properties'. The Ministry notifies specific benefits/ parity from time to time.

The Ministry has issued notifications granting registered OCIs further benefits as under:

1. Parity with Non-Resident Indians in the matter of inter-country adoption of Indian children;
2. Parity with resident Indian nationals in matters of tariffs in domestic air fares;
3. Parity with domestic Indian visitors in respect of entry fee for visiting national parks and wildlife sanctuaries in India;
4. Parity with non-resident Indians in respect of:
    1. Entry fees for visiting the national monuments, historical sites and museums in India;
    2. Practicing the following professions in India, in pursuance of the provisions contained in the relevant Acts, namely:
        1. Doctors, dentists, nurses and pharmacists;
        2. Advocates;
        3. Architects; and
    4. Chartered Accountants; and
    5. Entitlement to appear for the All India Pre-Medical Test or such other tests to make them eligible for admission in pursuance of the provisions contained in the relevant Acts.

7. Indira - Mujib Treaty, 1972

The Indo-Bangladeshi Treaty of Friendship, Cooperation and Peace was a 25-year treaty that was signed on March 19, 1972 to strengthen relations with Bangladesh, the newly established State. The treaty was also known as the Indira-Mujib Treaty as it was signed by Indira Gandhi and Sheikh Mujibur Rehman.

During the war of 1971, India provided extensive aid, training and shelter for the Mukti Bahini troops and people of Bangladesh that was fighting the Pakistan Army. More than 12 million refugees poured into India during 1971, increasing tensions between India and Pakistan. At the outbreak of the Indo Pakistan War of 1971, the Indian Army liberated East Pakistan leading to the establishment of Bangladesh. India's role in the independence of

Bangladesh led to the development of strong bilateral relations. The then-Indian Prime Minister Indira Gandhi along with Bangladesh's founding leader Sheikh Mujibur Rahman addressed before more than 500,000 people at Dhaka.

The Provisions

(i) The contracting parties solemnly declare that there shall be lasting peace and friendship between the two countries and each side shall respect the independence, sovereignty and territorial integrity of the other and refrain from interfering in the internal affairs of the other side;

(ii) The contracting parties condemn colonialism and racialism of all forms, and reaffirm their determination to strive for their final and complete elimination;

(iii) The contracting parties reaffirm their faith in the policy of non-alignment and peaceful co-existence as important factors for easing tension in the world, maintaining international peace and security and strengthening national sovereignty and independence;

(iv) The contracting parties shall maintain regular contacts and exchange views with each other on major international problems affecting the interest of both the states;

(v) The contracting parties shall continue to strengthen and widen their mutually advantageous and all round cooperation in the economic, scientific and technical fields, and shall develop mutual cooperation in the fields of trade, transport and communication on the basis of the principles of equality and mutual benefit;

(vi) The contracting parties agree to make joint studies and take joint action in the field of flood control, river basin development and development of hydroelectric power and irrigation;

(vii) Both the parties shall promote relations in the field of arts, literature, education, culture, sports and health;

(viii) In accordance with the ties of friendship existing

between the two countries, each of the contracting parties solemnly declare that it shall not enter into or participate in any military alliance directed against the other party. Each of the parties shall refrain from any aggression against the other party and shall not allow the use of its territory for committing any act that may cause military damage to or continue to threat the security of the other contracting parties;

(ix) Each of the contracting parties shall refrain from giving any assistance to any third party taking part in an armed conflict against the other party. In case if either party is attacked or threatened to attack, the contracting parties shall immediately enter into mutual consultations in order to take necessary measures to eliminate the threat and thus ensure the peace and security of their countries;

(x) Each of the parties solemnly declare that it shall not undertake any commitment, secret or open, towards one or more states which may be incompatible with the present treaty;

(xi) The present treaty is signed for a term of twenty-five years, and shall be renewed by mutual agreement;

(xii) Any differences interpreting any Article of the treaty shall be settled on a bilateral basis by peaceful means in a spirit of mutual respect and understanding.

Expiration of the Treaty

The two governments declined to renegotiate or renew the treaty when it approached expiry in 1997. Although initially received enthusiastically by both nations, the treaty with India became the subject of resentment and controversy in Bangladesh, where people saw it as unequal and an imposition of excessive Indian influence. Various issues such as, the dispute over water of Farraka Barrage, the delayed withdrawal of troops gave a doubt to Bangladeshis. Sheikh Mujib's pro-India policies antagonised many in politics and the military. The establishment of military regimes after the assassination of Sheikh Mujib sought to distance the country from India.

After Mujib's death, Bangladesh established diplomatic relations with Pakistan and other nations who opposed the creation of Bangladesh, like China and Saudi Arabia. Bangladesh started allowing Indian insurgent groups such as ULFA and PLA to operate from bases on its territory and DGFI started links with Pakistan's intelligence agencies. Bangladesh also alleged that India was supporting the Shanti Bahini insurgency in Chittagong Hill Tracts.

8. Who is an illegal immigrant?

An illegal immigrant is a foreigner who entered India without proper passport or travel documents or entered India with valid documents but remained beyond prescribed period permitted. A migrant is not necessarily a refugee. We have a number of ecological and environmental migrants.

Under the Indo-Bangladesh Treaty of friendship, cooperation and peace signed in 1972 (known as Indira-Mujib treaty and not renewed since it's expiry in 1997), India had agreed to take responsibility of all migrants who entered India on or before March 24, 1971. Thus according to this treaty, not anyone who entered India before the cut-off date is a *de facto* illegal immigrant. The Assam Accord signed in 1985 between the representatives of the Government of India and the leaders of the Assam agitation accepted the cut-off date of 24th March, 1971 for identification and deportation of illegal immigrants. The citizenship status of the children of those illegal migrants would, however, be decided by the provisions stated in section 3 of the Citizenship Act of 1955, which reads:

(i) A person born in India on or after 26th January 1950, but before 1st July 1987, is a citizen of India by birth irrespective of the nationality of his/her parents.

(ii) A person born in India on or after 1st July, 1987, but before 3rd December, 2004, is considered a citizen of India by birth if either of his/her parents is a citizen of India at the time of his/her birth.

(iii) A person born in India on or after 3rd December,

2004, is considered citizen of India by birth if both the parents are citizens of India or one of the parents is a citizen of India and the other is not an illegal migrant at the time of his/her birth.

Those migrants who came to India before the cut-off date of 24th March, 1971 would become legal citizens of India only upon going through the process of naturalisation.

Justice MC Chagla questioned the logic of setting a cut-off year for determining the nationality of an immigrant. He opined, "We have our Constitution, we have laws. There are decisions by the highest courts to indicate who is a national and who is a foreigner. Unnecessary complications have been introduced about the cut off year. What does it matter when a person comes to Assam if he is not a national but a foreigner? The year of entry does not change his legal status. Foreigners cannot remain on the electoral rolls, their names should be removed and precautions should be taken that they are not enrolled in the voters list".

No person shall vote at an election in any constituency if he is subject to any of the disqualifications referred to in Section 16 of the Representation of the People Act, 1950. [Section 62(2) of the Representation of the People Act, 1951.]

9. IMDT Act

On 2nd November 1978, the then External Affairs Minister, Atal Bihari Vajpayee had made a statement that "the Election Commission has also issued instructions to the electoral officers of the States and Union Territories concerned that if it is found that a large number of foreigners have managed to get their names registered in the electoral rolls, recourse should be made as per provisions of section 22 of the Representation of People Act, 1950 for getting the names of such persons deleted from the electoral rolls on the ground that they are not Indian citizens". The Act states that "A person shall be disqualified for registration in an electoral roll if he is not a citizen of India". This problem is further aggravated by the fact that even the names of deported foreigners are not deleted from the electoral rolls.

Higher judiciaries were too much concerned over Bangladeshi illegal immigrants coming to India. In 2005, a Supreme Court bench ruled Illegal Migrants (Determination by Tribunal) Act (IMDT) as unconstitutional with reference to Shri S. K. Sinha's report. It added that the impact of the aggression represented by large-scale illegal migrants from Bangladesh had made the life of the people of Assam wholly insecure. The panic generated thereby had created fear psychosis in Assam including other north-eastern states. In August 2008, the Delhi High Court dismissed a petition by a Bangladeshi national against her deportation. The High Court ruled that the illegal Bangladeshi immigrants pose a danger to India's internal security.

(a) The Background of the Act

The IMDT Act was enacted in 1983 in response to the Assam Movement 1979-1985 that began when the electoral rolls were being revised. Amid allegations that a large number of Bangladeshi Muslim immigrants were being included in the rolls, the Election Commission asked the Assam Government to identify constituencies with a big rise in the number of voters but the state allegedly dragged its feet on the issue. Some state that the electorate had grown by 10.2 per cent between 1970 and 1971, 10.42 per cent between 1971 and 1977 and by a further 10.3 per cent during the following few years.

The main demand of the Assam Movement was detection and expulsion of foreigners in the state. Its focus was on the Bangladeshis though according to some estimates they are only around 40 per cent of the immigrants, the rest being from the Hindi speaking region or of Nepali origin. It began as a secular movement of all the Assamese but always ran the risk of turning communal because of the religious slant some gave to it since most Bangladeshi immigrants are Muslims. The Nellie massacre of more than 300 Bangladeshis in 1983 did give it a communal angle. A VHP leader has even said that Bangladeshi infiltration is a Pakistani conspiracy to turn Assam into a Muslim state and that they "are supporting all kinds of terrorist activity"

('Staff Reporter', 2001). However, most AASU leaders have appealed to the people not to communalise the issue ("The Assam Tribune', July 15, 2005). Some of them even told the BJP recently that they would not tolerate such a communal slant.

The Act applies only to Assam. The rest of India has the Foreigners' Act 1946, which puts on the accused the onus of proving his/her Indian nationality. IMDT defines foreigners as those who settled down in Assam after March 25, 1971 and puts on the one who denounces a person the onus of proving that he/she is a foreigner. Because of it, many considered it ineffective (Bhattacharyya 2001: 154-155). The experience from 1962 until 1982 had proved them right. Five tribunals set up under the Act in districts bordering Bangladesh have, from January 1983 registered 423,021 cases, dealt with 65,000, have disposed of 23,420 (Editorial, The Sentinel, 16th December, 2004) and have till January, 2005 declared 12,424 persons illegal migrants under the Act. Only 1,538 of them have been deported ('Staff Reporter', 2005).

(b) A case for example

[In Nagaon district, a case of infiltration by a Bangladeshi national was detected by the police on 3rd February, 1998. The name of the person detected was Mohammad Kamaluddin. He was found loitering in Nagaon town.

On interrogation, Kamaluddin divulged that he hailed from Bangladesh and was born and brought up in the district of Moulabi Bazar (village-Chengrm, police station Barlekha), son of late Modorisin Ali. Kamaluddin procured a passport through illegal means on October 25, 1994, entered India, i.e., Assam and arrived at Murajhar in Nagaon district.

Kamaluddin was deported to Bangladesh via Mahisashan on 3rd February, 1998 itself. However, he re-entered India and filed a case (Civil Rule No. 2501 of 1998) in the Guwahati High Court challenging his deportation from India, stating that he was a citizen of India and a resident of Kapahbari, PO Murajhar, with landed property in that village.

Moreover, Kamaluddin claimed that he was enrolled as a voter and he even contested the 1996 election from No. 90, Jamunamukh Legislative Assembly constituency. He also claimed that he couldn't be deported from India without resorting to the provisions of the IMDT Act.

The state government contested Kamaluddin's claims and Advocate H. Rahman who appeared in the court on behalf of the state government, produced before the court a passport and a boarding pass of Pakistan International Flight seized from Kamaluddin.

The passport was issued in the name of Kamaluddin on November 2, 1994 by the Government of Pakistan and thereafter he travelled from Karachi to Dacca by Pakistan International Flight on November 7, 1994. The passenger ticket and baggage check - tag seized from Kamaluddin were also produced by Sri Rahman before the court.

In his oral judgement, Justice B.K. Sharma also vacated the stay order, passed earlier, on the deportation of Kamaluddin and said that Kamaluddin may be deported from India by the authorities immediately, while holding that Kamaluddin's petition also suffered from suppressing of material facts.

"Before parting with the record, I only express my displeasure and annoyance with regard to the casual and cavalier manner in which voters list is prepared/made in Assam. On the basis of such an incorrect voters list, a person was allowed even to contest the election ...," said Justice Sharma. ('The Assam Tribune' of 11th July, 2000).

In police station, proper staffs were not available for investigating the case under this Act. Police also did not have the power for search, seizure and arrest.

Mostly during trial, even though the Bangladeshi was present but the complainants were found absent because of being harassed in running to court several times. This Act encountered a strong opposition and was proved a wasteful exercise to hunt the Bangladeshis without resources. All the Bangladeshis who came to Assam before 24th March, 1971 as per Rajiv Gandhi accord were given Indian citizenship yet the practical fact in the field is that those all who came to Assam were only Muslims.

The migrants and their supporters found IMDT Act to be beneficial to them and they wanted this Act to be extended to other border states in lieu of Foreigners Act. The continuance of IMDT Act was a wasteful exercise and it was felt that this should be repealed. In Foreigners Act, proving citizenship was on the accused only. North-east states suffered for years because of influx of migrants from Bangladesh, there was uproar from the masses to scrape IMDT Act, and the demand was raised for deporting them under Foreigners' Act, 1946. A working group on border management appointed by Indian government headed by Dr. Madhav Godbole also recommend for repeal of IMDT Act, yet section 9(c) of the report was not made public. The IMDT Act was having following flaws:

1. It discriminated strongly against Assam, as it was only applicable for this state, whereas in all other states, Foreigners' Act, 1946 dealt with foreigners only.
2. The Act was so defective that detection and deportation became impossible and the courts/tribunals were found to be not working which went in favour of the accused.
3. No citizen used to come forward to pay the fees for being a complainant and government never made any effort from their side to find out as to where the migrants are available and made any effort to apprehend them.
4. As it was decided that no migrant would be deported from Assam, other migrants available in various states started converging to Assam for this purpose.
5. The IMDT Act became the guardian of illegal migrants and started protecting them as minority citizens and they got all benefits of getting their rations cards, voter cards and mutating land and properties in their names.

(d) Finally, the IMDT Act was struck by the Supreme Court in a verdict of 12th July 2005, stating that a separate law was not required for detecting foreigners in Assam. It also ordered for closure of all such tribunals opened under the IMDT Act. The Supreme Court further directed that the case pending with IMDT tribunals should be transferred to Foreigners Act courts. It directed government of Assam, taking into consideration of such large influx from Bangladesh, to immediately deal with them under Foreigners Act. This order of Supreme Court, repealing IMDT Act, was not liked by the migrants as they were in large numbers in Assam. They started protesting against it. The Congress then wanted to control the damage done by the Court's decision to its 'vote bank' politics. It set up a committee of Group of Ministers to study the ruling and decide on further action. The GOM decided that rather than bringing the IMDT Act in another form, it was better to make use of the provisions under the Foreigners Act and set up tribunals for determination of migrants' status. Central government invested more than Rs. 300 crores for these Tribunals. The cost of expulsion was as high as Rs. 20 lac per head. In 2003, the DGP Prakash Singh said at Guwahati, "what a joke it was, the persons thus expelled from Indian territory, again managed to enter in India." ('The Silent Invasion', p. 153).

(e) Abdul Mujib Mazumdar (a spokesperson of Bangladeshis in Assam) reportedly drafted these defective IM (DT) Act and later on, he became a senior Cabinet Minister in Government of Assam. The whole Assam government missionaries were only interested to have this Bangladesh lobby with them for their survival and political game. Whether it is Congress, or BJP, or the Muslim League, or even ULFA, no political party protested about presence of Bangladeshis in their territory.

(f) The Cabinet Committe on Political Affairs, chaired by

Prime Minister Manmohan Singh on February 10, 2006, dropped the idea of enacting a legislation in lieu of the controversial Illegal Migrants (Determination by Tribunals) Act and decided to amend the Foreigners' Act to ensure that anybody whose citizenship is in doubt gets a 'fair hearing'. In effect, it means that tribunals would be set up in Assam under the Foreigners Act, 1946, as was the case when the IMDT Act was in force, to examine the veractity of complaints against suspected Bangladeshi migrants. A tribunal hearing is, however, not mandatory anywhere else. This decision by the Cabinet Committee on Political affairs was reportedly taken, after a recommendation from the Congress government in Assam.

(g) Briefing the media after the Cabinet Committee meeting, Defence Minister Pranab Mukherjee said that henceforth, any person suspected of being an illegal migrant would be referred to a tribunal and be given an opportunity to present his or her case. The Foreigners Act has a provision for Tribunals, but not all cases are referred to these Tribunals. As the onus is on law-enforcing agencies to decide as to which cases should go through a judicial process, minorities felt a 'genuine citizen' is susceptible to deportation as a migrant.

(h) On December 5, 2006, the Supreme Court held the Foreigners (Tribunals for Assam) Order 2006, which puts the onus of proving a person a foreigner on the complainant as unconstitutional. Under the Foreigners' Act, 1946, the burden of proof that one is not a foreigner lies on the person who is alleged to be so. The 1964 order was amended in 2006, making it inapplicable in Assam. The Supreme Court said, "It appears that the 2006 order has been issued just as a cover-up for non-implementation of the directions of this court".

In their petition, Sonowal and Charan Chandra Deka contended that the Act was quashed, as it put on the state/complainant the onus of proving that a person was an illegal migrant for the provision that had been held illegal was incorporated in the amended Foreigners' Act. Agreeing with the submission, the Bench said:

The earlier decision referred to the relevant material showing that such uncontrolled immigration into the northeastern states posed a threat to the integrity of the nation. What is therefore, called for is a strict implementation of the directions of this court issued in Sonowal case, to ensure that illegal immigrants are sent out of this country. We have to once again lament with Sonowal that there is lack of will in the matter of ensuring that illegal immigrants are sent out. The Bench further observed, "Instead of obeying the mandamus issued essentially in the interest of national security and to preserve the demographic balance of a part of India that is Bharat, and implementing the 1964 order in Assam in letter and spirit, the authorities have chosen to make the 1964 order itself inapplicable to Assam Adequate facts, nay no fact, is pleaded to justify such apprehension. It is not explained how Indian citizens would suffer if the 1964 order is enforced. Nothing was also shown at the time of arguments to persuade us to come to a conclusion that the 1964 order worked harshly on anyone who was sought to be proceeded against under the Foreigners' Act and under that order. The present exercise is therefore, seen to be not a commendable attempt to evade the directions issued by this court earlier round".

(i) Quashing the amendment order 2006, the Bench imposed costs of Rs 25,000 payable to the petitioners as counsel fee (DN Bezboruah, 'Illegal Migration from Bangladesh', ed. BB Kumar, Astha Bharti, Delhi, 2006, p. 53).

(j) On 5th December 2006, the Supreme Court further held that the burden of proof lies on the foreigners itself. Bangladesh has violently denied about such migration of their population to India, which created terrorist problem not only in north-east, but in most parts of the countries where these migrants settled. Mr. L K Advani, the then Deputy Prime Minister of India, while addressing senior officials on 8th January 2003 asked them to locate and throw out 20 million Bangladeshis since they posed serious threat to the internal security of the country. After the Assam accord, the agitation stopped and the fencing in Assam-Bangladesh border started which is now more or less complete excluding the riverine part.

What was the achievement of IM(DT) Act?

1. Total enquiries (against suspected illegal migrants) —3,02,554
2. Enquiries referred to the Screening Committee —2,96,564
3. Enquiries reports referred to the IM(DT) Tribunals —31,264
4. Personal declared as illegal migrants by the IM(DT) Tribunals —9625
5. Number of illegal migrants expelled —1,461

Central Government invested more than Rs 300 crores for these Tribunals. The cost of expulsion was as high as Rs. 20 lac per head. In 2003, the D.G.P. Prakash Singh said at Guwahati, "what a joke it was, the persons thus expelled from Indian territory, again managed to enter in India." ('The Silent Invasion', p. 153).

No person shall vote at an election in any constituency if he is subject to any of the disqualifications referred to in Section 16 of the Representation of the People Act, 1950 [Section 62(2) of the Representation of the People Act, 1951).

11. Assam Accord (Memorandum of Settlement), 1985

Concluding six years of agitation in Assam over the vexed issue of illegal migration, the Government of India signed a Memorandum of Settlement with the leaders of the AASU and the AAGSP in the wee hours of India's thirty-eighth Independence Day. Signed in the presence of (and at the personal initiative of) the then Prime Minister, Rajiv Gandhi, on 15th August, 1985, debate continues about the success of the Accord and the fulfilment of the Accord provisions. Indeed, the Centre has convened a tripartite meeting with the AASU leaders on a number of occasions to discuss the Accord. The discussion continues 28 years after the Accord was signed. Excerpts are provided below.

Government have all along been most anxious to find a satisfactory solution to the problem of foreigners in Assam. The All Assam Students Union (AASU) and the All Assam Gana Sangram Parishad (AAGSP) have also expressed their keenness to find such a solution.

The AASU through their Memorandum dated 2nd February, 1980 presented to the late Prime Minister Smt. Indira Gandhi, conveyed their profound sense of apprehensions regarding the continuing influx of foreign nationals in to Assam and the fear about adverse effects upon the political, social, culture and economic life of the state.

Being fully alive to the genuine apprehensions of the people of Assam, the then prime minister initiated the dialogue with the AASU/AAGSP. Subsequently, talks were held at the prime minister's and home minister's level during the period 1980-83. Several rounds of informal talks were held during 1984. Formal discussions were resumed in March, 1985.

Keeping all aspects of the problem, including constitutional and legal provisions, international agreements, national commitments and humanitarian considerations, it has been decided to proceed as follows:-

(a) Foreigners Issue

1. For purposes of detection and deletion of foreigners, 1.1.1966 shall be the base data and year.
2. All persons who came to Assam prior to 1.1.1966, including those amongst them whose names appeared on the electoral rolls used in 1967 elections shall be regularised.

3. Foreigners who came to Assam after 1.1.1966 (inclusive) and up to 24th March 1971 shall be detected in accordance with the provisions of the Foreigners Act, 1946 and the Foreigners (Tribunals) Order, 1964.
4. Names of foreigners so detected will be deleted from the electoral rolls in force. Such persons will be required to register themselves before the Registration Officers of the respective districts in accordance with the provisions of the Registration of Foreigners Act, 1939 and the Registration of Foreigners Rules, 1939.
5. For this purpose, Government of India will undertake suitable strengthening of the government machinery.
6. On the expiry of a period of ten years following the date of detection, the names of all such persons, which have been deleted from the electoral rolls, shall be restored.
7. All persons who were expelled earlier, but have since re-entered illegally into Assam shall be expelled.
8. Foreigners who came to Assam on or after March 25, 1971 shall continue to be detected, deleted and practical steps shall be taken to expel such foreigners.
9. The Government will give due consideration to certain difficulties expressed by the AASU/AAGSP regarding the implementation of the Illegal Migrants (Determination by Tribunals) Act, 1983.

(b) Safeguards and economic development

Constitutional, legislative and administrative safeguards, as may be appropriate, shall be provided to protect, preserve and promote the culture, social, linguistic identity and heritage of the Assamese people. The government takes this opportunity to renew their commitment for the speedy all round economic development of Assam so as to improve the standard of living of the people. Special emphasis will be placed on education, science, and technology through establishment of national institutions.

(c) Other Issues

The government will arrange for the issue of citizenship certificates in future only by the authorities of the central government.

Specific complaints that may be made by the AASU/AAGSP about irregular issuance of Indian Citizenship Certificates (ICC) will be looked into.

The international border shall be made secure against future infiltration by erection of physical barriers like walls, barbed wire fencing and other obstacles at appropriate places. Patrolling by security forces, on land and riverine routes, all along international border shall be adequately intensified. In order to further strengthen the security arrangements, to prevent effectively future infiltration, an adequate number of check posts shall be set up.

Besides the arrangements mentioned above and keeping in view security considerations, a road all along the international border shall be constructed to facilitate, patrolling by security forces. Land between border and the road would be kept free of human habitation, wherever possible. Riverine patrolling along the international border would be intensified. All effective measures would be adopted to prevent infiltrators crossing or attempting to cross the international border.

It will be ensured that relevant laws for prevention of encroachment of government lands and lands in tribal belts and blocks are strictly enforced and unauthorised encroachers evicted as laid down under such laws.

It will be ensured that the relevant law restricting acquisition of immovable property by foreigner in Assam is strictly enforced.

It will be ensured that Birth and Death Registers are duly maintained.

Under the existing Foreigners Act 1946, there is enough provision for identification, detention and deportation of illegal immigrants and thus no new mechanism is required, Minister of State for Home Mullappally Ramachandran told the Lok Sabha in March 2013. He was replying to a private member's bill introduced by Baijayant Panda, which sought to identify and deport illegal immigrants from the country. The minister admitted that there was a big problem of illegal immigration from neighbouring countries, particularly Bangladesh. He said the bill seeking regular judicial procedure for dealing with the problem would further delay the process of identifying, detailing and deporting illegal immigrants.

The government in March, 2013 ruled out any fresh legislation to deal with the issue saying stringent mechanisms were already in place.

UNITED NATIONS CONVENTION AGAINST TRANSNATIONAL ORGANISED CRIME AND THE PROTOCOLS THERETO

Mr. Kofi A. Annan, the then the Secretary General of the United Nations, in the millennium summit of the Heads of sub-States meeting at the United Nations in September, 2000 reiterated that the trafficking of persons particularly women and children for forced and exploitative labour, including for sexual exploitation is one of the most egregious violations of human rights. He argued the member States to work against trans national organised crimes and punish trafficking in persons, specially women and children. Bangladesh being a member of United Nations convention against trans national organised crime had only reservation that People's Republic of Bangladesh does not consider itself bound by paragraph 2 of the said Article 35 of the convention. The Article 35, Para 2 describes as follows: - "Any dispute between two or more State parties concerning the interpretation or application of this convention that cannot be settled through negotiation within a reasonable time, shall, at the request of one of those State parties be submitted for arbitration if 6 months after the date of request for arbitration, those State parties may refer the dispute to the International Court of Justice by request in accordance with the statute of the court". This is about settlement of disputes between two State parties. Excluding this reservation, Bangladesh was totally in agreement with the convention against trans-national organised crimes. Some of the crime pattern contained in the United Nations resolution is given as under:

1. Article 5-Criminalisation of participation in an organised criminal group

Agreeing with one of more other persons to commit a serious crime for a purpose relating directly or indirectly to the obtaining of a financial or order material benefit and, where required by domestic law, involving an act undertaken by one of the participants in furtherance of the agreement or involving an organised criminal group.

Organising, directing, aiding, abetting, facilitating or counselling the commission of serious crime involving an organised criminal group.

2. Article 16-Extradition

This article shall apply to the offences covered by this Convention or in cases where an offence involves an organised criminal group and the person who is the subject of the request for extradition is located in the territory of the requested State Party, provided that the offence for which extradition is sought is punishable under the domestic law of both requesting State Party and the requested State party.

If the request for extradition includes several separate serious crimes, some of which are not covered by this article, the requested State Party may apply this article also in respect of the latter offences.

3. Article 17

States parties may consider entering into bilateral or multilateral agreements or arrangements on the transfer to their territory of persons sentenced to imprisonment or other forms of deprivation of liberty for offences covered by this Convention, in order that they may complete their sentences there.

PREAMBLE

Article 8: Repatriation of victims of trafficking in persons .

The State Party of which a victim of trafficking in persons is a national or in which the person had the right of permanent residence at the time of entry into the territory of the receiving State Party shall facilitate and accept, with due regard for the safety of that person, the return of that person without undue or unreasonable delay.

Article 9: Prevention of trafficking in persons:

States Parties shall establish comprehensive policies, programmes and other measures (a) To prevent and combat trafficking in persons; and (b) To protect victims of trafficking in persons, especially women and children, from revictimisation.

States Parties shall take or strengthen measures, including through bilateral or multilateral cooperation, to alleviate the factors that make persons, especially women and children vulnerable to trafficking, such as poverty, underdevelopment and lack of equal opportunity.

States Parties shall adopt or strengthen legislative or other measures, such as educational, social or cultural measures, including through bilateral and multilateral cooperation, to discourage the demand that fosters all forms of exploitation of persons, especially women and children that leads to trafficking.

Article 15: Settlement of disputes:

States Parties shall endeavour to settle disputes concerning the interpretation or application of this Protocol through negotiation.

General Provisions

Article 6: Criminalisation : Each State Party shall adopt such legislative and other measures as may be necessary to establish as criminal offences, when committed intentionally and in order to obtain, directly or indirectly, a financial or other material benefit: (a) The smuggling of migrants; (b) When committed for the purpose of enabling the smuggling of migrants: (i) Producing a fraudulent travel or identity document; (ii) Procuring, providing or possessing such a document.

Article 11: Border measures: Without prejudice to international commitment in relation to the free movement of people, States Parties shall strengthen, to the extent possible, such border controls as may be necessary prevent and detect the smuggling of migrants.

Each State Party shall adopt legislative or other appropriate measures to prevent, to the extent possible, means of transport operated by commercial carriers from being used in the commission of the offence established in accordance with Article 6.

Article 18: Return of smuggled migrants: Each State Party agrees to facilitate and accept, without undue or unreasonable delay, the return of a person who has been the object of conduct set forth in Article 6 of this Protocol and who is its national or who has the right of permanent residence in its territory at the time of return.

Each State party shall consider the possibility of facilitating; accepting the return of a person who has been the object of conduct set forth in Article 6 of this Protocol, and who had the right of permanent residence in its territory at the time of entry in to the receiving State in accordance with its domestic law.

GENERAL PROVISIONS

Article 11: Security and preventive measures : In an effort to detect, prevent and eliminate the theft, loss or diversion of, as well as the illicit manufacturing of and trafficking in, firearms, their parts and components and ammunition, each State Party shall take appropriate measures: (a) To require the security of firearms, their parts and components and ammunition at the time of manufacture, import, export and transit through its territory, and (b) To increase the effectiveness of import, export and transit controls, including, where appropriate, border controls, and of police and customs transborder cooperation.

As Bangladesh is a Party to this Preamble and this protocol of the United Nations and the general provision mentioned in this notification, we must take up with Bangladesh at proper level giving them proofs of their nationals migrating to India and the arms, ammunition and drugs entering into India from Bangladesh. The matter can be taken up with International Court of Justice if however, Bangladesh does not agree with such of our complaints giving enough proofs and material.

10

Main Deduction/Implications and Recommendations

It is imperative that a proper border management system has to be followed to take stock of the following hindrances and situations faced at the border, which help the migrants and militants to penetrate through the gaps.

Over Population in the Border Areas

We have number of villages very close to the international border and some of them are ahead of the fencing within 150 yards from the international boundary. The density of population of such villages has gone up to 800 whereas the density of population in north-east is between 400 to 500 per sq km and it is less in India. When these migrants cross over from Bangladesh to the extreme border villages that are in overpopulated area having a porous border, it is difficult to identify, locate and apprehend a Bangladeshi militant / migrant. In few cases, it has been seen the children of such villages which are very close to international border, were studying in Bangladesh schools. These overpopulated villages on other side of the fencing will remain a grave danger and will be helpful to the migrants in getting a proper shelter and to evade being apprehended by Indian security forces, as they can easily run away to Bangladesh.

Indifferent Attitude of Border Population

The crimes in the border, the illegal crossing in the border including cattle smuggling, is very well organised through criminals and touts operating both sides of the border; mostly the dacoits, criminals, undesirble elements and smugglers have settled since long both sides and they have family relationship. They are involved in organising crimes in border areas and consequently they do not like the border guarding forces and other security agencies operating in the border. None of the border villagers will ever come forward to divulge anything about migrants coming over to their side from Bangladesh or about the top smugglers as they are a party to these unlawful activities and will never be with our border guarding forces.

Difficulty in Identifying Bangladesh Nationals

Any Bangladeshi penetrating to Indian side from nearby area, i.e., border district of Bangladesh will go unnoticed by the security forces because their behavioural pattern is the same, they speak the same dialogue, have the same culture, and wear the same dress. It is very easy for them to obtain an identity card from their link persons in Indian side to prove that they belong to India. They speak both in Assamese and Bengali and these are the languages, which are spoken in Indian side of the border. It is understood that, at times, touts inside Bangladesh, before their departure to India are handing over the identity cards and ration cards to them on payment and they know the routes guided by the touts and the techniques to cross the border.

The Porous Border

We have various rivers, nullahs, hills, forests, gaps in the fencing, enclaves, adverse possession lands, unmarked boundary (Tripura Border), missing boundary pillars, missing sub-pillars and submerging of fencing during monsoon. The climate, particularly in Meghalaya border, in Khasi, Jaintia and Garo Hills during winter becomes so foggy that one cannot see for 10 yards even during day time, and thus, the crossing is very easy. Char islands cannot be fenced, the Brahmaputra and the Padma cannot be fenced, and there are so many low-lying areas where fencing is not possible. The delay in lighting the border fencing areas with more than 3000 villages coming within 150 yards of the border from the IB in Indian side pose numerous problems. Flooding of the border areas makes it very easy for migrants to cross. It is an impossible task for the border guarding forces to secure every inch of the border during monsoon and winter, particularly in night hours and when few of the BOPs have to be withdrawn because of the threat from the floods.

There are places in Indo-Bangladesh border where even HHTI, BFSR and LORROSS will not work, even the sensors become ineffective to some extent during flood and kilometres-after-kilometres of fencing is washed away due to the climate and the fury of nature every year. Therefore, the porousness of the border will remain for years to come and the proverb 'seal the border' is not possible on the ground and such a vast border cannot be protected giving zero effect for migration.

Problem faced for deportation of Bangladesh Nationals

The Bangladesh border guards in most of the cases, when contacted through the authorised check post, take time to confirm about the person's address in Bangaldesh who is been handed over to them after being ordered so by various Indian courts. In almost all the cases, the reply comes from them after few months that such a person does not exist in Bangladesh and he is not a Bangladeshi at all. For them, he is a Bengali speaking Indian Muslim and they refuse to accept. That way, any Bangladeshi migrant can speak in Bengali and some in Assamese. In the whole of West Bengal, Tripura, Khasi border, Karimganj border, Cachar border, the local dialect is Bengali and only in Dhubri belt of Assam border both the Assamese and Bengali are prevalent. It is easy for the BGB and the government of Bangladesh to refuse to accept any Bangladeshi when handed over to them.

In the case of pushing back of Bangladesh migrants, when they are apprehended at the borders, the BSF push them back and the BGB catch them and lodge a protest that India is trying to push Bengali Muslim Indians to Bangladesh and they again push them back to India. Similarly, the problem of feeding such Bangladeshi nationals who will have to be pushed back and for giving them accommodation is a big administrative task for both border police and for BSF, or that way, for any other state government or any other state's police, who bring them up to Bangladesh border to send them back.

I have personally witnessed this situation several times in Assam and Meghalaya border where such Bangladeshis are waiting for months to be pushed back to Bangladesh but without any result.

This situation will continue and there is only one solution that without obtaining any receipt of handing over such Bangladeshi persons, they should be pushed back at night through various gaps and never be allowed to enter into India. This has to be done as a policy matter. If we take up the case with the Bangladesh government or that way with BGB, it will be fruitless.

Problem of Fencing

The total fencing along Indo-Bangladesh border will be an eyewash as a large portion of it will be submerged under water and will be washed away in low-lying areas during monsoon because the border rivers change their course every year. This will involve a lot of expenditure for its maintenance and repair. The border floodlights may be successful in Jammu, Punjab, and J & K border where the rainfall is less, but in Indo-Bangladesh border, particularly in Meghalaya and Assam, where the rainfall is maximum, the floodlights will not work properly and will remain dark for months together. It requires a full-fledged engineering department, both civil and electrical, with sufficient material and funds, availability of resources and storing places under the border guarding force itself, which will be responsible for its repair and maintenance throughout the year. Necessary power of sanction to such field commanders of the border guarding force at a proper level be given so that there should not be any delay in the repair of the border fencing and the border floodlights. The extensive rainfall will result in large stretches getting waterlogged and vegetation under growth will come up immediately after the monsoon and the concrete base of the fencing will give away at various places. Repair of such portion and removing the under growth of whole of the fencing has to be made afresh in few places. The complete Indo-Bangladesh border areas, which get maximum rainfall, will cause the fencing to get rusted and damaged even within one year of its commissioning. This fencing has also created more enemies for us than friends as all the Indian villagers, ahead of the fencing, remain inclined towards Bangladesh, and more or less, they find it easier to have relations with Bangladesh villagers rather than come through our check gates which remain closed from six PM to six AM. Practically, all such villages ahead of fencing, are now under the control of Bangladeshi criminals. Fencing has come up as a cultural bar between villages at both sides of the border due to their having similar ethos and traditions and many of them being related to one another since ages. Unlike that of western border, fencing at Jammu Sialkot border, where civilians from both sides do not try to meet each other, Indo-Bangladesh border fencing is quite different. I have seen villagers coming close to borders to talk and meet at Hilly, Dawki, Chaudhurihat and Radhikapur.

Criminals, Security Forces and Political Nexus at the Border

Everywhere in Indo-Bangladesh border, the undesirable elements from both the sides and touts have their link with few security personnel, border police personnel, border political leaders and border administrative agencies. This helps the migrants to easily escape apprehension, as the touts in Indian side very easily manage valid identification cards and ration cards from administrative officers. Even though the places where migrants take shelter in border villages are known to security officials, but for varius reasons they are not being apprehended as it is all managed, much before their entry through these lacunaes in our own administration. These illegal migrants in border areas are guided from their hideouts to reach various destinations in India mostly in Odisha, Bengal, Assam, Bihar, MP, and UP. Some of them are now coming through authorised checkposts with fictitious documents which they manage to get before their entry to India after bribing officials in Indian side. It is a routine affair to be seen at Sutarkandi, Karimganj border, Dawkie in Meghalaya border, Dolu in Garo hills border and various checkpoints of West Bengal and Tripura also. Getting a fictitious passport from Bangladesh is very easy. Migrants, who are not successful in crossing the border through fenced area, try to spend money and come through proper check posts and vanish in India after reaching, going untraced.

Barbed wire cutting by cattle smugglers and militants for cattle smuggling is an old phenomen for the last 20 years or more and it is increasing day by day at these specific places. There is no order for Indian border guarding forces to open fire to smugglers and they only have to apprehend them. They take their cattle easily up to the border and the cattle are forced to enter Bangladesh in groups; the fencing is damaged and not only the cattle smugglers pass but along with them militants also try to cross the border both from India to Bangladesh and vice-versa.

There is no check in bringing thousands of cattle in trucks from Rajasthan, MP, Bihar, UP, Punjab and Haryana up to extreme border and none of the hundreds of check posts on national highway try to check these trucks nor they are checked by border district authorities or police while they are unloaded 10 to 15 kilometres away from the border.

This has resulted damage to the fencing evey day as at various places, gaps and openings are made in the fencing, which has to be then repaired.

Shelter provided to Indian and Bangladesh Criminals in Adverse Possession Areas and Enclaves

The Government of India has already taken up the case with the Government of Bangladesh for exchange of encalves and settling disputes over adverse possession cases. Yet, it will take some more time, and at present, the militants and criminals, including smugglers take benefit of these areas including the migrants for their safe entry and exit evading apprehension by security personnel. The Indian Parliament has not yet ratified the exchange of enclaves with Bangladesh and it will be decided after amending the Constitution to this effect. Until then, it is a haven for the migrants to get the shelter; so also for the militants and ISI agents to utilise them as their bases and hideouts at the border areas.

Zigzag Border between India and Bangladesh

The border between both the countires is not a straight line; it crosses through houses/ buildings, villages, mid-0stream of the river, in low-lying areas, in hilly terrain, inside reserve forests, within river Brahmaputra and river Padma, cutting across various char islands, having loops at places inside India and Bangladesh and slushy areas of Sunderbans. It helps migrants to cross-over and the border people use shortcut roads through these areas going straight from villages to villages. Thus, sanctity of the border is not maintained at all as crossing is very easy and it is more difficult to apprehend and detect the migrants.

Migrants change the profile of border areas

Since 1971, the profile and demographic pattern of all the border district of India towards Bangladesh have already undergone a massive change, particularly that of Nadia, Murshidabad, Maldah, West Dinajpur, Darjeeling, Jalpaiguri, Cooch Behar, Dhubri, Karimganj, Cachar, and Agartala. Everywhere, all along these borders, even very near to border BOPs, new mosques and madrassas have surfaced. No one knows wherefrom the funds have come. The proportional ratio to the increase in Muslim population with that of increase of madrassas in border areas does not match. The noticeable increase of madrassas and mosques are much higher in numbers in Karimpur of Nadia, Jalangi of Murshidabad, Khurka, Kaliaganj, Karan-Dighi, Hamjapur in West Dinajpur, Changrabandha in Cooch Behar, Dhubri, Cachar, Karimganj in Assam and Udaipur border of Tripura.

What I have seen personally in 1972 and 1973 in Kaliaganj, Raiganj, Khurka, Bora, Kadirganj, Patagora, Hoptiyagach, Kumargach, Dhaneerhat, Chopra, Hilly, Chakram, Balurghat, Bhimpur, Govindpur, Sidhai, Gitaldah, Punchdhwaji, Karela, Sahibganj, Changrabandha, Chowdhuryhat border areas is that they now bear a completely different picture of the border after major migration took place from Bangladesh to these areas. The locals helped them to enter, gave them shelter, sold them land and properties. Village football fields, cattle grazing fields, government lands and reserve forest areas were converted to household properties of these migrants who manipulated by various means in settling in border areas and there numbers were swollen more than the ethnic local people, who were staying there before 1971.

Getting Cheap Labours and Helps from Migrants

A Bodo will never go to the field and work, no Assamese will work in tea garden, no Manipuri will ever pull a rickshaw. Excluding sowing the seeds of jute, the Indian border population hate to cultivate their land. The local people of Nagaland, particularly in Dimapur, Guwahati, Siliguri, Calcutta, Cooch Behar, Agartala, Karimganj, Mizoram, and Manipur never go for physical labour work with the contractors in construction activities. No Khasi or Jaintia will ever like to work in limestone mines and coalmines, including Garos of Meghalaya. People all over India even in Bombay, Delhi and Jammu prefer to keep house cleaners in a cheaper rate employing these Bengali migrants. Bangladeshi migrants for their survival and their future, the future and security of their children and a place to live in are providing their services for all these menial jobs at a very cheap rate. The Assamese will never go for physical labour in their lifetime. We Indians, as a race want help in our homes for cooking and other jobs and the middle class family cannot afford to engage locals by giving them more money and the locals charge more to do this type of work. It helps the migrants to get a lower level job easily and they get full security, are able to provide education, better job opportunity to their children and plan for their next generation.

Migration getting easier because of relation of families both side of the International Borders: Until today, marriages are being solemnised between Indian border villagers and Bangladesh border villagers as a routine case as the crossing is easy at the borders and as there are number of gaps in fencing. It is obvious that family relations are maintained at both sides of the border as a number of villages are positioned ahead of the fencing. The new families, after marriage, take their own stand to settle, whichever side they feel like. It is seen more in Karimganj, Hilly, Agartala, Dawkie and Dolu borders.

Excessive flow of food items of public distribution system reaching border areas: If one visits to Chowdhuryhat, Dhubri, Dawkie, Bholaganj, Udaipur, Banpur, Gede, Metihari, Raskhoa, Hilly, Hathkhola and Sundarbans, it will be noticed that the business persons have captured these border markets in a greater way and are profited day by day. The inflow of sugar, kerosene oil, cycle parts, phensidryl, cattle and medicines to extreme border haats in a huge quantities usually give an indication that all these materials are sent to Bangladesh. These PDS items are pilferaged from hinterland by district officials. They sell these to businessmen, who carry them easily up to border villages, where they obtain registration for opening of shops in border areas and easily pass it at an inflated rate to Bangladesh and get maximum profit. A border village may be having 500 to 600 members but the PDS items will be coming for more than 50,000 to 60,000 people by the businessman located in these villages.

This is continuing since ages and there is no respite to this as there is a demand of food materials in Bangladesh.

Cultivation of adverse possession land - Few of the adverse possession land of Bangladesh in India are being cultivated fraudulently by these migrants. Migrants are employed as casual labours to cultivate by the landowners.

Losing natural resources in border areas and border districts: Poaching of limestone in Jaintia border, coal from Khasi and Garo Hills, of timber and forest material from Khasi, Jaintia, Garo, East Garo, West Garo, Tura are very common which one can observe everyday as thousands of Bangladeshis have entered reserve forest areas, occupied them, cleared them and have started cultivating the same. It is easy for Bangladeshi smugglers and touts to contact with these migrants settled in border areas, reccee and cut trees and remove stones very easily, and usually, it goes unnoticed. The timbers are cut and thrown into rivers/ nullahs in monsoon and they go to Bangladesh with heavy currents and cannot be seized.

Position of char islands in river Brahmaputra and Padma - Because of various char islands in thousands in Brahmaputra and in river Padma and that of emerging new char islands every year, the migrants find it as the easiest way for lebensraum and keep on shifting from char islands slowly and quietly to various cities after obtaining identity cards. These char islands are a boon to Bangladesh and a curse to India.

Missing border pillars: Every year border main pillars and sub-pillars either go inside the river or are washed away in heavy current during monsoon and also get uprooted. Smugglers also break some pillars intentionally. Thus, during monsoon and even after that, when the border remains open and its demarcation is not identified properly on the ground at various places because of non-availability of boundary pillars, the area is not properly secured by border guarding forces which helps the migrants to cross these missing boundary pillar areas.

Lack of development of border areas helps migrants to go unnoticed: If one looks at the release of 'border area development fund' to our various border states and its further distribution to border districts, it is too meagre an amount. One can find unavailability of markets in border areas, lack of health centres, unavailability of medicines, absence of doctors, lack of proper educational institutions, bad state of road communications, non-availability of potable water and the border areas plunged in darkness due to lack of power. These areas are not effectively administered or controlled by either state administrative authorities or central security agencies, particularly the border belt between one kilometre from the border up to 15 kilometres. Thus, the information and the intelligence of new migrants after their penetration from Bangladesh and their detection have become extremely difficult and they easily find their way through fields and jungles to interior areas without being noticed by any check post in between.

Order for not firing towards any person coming from Bangladesh even during night: In order to keep good relations with the Sheikh Hasina government, the border guarding force has been asked not to resort to firing at the border until and unless there is a threat to their lives. During night when the militants breach fencing to cross, it is very difficult for the border guarding forces to face the situation waiting for retaliation until they are fired at. This has resulted in a number of injuries to BSF personnel by militants, cattle smugglers and the migrants.

The fear of the forces in the border has already gone away with the result that migrants are taking more initiative to cross the border as they know it very well that the BSF will never fire at them and so there is no threat to their lives, and they can run and take shelter in Indian side after crossing the border even during day time.

We have a number of women and children trafficked from Bangladesh to India for immoral purpose and prostitution in Calcutta, Delhi, and other metro cities. These keep on increasing because of laxity at the border as the BSF is unable to stop these infiltration for the fear of official action against them if they resort to firing. A number of BSF personal were court martialled, have lost their services because of firing and killing the migrants; the punishments have spread as a wild fire among all BSF constables posted at the border to remain defensive as a result of which the smugglers, militants and migrants have become more offensive in the border. Thus, they make full use of this demoralisation in the rank and file of BSF personnel deployed at the border and mutely allow cross over of the migrants to India to take refuge with sympathisers and their relatives at this side of the border.

As an example, 152 battalion of BSF deployed at Nadia-Bangladesh border, has apprehended 28 Bangladeshis at Gobardha border on 27th June, 2013 night while coming from Bangladesh (PRO BSF).

Ambiguity of jurisdiction of border areas by the border guarding forces - The jurisdiction of BSF in Gujarat is of 50 kilometres; in J & K, the whole of state; in West Bengal, it is five kilometres; and in Meghalaya, it is 15 kilometres. When the battalion changes from western sector to eastern sector, the troops are not briefed properly about their jurisdiction areas and in most of the cases, the BSF is now engaged in looking after the fencing and securing just one kilometre away the border. Practically, it has become a fencing guard force.

Few of the border police stations in Indo-Bangladesh border have women police wing with them. Recently, the BSF have raised one 'Mahila Battalion' for whole of western sector and eastern sector but they are not sufficient to cope up with the task. Mostly, during the incursion of migrant women and children, particularly girls, it is very difficult to apprehend them by male forces and to interrogate them. They are supposed to be handed over to the police station much before evening hours and they cannot be interrogated without the presence of another woman employee and cannot be held in custody during night hours. Similar case is with the smugglers and the criminals, who use these women migrants for exploitation, and there were charges against border guarding security personnel of ill-treating women and border personnel have suffered in enquiries and consequently, nobody takes interest in apprehending any woman migrant, or for that matter, any girl or child coming from Bangladesh. In Assam border, and that also of Tripura and Mizoram, the local administration is more or less defunct. The same has also been seen in Mankachar, Mahenderganj, Dolu, Dawkie, Garo hills, Khasi, Jaintia belts of Meghalaya. If one visits to a border police station, you hardly find sufficient forces. The border police stations have inadequate staff, the custom officers at the border face security problem in guarding the seized items and its transportation because of the poor condition of border roads, practically unfit for vehicular traffic. Thousands of precious logs/timbers, both of sal and teak, seized in the whole of Meghalaya border while being transported to Bangladesh, after being poached from Indian forests, have been lying for more than 10 years in the border areas, and they are just getting destroyed due to heavy rain and in the process, the government exchequer suffers.

Even if some unscrupulous elements, criminals, smugglers, or touts are apprehended and are produced before the court, the border population, who are witness to all this, fail to turn up in the court on due date as they do not get any transport costs or money to feed themselves while appearing before the court. Most of these border villagers are a party to the smuggling and are hands in gloves with such touts giving shelter to migrants coming from Bangladesh.

The border population, in most of the cases related to entry of migrants are against their apprehension and do not provide any help to the security agencies. The presence of such migrants very close to our side of borders help the ISI agents and extremist elements and militants escaping to Bangladesh in providing proper direction and lead them up to the border. When there was pressure by Sheikh Hasina government on the Bangladesh Police and Bangladesh border guards to apprehend Indian militants operating in their side, and for apprehending such fundamentalists who are training them in various training camps close to the border, they easily trespassed into India and took shelter here.

During BDR Mutiny in 2009, few mutineers crossed over to India and took shelter in places arranged by Indian insurgents groups. Our legal system is full of loopholes and they always come handy to the migrants passing over to this side. If a migrant is coming along with smuggled or contraband items and is produced before the customs, the customs only seize the contraband items and release the apprehended person. Similarly, if he/she is handed over with seized items to the local police, the migrant, who may be a criminal, is released and brought to the border so as to be pushed back although no one knows whether he is really pushed back or again enters India vanishing thereafter.

Consequent to the Indo-Bangladesh border agreement of 1974, joint Indo-Bangladesh guidelines were framed in 1975 for both the border guarding forces of India and Bangladesh to prevent trans-border crimes and illegal migration. It also states that no border guarding force will construct any permanent or temporary structures including trenches within 150 yards of the international border.

On this pretext, Bangladesh border guarding force always refused to permit BSF to construct barbed wire fencing within 150 yards of the border stating the fencing to be a defence installation. They have gone even to the extent of opposing construction and repair of roads within 150 yards. Whereas, neither the roads nor the fencing will pose any security threat to Bangladesh and the Indian fertile land falling within such a big stretch of 150 yards in width is a great economic loss to both India and the border citizens; consequently, most of the villagers in this no-man's land have become stateless citizens indirectly. We have more than 3000 villages within 150 yards of Indo-Bangladesh border; as this zone remains cut-off from six PM to six AM, all this villagers are left at the mercy of Bangladesh criminals during night hours since no help can be rendered to them.

Practically, if Bangladesh really wants to stop their migration to India, it must help in the Indian construction of border fencing on the international border. It is a good sign that commerce ministers of both sides have agreed to expand the trade between India and Bangladesh for which 13 checkposts/trade points have been modernised by the MHA border management group along with the cooperation of the MEA, the Ministry of Commerce and the North-East Council (MHA progress report of 2011/2012).

The informal trade, which helped the smugglers, particularly in cattle smuggling, requires to be addressed and the general instruction to remove the border guarding forces for deployment during election duties, other internal security duties, and counter-insurgency operations at times, which is against the recommendation of the Group of Ministers' finding, has to stop.

The migration cannot only be minimised by making a barbed wire fence. It requires tremendous effort and active role of the central government and the state government, the North-East Council and all border-deployed administrative agencies to first strengthen the basic infrastructure on the borders. Creation of police outposts, road communications (also the lateral roads), legalising all border trades, mobilising border population in support of the government agencies, providing employment to border youths, removing the health hazards and solving educational problems of the border population should be taken up seriously. The inclination of the border population in all the border districts is in favour of the migrants. The gap between the public and the government machineries deployed at the border must end soon. In comparison to various sanctions for the states from the centre/the Planning Commission, the portion of BADP which is coming for north-eastern states, are too meagre. It has to be 10 times more than what has been givien in 2012 as the border states are not coming forward themselves for development of border areas.

Few insurgent camps during the present regime of Sheikh Hasina were demolished and some of the north-east insurgent groups operating very close to the border were removed from the border areas of Rajshahi, Khulna, Dinajpur, Rangpur, Kustia, Rangamati, etc. Yet, there is every possibility during Begum Zia's regime, if she comes to power in 2014, Bangladesh will again be a cause of worry to India. Our insurgent groups supported by ISI and the fundamentalist parties of Bangladesh will become a deadly combination for carrying out subversive activities against India. Therefore, the defensive posture of the border guarding force will never succeed in the border.

Few political parties from Bangladesh who are getting funds from various developed countries and western countries are diverting these aids for promoting terrorism in India and helping north-east insurgent groups, fundamentalist Muslim groups in Assam and Indian Mujahideen in the hinterlands.

Until and unless the border population will not repose their faith and trust on the government, they will never help in apprehending illegal migrants. They do not have faith on our border guarding forces as these forces remain at a place for two to three years and do not understand their language and culture and by the time, in case, they begin understanding the local people, they get changed; a new group arrives, a vacuum is created and continuous liaison breaks.

The border is always inhospitable and the administrative missionaries deployed in Indo-Bangladesh border are always under constant mental stress. Yet in national interest, their welfare has to be looked into along with that of the ethnic local border population so as to preserve their culture, tradition, language, festivals and ethos.

Ending Corruption

Corruption in border is rampant, be it with the border guarding force or the district administration, the PHD, the health service or to that way, with the politicians. Corruption is the root cause for the entry of migrants from Bangladesh. Considerable money is transacted in exchange of drugs, arms, ammunitions, coal and personnel from both sides of the border and a number of transactions of fake Indian currency notes are being made in border areas. There is huge smuggling of coal and timber from Meghalaya to Bangladesh, both through Assam and Meghalaya border. These extra funds generated due to the smuggling of items are also linked to insurgency and terrorism, which has to be nipped in the bud. Accelerated economic development through proper coordination of various corporates and banks needs to be planned. Even though security forces are responsible for physical stoppage of migration at the border, but adequate and parallel socio-economic development of north-east border is a major issue which has to be looked into by the North-East Council and the 'Donor Ministry' of Government of India in consultation with all the seven north-east states. These seven states should not be left isolated nor should be segregated from other states. All insurgent groups are having support of a political party, openly or secretly. This emboldens insurgent groups in keeping a check on the efficiency of the administration. Various awareness programmes should be launched for the north-east people who are treated by mainlanders as foreigners. They should be brought psychologically closer to India and must think mentally that they are a part of India, which does not exist now in Manipur. We have parallel governments in Nagaland and Manipur where the NSCN-IM and the MPLF (the combine effort of UNLF, PLA and Pro-Pak) are calling the shot. Administration of north-east requires to be handled in a very different way instead of the present position of the bureaucrats remaining away from here for most of their tenure in plush postings, like that of Delhi in various ministries and semi-government institutions.

The infiltration is continuing because of the support from the politicians, the local Muslims and the early-settlers from Bangladesh. It also continues because of lack of interest of local workers for doing menial jobs not only in border region, but also in most of the metro cities of India. There should be a cut off date to be fixed, not necessarily 25th March 1971, but may be from the date of commencement of 2011 census, so that those who came after that should be detected and sent out / deported / pushed back. It requires a political will. The vote factor should not come in the way and must be sacrificed in the interest of nation's security. The attacks on non-Assamese in Assam, the gunrunning, the drug trafficking and the communal violence supported by ISI must be detected and Indians involved with these crimes should be punished. ISI supports have gone tremendously to the manual labours of Bangladesh Muslims who have migrated to north-east. We will have another Bosnia or Kashmir, which can play havoc in Assam, and this significant factor should not go out of mind of security advisors to the nation.

As a policy, both Pakistan and Bangladesh, to help exfiltration of their militants and their personnel, have allowed their ex-Army, ex-Ranger, ex-BDR and ex-Police personnel settle in border areas; they are very aggressive and cultivate their land up to the last inch of their side of the border. To counter this, we should also allow our ex-service members to be given cultivable land available in the border areas so that they will be our eyes and ears and forewarn the security agencies.

Modernisation of north-east police is a big task. The North-East Police Academy (NEPA) at Shillong has received some funds recently for its modernisation. It is controlled and looked after by the Ministry of Home Affairs. More emphasis on border management and security management topics should be inculcated in the curriculum by the faculties. Even though the location of UG camps in Bangladesh are known to our security agencies and several times, the list of such camps were handed over to BGB authorities by BSF in various border meetings, yet we may go to the extent of neutralising some of the camps in Bangladesh by some other methods like the one made use of by USA to wipe out Osama Bin Laden. It was again on 15th November, 2012 that BSF handed over list of 55 Indian militants' camps in Bangladesh to BGB authority (TOI of 16th November, 2012).

A greater transparency and information dissemination between all sister security agencies in the border is required. The accurate information of availability of weapons with Muslim fundamental organisation in north-east and unauthorised madrassas coming up in Nadia, Murshidabad, Dhubri, Karimganj, Cachar belts have to be brought to the notice of both state governments and central government and action should be taken against such activities instead of just filing the report in a folder. Recently, on 13th November, 2012, a riot took place at Tehatta border tehsil of Nadia district between the locals and the Muslim migrants (TOI of 14th November, 2012).

The unhindered, accurate and unreserved flow of information and intelligence from the lowest formation up to the highest formation must reach easily. Action-oriented intelligence inputs have to be given first to those agencies that are deployed in the field in that particular area/zone. North-East Council, which is a part of DONER, should also help more the border districts by giving priority, rather than providing funds to other districts for development. The functioning of NEC should be transparent and weightage should be given to those blocks, which are lagging behind, particularly to the health and education aspects of the youth of border villagers and the women in the border areas. The ISI has already made deep inroads into north-east states with the help of the Muslim migrants and its settlers all over the country. A well coordinated massive operation not only in north-eastern border but also in West Bengal border by the security forces have to be carried out to stop the migration in the gaps of the riverine border, the low lying border, the unfenced areas and the fenced areas without floodlight. In an article (clout of communal forces in Bengal worries CPM, TOI of 12th November, 2012), it has been mentioned that in last Jangipur Lok Sabha elections, 4 per cent votes went to WPI (political wing of Jamat-e-Islami Hind) and 3 per cent votes went to SDPI (former members of popular front of India, a confederation of Muslim organisations).

The muddle, strategic, psychological, communal, ethnic, religious, administrative, social and political scene in the north-east is a fact and it is due to immigration from Bangladesh only. All concerned, that is to say, Indian underground elements/insurgents, politicians, bureaucrats, students, youths and the people from all community should co-operate for development of the border region and work as a common force failing which the border will be eternal ferment devoid of peace and will be victim of the evil design of Pakistan.

We are now living in the age of migration which has become a source of conflict in states having border with Bangladesh. However, millions of Bangladesh migrants cannot be deported but temporary work programme and permission for inner line permit can be issued to them. There is no possibility of sealing the Indo-Bangladesh border and even in future, no one will be successful in sealing the border completely. There cannot be any effective mechanism to deport all illegal migrants now. What can be done to bring down the conflict in riot-prone areas is that the illegal settlers be fast removed from ethnic and tribal belts. There is a requirement of effective administration in BTC, Dhubri, Goalpara, Karimganj districts of Assam. Every state must come forward to detect the Bangladesh illegal migrants and delete their names from the electoral list whereever they were entered fraudunently, and those, who came after 2011 census, have to be deported fast by force. Provisionaly, as per 2011 census of Assam, the population has increased to 3,11,69,272. Dhubri has recorded the highest decadal growth of 24.4 per cent because of the migration and polygamy, which is observed routinely among the migrants. Mori Gaon has recorded 23.39 per cent decadal growth, Goalpara 22.74 per cent, Nagaon 22.09 per cent, Hailakandi 21.44 per cent, Karimganj 20.74 per cent, Barpeta 21.4 per cent, Dhemaji 20.30 per cent, Cachar 20.17 per cent, and Laxmipur 17.06 per cent, which include a number of Bangladeshi Muslim migrants who were forcibly removed from Arunachal Pradesh and entered Laxmipur.

As an instance, AIUDF secured 18 seats in 2011 Assembly elections. In 2006, this party led by Badruddin Azmal had only nine seats. He is having an eye of improving his position in the coming elections as the voters are all the migrants. It is high time that firm steps be taken to implement the Assam Accord for safeguarding the interests of ethnic tribals and ethnic people in Assam, otherwise, Assam will be annexed to Bangladesh in near future. There should be very prompt deportation in detected cases and all such political and fundamentalist organisations who favour illegal immigrants, anywhere in the country, must be banned in national interest. Action should be taken against forces destabilising the country and those fundamentalist organisations, in border areas, have to be identified, who are raising provocative, sensitive, religious campaign/slogans. The society must stop giving shelter to Bangladeshi migrants and no work should be offerred to them. There should be a collective and complete economic blockade to all such immigrants.

The political parties should not go for number game but help in prompt detection of Bangladeshis by their 'karyakartas'. People of Assam have lost their faith in government and what transpires now is that, there may be another such incident like Nielle Massacre or that of Kokrajhar, in near future as Kokrajhar, to this day, is boiling.

The illegal immigrants have started wielding enormous political power in Assam. The Muslims have now become majority in 11 out of 27 districts of the state and can determine the result of 54 out of 126 constituencies in the local assembly in coming elections.

They have become a poltical force and the indigenous population is apprehensive of losing their identity and culture. It has omenous implications for 'national security' and 'socio-economic stability' of the county as a whole.

The ISI is using migrants as conduits to ferry terrorists and arms to India and crippling the economy in north-east. There may be another Kashmir like situation to be faced in Assam where permanent deployment of Force has to be made ('Niti Central' of 31st October, 2012). Shri Tarun Gogoi, the present Chief Minister of Assam has stated on 3rd November, 2012 in the Press Club of India, Delhi that the migration has declined since 1991. If we study

Bangladesh's situation now, the fundamentalists are raising their heads again and it was reported that on 29/30, September, 2012, the 100 year old Buddhist monastery with 23 Buddhists and Hindu temples were burnt at Cox's Bazaar, Ramu, Patiya, Ukhia, Taknaf in Chittagong. A number of houses were burnt by 25 thousands BNP, Awami League, JEI activists.

They went to the extent of destroying the Navarun Shangha Durga Mandir, and Matri Mandir at Jelepara, Ukhiya in Chittagong and it was reported that, even Bangladesh Army was also involved in this incident (ACHR Press Release of 1st October, 2012 and ABC news of 30th September, 2012)

Pakistan's Bangladesh Plan is to create a Mughlistan in Indian continent. The Mughlistan will connect Pakistan to Bangladesh through India as reported by MRI Jahangir Nagar University of Bangladesh. The task will be performed jointly, by the ISI and the DGFI. This will take whole of Kashmir, portion of Jammu, and then Mewat area of Haryana, UP, Bihar, West Bengal and Assam. Perhaps, the result of 2011 census in these areas will be an eye-opener.

In 2001 census, the percentage of Muslims in Assam and West Bengal border districts were as follows:-

1.	Barpeta	59%	Birbhum	35.08%
2.	Bongaigaon	39%	CoochBehar	24.24%
3.	Cachar	36%	Jalpaiguri	10.78
4.	Daraang	35%	Malda	49.72%
5.	Dhubri	74%	Murshidabad	63.67%
6.	Goalpora	54%	Nadia	25.41%
7.	Haila Kandi	57%	North 24 Paraganas	24.22%
8.	Karimganj	52%	South 24 Paraganas	33.34%
9.	Nagaon	51%	North Dijanjpur	47.36%
10.	Marigaon	47.5%	South Dinajpur	24%

The whole of West Bengal had 25 per cent Muslims in 2001 census. There will be an increase of minimum 10 per cent in Muslim population, which is antipicated in the census of 2011, and this will also add few more Muslim majority districts in Assam very soon.

The total population of West Bengal is 91,347,736 and it has 30 per cent Muslims.

The following table lists the total Muslim population of Assam from 1871 to 2011:

Year	*Muslim Population of Assam*
1871	86,193
1901	5,05,197
1911	6,30636
1921	8,67795
1931	12,66243
1941	16,96978
1951	19,81857
1961	27,42295
1971	35,92124
1991	63,73204
2001	8240611
2011	9765600 (if verifications have been correctly made by census 2011)

The total population of Assam is now 3,11,69,272 as per 2011 Census. 35 per cent of Assam population are Muslims now.

In the beginning of October, the Border Security Force and the BGB, both the border guarding forces, met at Silchar border, Sutarkandi to finalise the solution of all the adverse possession land cases between India and Bangladesh in the north-east. The work was supposed to start from December, 2012 again. Yet time will tell whether this will end. It may not be solved, as Bangaldesh will never agree to give away even one inch of Indian land under their adverse possession, like at Boraibari, where they had killed 16 BSF personnel in the year, 2001.

Statements of few noted leaders about 'Illegal Immigration'

"Illegal migrants fuel tension". Hangra Mohilari, BTC chief. ('Seven Sisters Post', 25.7.2012)

"The newly floated militant organisation United Muslim National Army (UMNA) under the chairmanship of Ramjan Islam was responsible for the clashes in the three districts of western Assam". By all Ex-BLT Welfare Society ('Seven Sisters Post', 1.8.2012).

Assam is famous in history as being one of the few regions that was never conquered by the Mughals. The mighty Ahoms managed to thwart every single intrusion by the Islamic armeda. The same region is home to over 81 lakh Muslims (2001 census), who comprise over 31 per cent of the total population—Shri Jaleswar Brahma, Gen. Secretary of Janajati Faith and Culture Protection Forum.

Flush out illegal Bangladeshi immigrants - Naga Hoho.

"The 12000 refugees who are identified by the Government of Assam on the basis of their land records will be re-examined by by BTC administration before allowing them for rehabilitation." Hangrama Mohilari, BTC Chief ('Asomiya Pratidin', 19.9.2012).

"The unabated infiltration of Bangladeshis is the route cause of the clashes in BTAD. The State government as well as the central government do not have political will to check infiltration." National Council of Churches of India ('Asomiya Pratidin' 29.7.2012).

Mohd. Mijarul Quayes, Foreign Secretary of Bangladesh (during his visit to Guwahati) said, "India has never raised the issue of illegal infiltration from his country with Dacca". ('The Sentinel', 4.8.2012).

Shri Tarun Gogoi, chief minister had given a statement that "the involvement of Bangladeshis is not possible, there is no proof of it. How the infiltrators, coming from Bangladesh will do such work? This is the act of miscreants only. There may be some third force behind it".

"Assam is like a volcano which may burst anytime and anywhere. Both the internal and external forces are active here" ('Dainik Purvoday', 8.8.2012).

Shri J B Patnaik, Hon'ble Governor of Assam: - "Influx of illegal immigrants hasn't stopped. How can you say that there is no immigration, when the border is porous and in places one-half of a village lies on the other side of the border?" ('Seven Sisters Post', 13.4.2012).

Shri P. Chidambaram, the then Union Home Minister:- "There is no denying fact that there is illegal immigration but influx (from Bangladesh) has gone down very sharply" ('The Sentinel', 4.8.2012). Again he said that "we should learn to live together".

Shri Badaruddin Ajmal, AIUDF Chief– "To whom Hagrama terms Bangladeshis; they live here in Assam even before his birth". ('Dainik Purvoday', 26.07.2012).

Shri Rockybul Hussain, Forest Minister, Government of Assam – "Involvement of Bangladeshi elements behind the clash is baseless allegation" ('The Assam Tribune', 26.7.2012).

Smt. Mamata Banerjee, CM of West Bengal (When more than 15,000 Bangladeshi Muslims left Assam and arrived at Cooch Behar, WB for seeking refuge there.)—"I will give shelter to the refugees coming to West Bengal from Assam."

The Group of Ministers (GOM), in NDA Government, after a detailed survey produced the report and said the Bangladeshi infiltrators are more than 1.27 crore in the country. A report of 'The Sentinel': a prominent daily newspaper of north-east, published the abstract of the "central government report on illegal infiltrators entered in India"- "More than 15 million illegal immigrants are reported to have entered India over the last five decades from Bangladesh, an intrusion that has completely changed the demography of large parts of Assam, Meghalaya, West Bengal, Tripura, and Bihar. This has been observed in a 135-page report of the Group of Ministers (GOM) headed by Union Home Minister L.K. Advani and submitted to the Government recently". "The report notes: 'Today, we have

15 million Bangladeshis, 2.2 million Nepalese, 70,000 Sri Lankan Tamils and about one lakh Tibetan migrants living in India. Demographic changes have been brought about in the border belts of West Bengal, Tripura and Meghalaya because of large scale illegal migration. Even states like Delhi, Maharashtra, Bihar and Rajasthan have been affected."

"Rampant encroachment of land by illegal migrants identified as one of the main cause of the conflagration of violence in the area." B.B. Jamatia, President of Janajati Faith and Culture Protection Forum.

The State Home Minister in UPA Government, Shri Shree Prakash Jaiswal informed the Parliament that more than 1.57 crore Bangladeshis are living in India.

Shri Jaideep Saikia stated in his book "Terror Sans Frontiers" pp. 152-153 "a serious possibility exists that Islamist Fundamentalists in the region are seeking to carve out an Islamic homeland comprised of the present-day Bangladesh and parts of Myanmar and north-east India. The fact that the ULFA and such other groups are not stepping on US interst immediately should not be viewed as tantamount to not doing so in the future. Indeed, the linkages which the ULFA has with the Islamist forces in the region and the ISI-DGFI are well on the way to prove that the ULFA has joined the global club of terror".

The sun may shine as the Bangladesh is set to deport Anup Chetia to India shortly. Shri R K Singh, Ex-Home Secy., Government of India informed media that after six rounds of talks with Bangladesh, it had some effect. Bangladesh Government had shifted Anup Chetia from Raj Shahi Jail to Kasimpur Jail nearer to Dhaka for smooth deportation process. Anup Chetia was arrested at Dhaka on 21st Dec., 1997. There is possibility that Anup Chetia may be released from Indian jail after he is received from Bangladesh to initiate peace talks. The Government of India will also be asking Lakhi Prasad Goswami and Babul Sharma who were also arrested with Anup Chetia for their deportation from Bangladesh (TOI, 30th June, 2013).

The government will bring a constitutional amendment bill in parliament during the fourth coming monsoon session beginning on 5th Aug., 2013 for implementation of the Indo – Bangla land boundary agreement. The Home Secretary level talks were held on 19th July, 2013 in Delhi and conveyed this to Bangladesh government. The bill will be introduced for implementation of Indira–Mujib pact of 1974 implementing territory swap of various enclaves. The approval is hanging in fire as the government lacks two-third majority in parliament. Bangladesh has already been told very clearly for deportation of ULFA General Secretary Anup Chetia currently lodged in Bangladesh jail (TOI 20th May, 2013). Both India and Bangladesh has agreed on Chetia's deportation. Bangladesh denied the deal but agreed to swap Chetia in getting two Bangladeshi criminals Subrata Bain and Sajjid Hossain from Indian jails. Both sides also discussed about firing in Indo-BD border by BSF, drug smuggling, cattle smuggling, smuggling of counterfeit notes and fencing at the border. Colonel Obeidul of Bangladesh team, being asked informed that BGB has permitted BSF to go ahead for construction of fencing in 57 unfenced patches out of the fresh list of 115 patches provided by BSF, lessening the earlier list provided to them.

Afmza Khatun, a girl of nine years was handed over to DG BGB of Bangladesh General Aziz Ahmad by BSF on 14th Sep., 2013. Her mother Manowara Begum died in disease and her brother was sent back to Bangladesh after conviction of two years and fine of Rs 10,000. They entered India from Bangladesh in January, 2009 through south Dinajpur border. Afmza was adopted by Addl. DG BSF Shri B.D. Sharma and given education in Nadia district of WB.

Government of India has approved to supply 250 MW of electricity to Bangladesh from 5th October, 2013 when it will be plugged from Delhi.

Bangla violence may spill into NE, feel intel agencies

India's internal security establishment is worried over the political uncertainty and incessant violence in Bangladesh.

It is being suspected that the unabated violence may have a spillover effect in the northeast as there are reports of religious minorities in Bangladesh being targeted. This, sources say, could see retaliation on minorities in troubled states like Assam and revive a situation similar to May-June 2012 when it saw raging riots. In an electoral year, this could further spill over to the rest of the country, say sources.

Trouble is also being expected on the Indo-Bangla border as well, with the religious right in Bangladesh suspected to be injecting new energy in their ties with Pakistan terror groups to gain greater strength to prolong the battle inside their country.

There have been reports of religious minorities being targeted in Bangladesh's Satkhira. Jammat-e-Islami leader Abdul Qadir Mullah, hanged on December 12 for war crimes in 1971, hailed from this region. Sources say in Assam there are already divisions among the native population and Muslims, most of whom have migrated from Bangladesh over the years, and this taking a communal colour could not be ruled out.

According to sources in the security establishment, it's no more a matter of whether the Sheikh Hasina-led Awami League, known to be friendly to New Delhi and harsh on anti-India terror groups, wins the January poll. "What's more important is that free and fair elections happen and a legitimate government is established. If Bangladesh Nationalist Party (BNP) and its chief Khaleda Zia (perceived not to be all that friendly to India) boycott the poll, hardline groups aligned to it would continue to foment violence and unsettle the government," said an intelligence official.

BNP and JeM have refused to participate in the elections until they are held under a neutral government. They have not even filed nominations with elections to go in just over a fortnight, leading to a situation where the Awami League would win unopposed. Sources say this would escalate the violence further and increase problems for India as there are signs of Pakistan fishing in troubled waters.

While Pakistan's interior minister Chaudhry Nisar Ali Khan has called it a "judicial murder" for Mullah's loyalty to Pakistan, LeT's Hafiz Saeed has blamed India for his hanging as well as the violence in Bangladesh.

Violence over shadowed bangla polls on 5th January 2014 and 8 persons were killed in nationwide violence called by BNP and Jammat-e-Islami. Very few voter turnout was recorded. Ruling Awami League sealed win as opposition boycotted the elections. Most voters preferred to say at home fearing violence during the polling in 147 out of the 300 constituencies in 59 districts of Bangladesh. Candidates in other constituencies were declared un-opposed. Opposition cadres set over 200 polling stations on fire. As per BNP, it was one sided polls. The chief election commissioner Kaji Rassibuddin Ahmad had declared the polls were fair. A total of 390 candidates, mostly from the Awami League and its ally Jatiya party, conferred 147 seats and 95 seats went to? Awami League, 12 seats to Jatiya party and 13 seats to independent candidates. Seikh Hasina won from Gopalganj and Rangpur constituencies. General Bikram Singh, the present army chief, had also stated in february 2014 that Bangladesh Migrants are a threat to India's security.

References

Sadique Khan, *The Question of Lebensraum* as published in the *Holiday Weekend of Bangladesh* dt. 18 Jan 1991.

Dhaka Courier, 22 November 1991.

VIK Sarin, *India's North-East in Flames*.

Shri SL Sakhder during the conference of Electoral Officers held at Ootacamund from 24-26 September 1978.

Rajmohan Gandhi, *The Wounds of Indifference*.

Myron Weiner, *Sons of the Soil*.

The Times of India, 03 November 2012.

The Times of India, 13 November 2012.

Islam 1992

Ibid (9) above

Ibid (9) above

Ibid (9) above

Ibid (9) above

Ibid (9) above

Myers 1993

Bangladesh-India border not strict, admits BSF chief IANS, Jalandhar August 29, 2012

Quoted from an electioneering campaign speech delivered on 10 February 1983 by Abdul Ghani Khan Choudhury at Mairabari while campaigning for the Congress (I) candidate. pp. 4.

Hiranya Kumar Bhattacharya, The *Silent Invasion*, Spectrum Publications, 2001.

PIB Press release, 12 December 2012.

Press Trust of India, 12 April 2012.

Border firing, drugs feature in DG-level talks between BSF and BGB in September 2012.

Seven Sisters Post 13 April 2012.

Also references drawn from below mentioned articles:-

Illegal Immigration from Bangladesh has turned Assam explosive by Mayank Singh of 31 October, 2012

The changing climate of Bangladeshi Migration to India by Manish Vaid and Tridivesh Singh Maini of 23 March, 2013.

India's Mexican problem by Palash Ghosh of 6 Feb, 2012 in Int. Business Times.

ISI, DGFI plan to bleed India using Bangladesh Migrants-rediff.com

Climate change and conflict in migration to Assam (India) by Casey Gugoff of Dec- 2011

India – BD restoring Soverignty on neglected borders- By S K Jha and K Lakhman.

Delema of gurading the India – Bangladesh border by N S Jamwal of Jan, 2004

Bangladesh India Ink border deal by Haroon Habib of the Hindu of 30 Jul, 2011 Dhaka

ANI of 10 Nov 2012- India Bangladesh disucss issues relating to security, border management, Shinde's statement.

Management of India – Bangladesh border by Mansi Mehrotra of 8 May, 2009 of CLAWS

India Bangladesh border manangement by Pushpita Das of IDSA of 28 May, 2009

India Bangladesh border management of times of Assam of 15 May, 2012 by Swadesh Roy

MHA Annual report 2011- 12

MHA's Report on release of BADP for 2012- 13

Enclaves and Adverse possessions of 27 Dec, 2010 by Pushpita Das

Illegal Immigration in India Wikipedia- The free Encyclopedia

Enviornmentally induced migration from Bangladesh to India by Sarfaraz Alam of IDSA of July, 2003

RNP Singh- Bangladesh Decoded

Mughalistan – Bengal Genocide (WWW.Bengalgenocide.com)

Indian borders- threats and challenges – Border Darshan

India Bangladesh restoring Soverignty on neglected Borders by Kanchan Lakhman and Sanjay Kumar Jha

Transborder identities by Dr. Subhakanta Behera

Managenent of India Bangladesh border by Mansi Mehrotra

Bangladesh Wikipedia, the free encyclopedia.

Census of India 2001

IMDT Act is the biggest barrier to deportation.Supreme Court. (The Hindu)

Illegal Bangladeshi immigrants threat to India (Court).

World Bank Report

Trafficking in Bangladeshi women and girls by Bimal Kanti Paul, geographical review.

Illegal Bangladeshi migration to India, impact on internal security by Anand Kumar. 7 May 2010.

Bangla migration to India largest in developing world by Kounteya Sinha. 13 September 2013.

Bangladeshi migration to India largest in developing world. News UN report London 15 September 2013.

Illegal Bangladeshi immigrants threat to India. Court. IANS12 August 2008 New Delhi.

Great Bangladesh Wikipedia.

Indian Mexican problem. Illegal immigration from Bangladesh. Palash Ghosh.

The illegal Bangladeshi immigrant, Do the bogey man numbers add up? Sandip Roy 16 August 2012.

Illegal migration from Bangladesh, threat to India's internal security-N Manoharan. 18 September 2013.

Illegal Bangladesh immigrants-Threat for India's security-Feroz Khan.

Bangladeshi migrants pose threat to internal security. Rediff. com 18 April 2008.

Illegal Bangladeshi migration to India - impact on internal security. by Anand Kumar. January 2011.

Illegal migration as a threat to Indias Internal Security of Hindu Samhati-8 August 2012.

Appendix

1. Treaty of Yandaboo

[The Treaty was concluded between the King of Ava (present Myanmar and thereabouts) and the British on 24th February, 1826. Under the aegis of the Treaty, Assam was handed over by Burma (which was "temporarily" in control of Assam) to the British. It would be of interest note for the reader that the United Liberation Front of Asom has prefaced its demand for a sovereign Assam on the basis of this Treaty, stating that Assam was not a part of India before the Treaty and should, therefore, be reinstated to it independent status after the departure of the British.]

TREATY of PEACE between the HONOURABLE EAST INDIA COMPANY on the part, and HIS MAJESTY the KING of AVA on the other, settled MAJOR-GENERAL SIR ARCHIBALD CAMPBELL, K.C.B., and K.C.T.S., COMMANDING the EXPEDITION, and SENIOR COMMISSIONER in PEGU and AVA; THOMAS CAMPBELL ROBERTSON, ESQ., CIVIL COMMISSIONER in PEGU and AVA; and HENRY DUCIE CHAD, ESQ., CAPTAIN, COMMANDING BRITANNIC MAJESTY'S and the HONOURABLE COMPANY'S NAVAL FORCE, on the part of the Honourable Company; and by MENGYEE-MAHA-MEN-KYAN-TEN WOONGYEE, LORD of LAYKAING, and MENGYEE-MARA-HLAH-THUO-HAH-THOO-ATWEN-WOON, LORD of the REVENUE, on the part of the King of Ava; who have each communicated to the other their full powers, agreed to and executed at Yandaboo in the Kingdom of Ava, on this Twenty-fourth day of February, in the year of Our Lord One Thousand Eight Hundred and Twenty-six, corresponding with the Fourth day of the decrease of the Moon Taboung, in the year One Thousand One Hundred and Eighty-seven Gaudma Era, 1826.

Article 1

There shall be perpetual peace and friendship between the Honourable Company on the one part, and His Majesty the King of Ava on the other.

Article 2

His Majesty, the King of Ava renounces all claims upon, and will abstain from all future interference with the principality of Assam and its dependencies and also with the contiguous petty States of Cachar and Jyntia. With regard to Munnipoor it is stipulated, that should Ghumbheer Sing desire to return to that country, he shall be recognised by the King of Ava as Rajah thereof.

Index

J

N

O

P